VERIFICATION IN AN AGE OF INSECURITY

VERIFICATION IN AN AGE OF INSECURITY

THE FUTURE OF ARMS CONTROL COMPLIANCE

Philip D. O'Neill, Jr.

OXFORD
UNIVERSITY PRESS

OXFORD
UNIVERSITY PRESS

Oxford University Press, Inc., publishes works that further Oxford University's objective of excellence in research, scholarship, and education.

Copyright © 2010 by Oxford University Press, Inc.
Published by Oxford University Press, Inc.
198 Madison Avenue, New York, New York 10016

Library of Congress Cataloging-in-Publication Data

O'Neill, Philip D., Jr., 1951-
   Verification in an age of insecurity : the future of Arms Control Compliance / Philip
D. O'Neill, Jr.
      p. cm.
   Includes bibliographical references and index.
   ISBN 978-0-19-538926-5 (hardback : alk. paper)
   1. Weapons of mass destruction. 2. Nuclear arms control.
   3. Nuclear disarmament—International cooperation.
   4. Nuclear nonproliferation—International cooperation. I. Title.
   KZ5675.O54 2009
   341.7'34—dc22   2009027995

Note to Readers:

This publication is designed to provide accurate and authoritative information in regard to the subject matter covered. It is based upon sources believed to be accurate and reliable and is intended to be current as of the time it was written. It is sold with the understanding that the publisher is not engaged in rendering legal, accounting, or other professional services. If legal advice or other expert assistance is required, the services of a competent professional person should be sought. Also, to confirm that the information has not been affected or changed by recent developments, traditional legal research techniques should be used, including checking primary sources where appropriate.

*(Based on the Declaration of Principles jointly adopted by a Committee of the
American Bar Association and a Committee of Publishers and Associations.)*

TABLE OF CONTENTS

For the sake of our children

CHAPTER I

INTRODUCTION: RISKY BUSINESS

The 21st century tests, in new ways, the continuing quest to prevent and roll back the proliferation of weapons of mass destruction (WMD). Renewed political emphasis is evident in seeking arms control measures, as well as informal behavioral constraints.[1] Calibrated movement toward nuclear disarmament is again making legal process tools a valued element of our layered WMD defense.[2] An essential element of that process is the manner in which we verify agreements to control, limit, and disarm. Verification[3] is well recognized, both in principle[4] and politically, as "a key component of meeting our core objective for our nonproliferation policies—namely preventing rogue states and non-state actors from obtaining nuclear, chemical or biological weapons and their means of delivery."[5] It was equally embraced as an

---

1 For example, nuclear weapon states within the Nonproliferation Treaty Regime currently adhere to fissile material production and underground test ban moratoriums while they seek formal agreement in these areas.

2 *See, e.g.*, BRIAN JONES, INTELLIGENCE, VERIFICATION AND IRAQ'S WMD, Chapter 10 in Verification Yearbook (2004) ("The verification of a particular nation's compliance with its obligations under international agreements is one aspect of one element in a layered approach to defending against WMD. The overlapping elements are: to prevent or minimize possession; where this fails, to deter use; and, in the event of use, to reduce the effectiveness of the weapons.").

3 Verification can be generically defined as a process in which data are collected, collated and analyzed in order to make an informed judgment as to whether a party is complying with its obligations. U.N. Report of the Secretary General, "Verification in all its Aspects, Including the Role of the United Nations in the Field of Verification," A/50/377 at p. 16 (22 September, 1995) *accessed at* http://www.un.org/documents/gn/docs/50/plenary/a50-377.html ("Verification Report of the Secretary General").

4 U.N. General Assembly 1996 resolution A/51/182 6 embraced the Disarmament Commission's recognition of Sixteen Principles of Verification (The U.N. Verification Principles"). Principle 2 states verification is an essential element in the disarmament process.

5 Paula A. DeSutter, Assistant Secretary for Verification, Compliance and Implementation, "The New U.S. Approach to Verification," Remarks at the Carnegie

essential element of the arms limitation and disarmament process in the superpower era, as it will be again in the continuing efforts of America, Russia, and others to reduce nuclear stockpiles. In short, achieving compliance with international agreements is a "pillar" of America's national strategy to combat WMD.[6]

Regardless of the adversary, though, the collection and analysis of information to detect noncompliance with agreements has been and still remains at the heart of the verification process. The objectives of that process include not only detection of cheating, but also deterrence and confidence building.[7] The process functions through monitoring to collect information. This tends to be an objective and intrusive process. But systems are calculated to facilitate informed, subjective judgments about the significance of the information that monitoring produces. While not an "aim in itself,"[8] the exercise of that expertise, in turn, positions an issue for a treaty compliance judgment with respect to either agreed terms, or even less formal arms control constraints. Today, that aim of the verification process remains the same. But the ability of verification systems to inspire confidence, induce adherence, and encourage participation[9] faces new issues arising from the emerging threats of sub-state actors and rogue regimes. Their potential acquisition and willingness to use such weapons became at once the preeminent collective security challenge to, and a strategic imperative of, our current era of insecurity.[10]

International Nonproliferation Conference "Sixty Years Later," panel on "The Future of Verification", Washington, D.C. (November 7, 2005) *accessed at* http://www.state.gov./t/vci/rlslrm157098.htm and http://www.nti.orgle.research/official_docs/dos.html.

6   *See* "National Strategy to Combat Weapons of Mass Destruction," NSPD-171 HSPD4 (unclassified version) (September 17, 2002) at p. 2 (Strengthened NonProliferation to Combat WMD Proliferation).

7   COMING TO TERMS WITH SECURITY: A HANDBOOK ON VERIFICATION AND COMPLIANCE, UNIDIR & VERTIC (June 2003) ("UNIDIR Verification Handbook").

8   See the U.N. Verification Principles, *supra* note 4 at Principle 2.

9   *See ibid.* at Principle 3.

10 *See, e.g.*, National Security Strategy 2002, at p. 1. *See also* Report of the Secretary-General's High Level Panel on Threats, *Challenges and Change*, "A More Secure

At the very outset of the Obama administration, America's secretary of defense identified North Korea and Iran as particularly vexing challenges in facing the "toxic mix"[11] of rogue nations, terrorists, and WMD. Compounding the problem was the increase in range of the missile programs of these countries and their related records of proliferation.[12] The WMD risks from rogues ranged from potential attack, to coercion, to otherwise deterring the U.S. from acting in its interests. The new American president characterized terrorist acquisition of a nuclear weapon as the "most immediate and extreme threat to global security."[13] As America's administration changed, a bipartisan Congressional Commission reported the sobering conclusion that it expects a terrorist attack with WMD in the near term.[14] At the same time, the U.S. made clear in late 2008, as a matter of declaratory deterrence policy, that we "will hold any state, terrorist group or other non-state actor or individual *fully* accountable for supporting or enabling terrorist efforts to obtain or use weapons of mass destruction, whether by facilitating, financing or providing expertise or safe haven for such efforts."[15] This represented a logical expansion of a presidential statement in 2006 that North Korea would be held "fully accountable" for nuclear transfers, whether to another state or terrorist organization. To this end,

---

World: Our Shared Responsibility," A/59/565 (December 2, 2004). ("Stopping the proliferation of [nuclear] weapons—and their potential use, by either State or non-State actions—must remain an urgent priority for collective security.") ("High Level Panel Report") *accessed at* http://www.un.org/secureworld.

11 Secretary of Defense Robert M. Gates, submitted statement to the Senate Armed Services Committee, at p. 3, January 27, 2009.

12 *Ibid.*

13 President Obama, Speech in Prague, Czech Republic, delivered April 5, 2009 ("Prague Speech"). Text of speech may be *accessed at* http://www.marketwatch.com/news/story/story.aspx?grid=9.7B61A1EE9A%2DAA02%2D.

14 *World at Risk: The Report of the Commission on the Prevention of Weapons of Mass Destruction Proliferation and Terrorism*, Vintage Books, at p. xv (New York 2008). ("Unless the world community acts decisively and with great urgency it is more likely than not that a weapon of mass destruction will be used in a terrorist attack somewhere in the world by the end of 2013.") ("World at Risk Report").

15 Gates, "Nuclear weapons and Deterrence in the 21st Century," speech delivered October 28, 2008 at the Carnegie Endowment for International Peace, transcript at p. 7 (emphasis added.) ("Gates Speech").

efforts at verifying the identity of enemies was given added impetus through pursuit of new technologies that could determine the forensic signature of a weapon.[16]

Apart from force employment doctrinal and practical measures, in the face of these dangers, America began to revisit the basic bargain in the Non-Proliferation Treaty ("NPT");[17] namely, to relinquish nuclear arms in exchange for nonproliferation by other states. The U.S. started to reconsider the need for nuclear weapons in earnest, perhaps for the first time since shortly after World War II. Over 60 years after we proposed the Baruch Plan[18] of international control over nuclear energy, some senior members of our defense establishment, on a bipartisan basis, now advocate eliminating them. These "new Abolitionists" urged the U.S. to move meaningfully toward establishing a "nuclear weapon free world."[19] This domestic political movement followed by almost a decade the U.N. General Assembly resolution urging specific steps to that end and the need for a new agenda.[20] As part of that path, there was express recognition that the "development of verification arrangements will be necessary for the maintenance of a world free of nuclear weapons . . . "[21] The U.N. stressed that underlying "the process towards the total elimination of nuclear weapons" would be a "non-discriminatory, multilateral and internationally and effectively *verifiable* treaty banning the production of fissile material for nuclear weapons . . .".[22] The resolution equally endorsed unconditional ratification without delay of the Comprehensive Test Ban Treaty ("CTBT"),

---

16 *Ibid.*

17 Text available at http://www.state.gov/t/isn/trty/16281.htm.

18 Text of the Baruch Plan presented to the United Nations Atomic Energy Commission, June 14, 1946, *accessed at* http://www.atomicarchive.com/Docs/Deterrence/BaruchPlan.shtml ("Baruch Plan").

19 *See, e.g.,* George Schultz, William Perry, Henry Kissinger, and Sam Nunn, *Toward a Nuclear Free World,* WALL ST. J., January 15, 2008, *available at* http://online.wsj.com/article/SB120036422673589947.html.

20 See, U.N.G.A. Resolution 54/54G, 69th Plenary Meeting, December 1, 1999 ("Nuclear-Weapon Free World Resolution").

21 *Ibid.* at Operational paragraph 17.

22 *Ibid.* at Preamble Paragraph 14 (emphasis added).

with continued observation of a moratorium on underground testing in the meantime.[23] Neither treaty has been ratified to date by America.

President Obama embraced in his electoral campaign the goal of eliminating all nuclear weapons as a central element in our nuclear policy. While he did not then address how or when to achieve it, the prospect of renewed efforts to ratify these treaties seemed likely. Immediately following his election, the European Union also began pushing again toward nuclear disarmament. It advanced various step-by-step initiatives, including a global ban on nuclear testing; embracing the dismantlement of nuclear bomb test sites; pushing for a universal inspection regime; and seeking a moratorium on the production of fissile material.[24] Thereafter, the U.S. President provided greater detail about American nuclear disarmament aspirations in his speech in Prague in April 2009. Characterizing the very existence of nuclear weapons as the "most dangerous legacy of the Cold War," the president observed:

> "[i]n a strange turn of history, the threat of global nuclear war has gone down, but the risk of nuclear attack has gone up. More nations have acquired these weapons. Testing has continued. Black market trade in nuclear secrets and nuclear naturals abound. The technology to build a bomb has spread. Terrorists are determined to buy, build or steal one. Our efforts to contain these dangers are centered on a global non-proliferation regime, but as more people and nations break the rules, we could reach the point where the unity cannot hold."[25]

Verification, of course, informs not only the substance of what rules are possible in meeting these risks, but also our judgments about adherence to them.

---

23 Testing in the atmosphere, outer space, and under water has long been banned under the 1963 Partial Test Ban Treaty. The text of the comprehensive treaty is found at 1456 United Nations Treaty Series ("U.N.T.S.") No. 24631.

24 *See* Steve Erdanger, *Europeans Seek to Revive Disarmament*, N.Y. TIMES, December 9, 2008.

25 Prague Speech, *supra* note 13. *See also* U.S. NATIONAL INTELLIGENCE COUNCIL, GLOBAL TRENDS 2025: A TRANSFORMED WORLD, NIC. 2008–003 (Nov. 2003) at p. 67 ("The Risk of nuclear weapon use over the next 20 years, although remaining very low, is likely to be greater than it is today as a result of several converging trends.") *accessed at* http://www.dni.gov./nic/NIC_2025_project.html. ("Global Trends Report").

The new American president expressly tied U.S. relinquishment of nuclear weapons to the existence of such weapons in the possession of others. Deterrence was linked in the initial declaratory policy statement only to them, and not to other types of WMD. With the recognition that reduction of our arsenal to the point of extinguishment will not be a quick process, the first step identified by President Obama is that of seeking a "new treaty that *verifiably* ends the production of fissile materials intended for use in state nuclear weapons."[26] There are dual focal points embraced in his approach: It was directed both at "more resources and authority to strengthen international inspections," along with real and immediate consequences for countries caught breaking the rules or trying to leave the NPT without cause.[27]

Other members of the Western defense establishment view the disarmament goal as extremely difficult to attain. The biggest hurdles seem two-fold: first, the proper scope of nuclear deterrence; and second, creation of the necessary political environment. In his initial public testimony for the new administration to the Senate Armed Services Committee, Secretary of Defense Gates clarified that "as long as the nations have nuclear weapons, the U.S. must maintain an arsenal of some level."[28] This position is consistent with America's legal obligation as a party to the NPT. Yet, this linkage of the nuclear deterrent only to that of others potentially represents too narrow a security policy in the view of many in the West. Indeed, a broader attitude toward deterrence was advanced in the U.S. Senate at the close of the century, and recognized at the end of the Bush Administration by Defense Secretary Gates. During the debate over ratification of the CTBT, our nuclear force was promoted as the guarantor of deterrence against *any* type of WMD attack. In particular, a lesson drawn from the first Gulf War was that Saddam Hussein decided against use of chemical or biological weapons on American troops because of our nuclear deterrent, coupled with a strong threat that we would use it.[29] As Senator Kyl

---

26   *Ibid.*

27   *Ibid.*

28   *See* Gates, *supra* note 11 at p. 7. *See also* Gates Speech, *supra* note 15 at p. 3.

29   *See, e.g.,* CTBT Senate Debate at p. S12534. Secretary Gates also confirmed the Iraqi example. *See* Gates Speech, *supra* note 15 at p. 4.

stated at that time in acknowledging the differences in post–Cold War conditions:

" . . . our nuclear weapons continue to serve as an essential hedge against a very uncertain future with both Russia and China. . . . *Equally important*, deterrence—backed by credible nuclear forces—remains the first line of defense against an even broader range of threats than in the past, including rogue states armed with weapons of mass destruction."[30]

An expansive American nuclear posture, if embraced as our WMD deterrent policy, would challenge the more narrow nuclear legal bargain of the NPT. This debate over the proper scope of nuclear deterrence seems destined to be revived as the new Administration moves toward revisiting ratification of arms control treaty regimes like the CTBT and Fissile Material Cut-off Treaty ("FMCT").

To explain, within the political spectrum comprising America's defense establishment, some adhere to the view that the key to disarmament realization requires a "fundamental transformation of the world political order."[31] As one group of experts concluded: "[T]he geopolitical conditions that would permit the global elimination of nuclear weapons do not currently exist."[32] As a result, their policy acceptance of the "zero option" nuclear disarmament proposal as a "long term goal" is conditional. Any policy shift toward a nuclear free world would necessitate maintenance of a nuclear deterrent. That deterrent would be "*appropriate to existing threats* until such time as verifiable international agreements are in place that could set the conditions for the final abolition of nuclear and other weapons of mass destruction."[33] Proponents of this view clearly embrace an expansive and continuing role for our nuclear deterrent. As a corollary, other adherents of this view also maintain international constraints on America's freedom of action to

---

30 *Ibid.* at p. S12535 (emphasis added).

31 *See, e.g.*, Congressional Commission on the Strategic Posture of the United States, Interim Report (December 15, 2008), at p. 9 ("Interim Strategic Report"). The 2009 Final Report may be *accessed at* http://www.usip.org/strategic-posture/final.html.

32 *See* Council on Foreign Relations Task Force Report No. 62, *U.S. Nuclear Weapons Policy*, April 2009 (CFR Press) ("CFR Task Force Report No. 62").

33 Interim Strategic Report, *supra* note 31 at p. 8.

defend itself would have to be resisted if they undermined our "ability to *verify* the reliability and effectiveness of [the] nuclear deterrent."[34] They contend the task remains to maintain, modernize, and sustain our nuclear forces until the need dissipates.[35] However, prior to the last election, Secretary Gates characterized as "bleak" the long-term prospect that our stockpile would continue to be "safe, secure, and reliable" without either a replacement warhead or physical testing.[36]

Regardless of the defensive scope encompassed by deterrence policy, verification demands became a two-edged sword by the turn of the century. It would be used not just for perfecting control or elimination of nuclear arms, but also for the preservation of their effectiveness while they exist to provide a deterrent. Nearly a decade following the Senate debate and rejection of the CTBT, many American nuclear policy makers continued to invoke verification as a critical need for maintaining the operational safety and reliability of our nuclear stockpile. Whether achieving continuing certainty about this goal will eventually require resumed physical testing still remains to be seen.[37]

Our threat definition in this century also portends a fundamental WMD defense policy shift. The contemplated shift from a focus on rational state actors bent on WMD deterrence and arms control to exploration of the prospect of disarmament, came amidst a rising concern over proliferating WMD accessibility to sub-state actors. Given the vast existing inventories of fissile material, chemical weapon precursors, and biological toxins, many security analysts believe it

---

34 John Bolton and John Yoo, *Restore the Senate's Treaty Power*, N.Y. TIMES, January 5, 2009, *accessed at* http://www.nytimes.com/2009/01/05bolton.html (emphasis added).

35 Interim Strategic Report, *supra* note 31 at p. 8 (citing the "Schlesinger Commission" recommendations).

36 Gates Speech, *supra* note 15 at p. 6.

37 Secretary Gates has stated that America would not need new physical testing to deploy a replacement warhead, since it was tested prior to the 1992 moratorium. But if there is no replacement program, then Secretary Gates maintains at some point a resumption in physical testing will be needed. *Ibid.* at p. 6.

as only a matter of time before some would fall into terrorist hands.[38] As the U.S. National Intelligence Council observed:

> "For those terrorist groups active in 2025, the diffusion of technologies and scientific knowledge will place some of the world's most dangerous capabilities within their reach."[39]

The concern that they could not be deterred from using such weapons, once possessed, impels the potential policy transformation toward disarmament to eliminate certain stockpiles, while reducing and better controlling others, so that they would not provide an accessible source for weapons for today's adversaries or those of tomorrow.

Yet, the challenges inherent in the contemplated WMD disarmament process would extend well beyond those encountered during the superpower bilateral arms control efforts of the Cold War. At the same time, the bedrock principle of action remains that existing and future arms control or disarmament agreements need be *verifiable*. President Reagan's political adage—"trust, but verify"[40]—retains continuing vitality, even as new threats emerged following dissolution of the "Evil Empire."

First, this change in the nature of our enemies yielded a shift in threat assessment. By late 2008, America's National Intelligence Council concluded that the risk of nuclear weapon use in the coming decades "is likely to be greater than it is today as a result of several converging trends."[41] Proliferation is foremost among those concerns, for erosion of the nuclear "taboo" is perceived to arise with the spread of nuclear technology and expertise. As the Congressional Commission on the Strategic Posture of the United States also observed in its December 2008 interim report:

> "It appears we are at a 'tipping point' in proliferation. If Iran and North Korea proceed unchecked to build nuclear arsenals, there is a serious possibility of a cascade of proliferation following. And as each new

---

38 *See* GLOBAL TRENDS REPORT, *supra* note 25 at p. 70.

39 *Ibid.* at p. 68.

40 Remarks on Signing the Intermediate Range Nuclear Forces Treaty, December 8, 1987, *accessed at* http://regan.utexas.edu/archives/speeches/1987/120887c.htm. Secretary Gates also recently endorsed the continuing importance of the need to verify arms control agreements. *See* Gates Speech, *supra* note 15 at p. 10 (answer to question).

41 *See* GLOBAL TRENDS REPORT, *supra* note 25 at p. 67.

nuclear power is added, the probability of a terror group getting a nuclear bomb increases."[42]

The nuclear terrorism threat is thus seen as being "strongly reinforced by proliferation." This conclusion is largely derived from the possibility that nuclear weapons might deliberately be passed on to terrorists, or stolen by them.[43] While this judgment is premised on twin threats of intentional or unintentional transfer, the risks arising from them are not necessarily the same. As one recent study on securing nuclear weapons concluded:

> "Conscious state decisions to transfer nuclear weapons or materials to terrorists are a small part of the overall risk of nuclear terrorism; hostile dictators focused on preserving their regimes are *highly* unlikely to hand over the greatest power they have ever acquired to groups they cannot control, in ways that might provoke retaliation that would destroy their regime forever."[44]

While the risk of intentional transfer is perceived as low, there is expert recognition that it is not nonexistent.[45] At the same time, intentional transfer to other rogue regimes, for money or a technology trade, is a less remote threat. Either way, though, the particular threat emanating from rogue regimes, such as Iran or North Korea, seems as susceptible to political inflation in gauging the security risks which any verification process must meet in seeking to disarm or control them, as it was with the Soviets.

In contrast, the prospect of nuclear or WMD theft through bribery, infiltration, coercion, or loss of control during the chaos of regime collapse, all are more highly plausible scenarios. They present a range of "militarily significant" risks. Open source material reveals a number of incidents where the security of nuclear material already has been breached. Troubling examples of this insecurity include both the attack

---

42   Interim Strategic Report, *supra* note 11 at pp. 4–5. *See also World at Risk Report, supra* note 14 at p. 18.

43   *Ibid.* at p. 9.

44   MATHEW BUNN, SECURING THE BOMB (2008) at p. XIV, *accessed at* www.nti.org/ e_research/cnwm/overview/cnwm_home.asp (emphasis added).

45   *Ibid.*

VERIFICATION IN AN AGE OF INSECURITY

in Pelindaba, South Africa in November 2007,[46] as well as the prior nuclear material seizures by Russian authorities in the 1990s, Georgian police in early 2006,[47] and most recently in Ukraine.[48] With access to weaponized fissile material, targeting by rogues or terrorists would likely be cities—not silos as in the Cold War. The delivery vehicle will be of little concern to them as long as it is effective, whether by suitcase, truck, ship, or otherwise. Given the proclivity for martyrdom missions, the safety of the weapons simply will not be a factor of high concern either for such adversaries,[49] as it is with other nuclear weapons states. Hence, traditional arms control measures, which focus on more easily verifiable "substitutes" for weapons, such as delivery systems, as well as safety, become less meaningful in guarding against WMD threats from sub-state actors.

Accordingly, the resulting vulnerability to such threats needs to be factored into any future nuclear weapon reduction or disarmament agreements, or WMD control regimes. In turn, the resulting verification tasks differ with circumstance. For example, the verification needs for an agreement with a North Korean regime in totalitarian control of its people are not the same as those with one losing its grip, or one in danger of collapsing. The same can be said of governmental upheaval or overthrow in Pakistan.[50] The resulting insistence on degrees of intrusion requires fresh consideration in any control or disarmament regime with respect to these unstable nuclear weapons powers. In each scenario, the inspection needs in a verification system can potentially vary.

---

46   South Africa stores weapons-grade enriched uranium there. For a description of the attack, see WORLD AT RISK REPORT, *supra* note 14 at pp. 13–14.

47   *Ibid.* at pp. 15–16.

48   *See, e.g.*, Levy, *Ukraine Says 3 Tried to Sell Bomb Material*, N.Y. TIMES, April 15, 2009, *accessed at* http://www.nytimes.com/2009/04/15/world/europe/15ukraine. html?ref=global-home. A nuclear trafficking database of incidents and significant events is maintained with respect to former Soviet republics and may be *accessed at* http:/www.nti.org/db/nistraff.

49   *See* K. BAILEY, WALL ST. J., October 12, 1999 (reprinted in Senate CTBT Debate at p. S12393).

50   *See, e.g.*, A. Sawyer, *Pakistan Strife Raises U.S. Doubts on Nuclear Arms*, N.Y. TIMES (May 4, 2009) *accessed at* http://www.nytimes.com/2009/05/04)/world/ asia/04nuke.html.

The degrees of intrusiveness could be structured for activation by differ-ent circumstantial triggers. This could be done in similar fashion to the tiered approaches to monitoring declaration accuracy and compliance in some WMD regimes.

The increasing risk assessment also extends to non-nuclear types of WMD, particularly biological weapons. Those weapons were originally viewed as having little military utility. Rather, military analysts and civilian officials in the U.S. perceived them as "unpredictable and potentially uncontrollable."[51] Given our lack of military experience with these weapons, the U.S. determined in the early 1970s that our acceptance of the prohibitions of a global ban on them would not deny us a "militarily viable option." As a result, the inability to verify the international treaty banning them was deemed to be less important.[52] Yet with the advances in bioengineering of the ensuing decades, a reassessment of military utility and threat is ongoing. The globalization of the life science industry increases the accessibility of pathogens that can be used for attack, even while they are studied for defensive purposes, including countermeasures. Indeed, in early 2003, the "Project BioShield Act" was passed in the U.S. to accelerate the process of research, development, and implementation of countermeasures against bioterror. Still, over five years later, in late 2008, a Congressional bipartisan commission concluded that "terrorists are *more likely* to be able to obtain and use a biological weapon than a nuclear weapon."[53] While radiological and chemical weapons also pose mass casualty potential, they are at significantly reduced levels of damage from the more potent capabilities of nuclear and biological weapons. Hence, the latter threats are and will continue to be our primary risk focus, both in accessing and seeking verifiable constraints on WMD.

Still, security analysts and the populace alike tend to focus on (and fear more) the potential emergence of new nuclear states through continu-ing erosion of the nonproliferation regime. The specter in this century

---

51   See the testimony of Fred Iklé, then director of the Arms Control and Disarmament Agency, before the U.S. Senate Committee on Foreign Relations, Hearings of the Prohibition of Chemical and Biological Weapons, 93rd Cong., 2nd Sess., Washington, D.C. (U.S. Gov't P.O.) at pp. 15–16.

52   *Ibid.*

53   WORLD AT RISK REPORT, *supra* note 14 at p. xv (emphasis added).

is a "cascade" of them.[54] Three potential sources are identified: those spawned by Iran's increasing nuclear capacity;[55] proliferation from the diaspora resulting from partial dismantlement of A.Q. Khan's proliferation network; or from transfers by rogues like North Korea. While the nuclear danger, particularly that arising from proliferation, is deeply ingrained in American citizens and increasingly others globally, the public warning bells from the biological weapons threat are really just beginning to sound. Meanwhile, development of an effective verification regime to enforce the multilateral ban over biological weapons remains elusive. As a result, some in the defense establishment continue to view the nuclear arsenal as the principal deterrent to the use of other WMD against the U.S. or its allies.

Today the verification issues resulting from the primary threats of nuclear and biological weapons are developing in a WMD arms-control legal environment whose structure and precedents were products of much different security strategies, and to some extent needs as well. While possession of nuclear weapons was limited, for example, in the 20th century during the superpower confrontation, the Non-Proliferation Treaty's asymmetric regime permitted non-weapon states to acquire nuclear know-how and infrastructure for peaceful use. That legal regime left a number of nations at the threshold of weaponization[56] as "virtual" nuclear powers. With relatively little effort today, a large number of countries could "break out" through treaty withdrawal to transform peaceful energy use through remaining technology buffers into a weapons program, at least where there is political will to do so. Even a primitive state like North Korea repeatedly exploded a nuclear device, which the United Nations Security Council condemned as a threat to international peace and security.[57]

Equally, the legal framework governing chemical and biological weapons of mass destruction left much to be desired in constraining their

---

54   *Ibid. See also* High Level Panel Report, *supra* note 10.

55   *Ibid.* at p. 70.

56   IAEA Director General, Dr. Mohamed El Baradei, *Nuclear Non-Proliferation: Global Security in a Rapidly Changing World*, (21 June, 2004) at p. 3 *accessed at* http://www.idea.org/NewsCenter/Statements/2004/ebsp004n004.html.

57   *See, e.g.*, U.N. Security Council Resolutions 1718 (2006) and 1874 (2009) *accessible at* http://www.un.org/documents/scres.htm.

acquisition and potential use by sub-state actors and irrational regimes. Indeed, the 1972 treaty[58] providing the centerpiece of the global biological weapons-control regime left out verification entirely, for traditional measures were simply regarded as ineffective.[59] Thus, only a generation ago American and Western policy makers were willing to outlaw biological weapons even where there was a gap in our ability to verify. While abandoning chemical and biological weapons by treaty, we retained our nuclear weapons, and they could be used in response to such attacks.[60] Yet, a little more than a quarter century later, the U.S. Senate rejected a largely verifiable comprehensive test ban on nuclear tests, where concealable low-yield tests were then beyond the ability of national technical means to monitor with certainty, even when used together with a complementary international regime; but that was also a situation where the viability of our nuclear arsenal might erode. With that rejection, we saw yet another aspect of verification's role reflected; that is, as an element of the ratification standard applied by the U.S. Senate regarding the propriety of entry into a WMD arms-control treaty.

In the current risky environment, verification methods continue to evolve with technological advances. They have been a focal point of analysis and development through decades of arms-control efforts, particularly in recent years. Still, even greatly improved seismological devices only measure the earth's vibration, not an event's compliance with a treaty's obligations. Signal identification has subjective components, introducing an element of uncertainty into judgments about events, particularly in uncalibrated areas. Yet, it is the ability to identify, not merely detect, that provides a key element of verification. Moreover, to date there has not been sufficient concurrent attention to changes in other underpinnings of verification that may be impelled by the shifting security paradigm. In short, how do new threats impact verification

---

58 Convention on the Prohibition of the Development, Production and Stockpiling of Bacteriological and Toxin Weapons and on Their Destruction, April 10, 1972, 2U U.S.T. 583, 1015 U.N.T.S. 163.

59 World at Risk Report, *supra* note 14 at p. xviii.

60 *See* International Court of Justice Advisory Opinion, Legality of the Threat or Use of Nuclear Weapons, 8 July, 1996 (A/51/218, annex), 35 I.L.M. 809 (1996).

needs that both facilitate agreement as well as allow our leadership to assess compliance—now and in the future? Framed differently, will our intolerance for uncertain compliance drive us toward enhanced verification approaches; or act as brakes to the WMD disarmament process or our ability to diffuse conflicts with Iran or North Korea? Should it? These issues are and will be among the basic elements of any policy analysis with respect to verification's future role in assessing compliance with WMD arms control and disarmament. In determining where we are headed, it is instructive to look backward at where we have been.[61]

---

61 See Verification Report of the Secretary General, *supra* note 3 at p. 59 ¶234 (Conclusion: ". . . In thinking through the design of verification regimes for future agreements, it will be important to draw on the lessons of past verification experiences as well as to reflect on the changes that are taking place in the world.").

CHAPTER II

THE EVOLUTION OF CERTAINTY

A. INTRODUCTION

In the post-Cold War era, the U.S. emerged from a military position of strategic parity to one of dominance. America's national strategy is to maintain substantial advantages in military strength against potential foes.[62] However, a recognized downside to U.S. relative dominance is that it impels others to seek to rely on WMD to counter that strength. In turn, America relies on its nuclear arsenal to deter any adversarial use of chemical or biological weapons. As the U.S. moves forward, exploring and evaluating nuclear and other arms-control agreements to serve its national security interests, America will continue to gauge treaty verification. Yet, just as the nature of threats to the U.S. changed with the end of the superpower confrontation, so too, demands on the ability to verify evolve in gauging what suffices. The content of historical verification standards began to shift at the end of the last century, which is well illustrated as part of the ratification standard by which the U.S. Senate rejected the Comprehensive Test Ban Treaty. The CTBT debate linked the various ways in which verification has been employed for decades as a measuring process; namely, whether (i) existing arms control constraints are being violated; (ii) our own nuclear deterrent is safe and reliable; and (iii) proposed arms control or disarmament agreements should be embraced. In each context, the measure of certainty or risk that the U.S. is willing to countenance reveals the demands to place on a verification scheme.

B. THE SUPERPOWER ERA

The history of American arms-control efforts for most of the second half of the 20th century reflected a bipartisan embrace of "adequate

---

62 *See, e.g.*, President Obama, Remarks of the President at the United States Naval Academy Commencement, May 22, 2009 ("We will maintain America's military dominance.") *accessed at* http://www.whitehouse.gov/the_press_office/Remarks-by-the President-at-U.S.-Naval-Academy-commencement.

verification" as the proper verification standard. Deviation from that standard was measured by "military significance" in making compliance judgments. The impact of cheating, or the prospect of it, on the overall balance of strategic forces of the superpowers gave content to the standard Today, America's nuclear establishment often continues to frame its verification debate in terms of the adequacy standard. But while this standard was linked to "parity" with the Soviet Union as the original security organizing principle, we effectively shifted from "significance" to "utility" as the gauge for the military measure of adequacy in an era of dominance. Our tolerance for risk, or lack of it, subtly changed because the demand of certainty became more rigorous with respect to verifying the reliability and safety of our nuclear deterrent. The prospect of further, substantial cuts in our nuclear arsenal will likely necessitate further reconsideration of the standard as well; that is, the deeper the cuts, the closer our return to parity, or the temptation of achieving it to our adversaries. In these circumstances, re-calibrating the metrics of advantage will be tied to our risk assessment. The accuracy of it, with potential deep cuts, will probably tighten the standard of certainty required of any verification process in its three uses. Also, the changing nature of the source of threats will likewise impact how rigorously we apply our evolving verification standard for risk tolerance as we strive for "effectiveness" in monitoring to make future compliance judgments.

(i) The Role of Parity

In the superpower era, our analytic approach to verification was premised on the assumption that if a new weapon was involved, there would be long lead time from development through testing, training, and finally, deployment. Once identified by national technical means, this allowed for timely reaction, such as military adjustment or, potentially, treaty termination or rejection. At that time, the assumption could be misplaced where the evasion of agreed-upon limits was quantitatively driven, rather than qualitatively—that is, more weapons of a particular type were retained than allowed, rather than modernized or replaced. The compliance failure was strategically insignificant, however, if it did not really impact the military parity of the treaty parties, which was the strategic organizing principle of action. After all, the superpowers' agreements were carefully calibrated and controlled to meet a bottom-line goal of "substantial equivalence" in overall force projection power. Equally, as long as our nuclear forces could fulfill their mission, marginal cheating was of no particular military consequence, and certainly not "significant" in compromising parity. The deviation still would be regarded as a violation, especially when assessed by a strict verification standard, which is simply asking whether or not there was a violation. In contrast, in the post-Cold War era, the measure of significance in verification became divorced from parity, for there was no longer parity with American military might. However, the resulting changes from that shift were not recognized, because while the U.S. paid homage to "adequate" verification, it shifted to "effectiveness" as the actual measure by focusing on the existence of a violation alone.

Our prior assumptions about verification processes were also tied to the Deterrence Theory; namely, that the prospect of certain nuclear retaliation provided a credible deterrent to an attack. That certainty could be relative yet effective in the superpower context. A surprise first strike at the force levels employed left a surviving retaliatory capacity too punishing to invite or chance. That risk remained certain. Today, with the expected future push to reduce the nuclear force levels of the U.S. and Russia considerably lower than those presently existing,[63] the range of acceptable certainty will likely be more constrained than in the past. A difference arises though from the legitimate expectation that the risk factor should be driven more by military than political significance, as sometimes occurred in the past, at least in circumstances where there is a diminished ideological component to our adversarial relationship with Russia and China.[64] Still, if disarmament eliminates nuclear forces at some point, either by design or erosion, then the countervailing force to deter cheaters becomes suspect. Consider if America had to rely only on its conventional superiority to deter employment of chemical weapons against our forces, as Saddam Hussein contemplated in the first Gulf War. We know from debriefing captured high-level

---

63   *See* Prague Speech, *supra* note 13.

64   That is not always the case with all potential nuclear foes now. For example, America is the "Great Satan" to Iran's theocratic leadership and it is a "rogue" nation in our view, for it fails to comply with basic norms regarding nuclear uses, proliferation, support of terrorists, etc.

Iraqi officials that our threat to employ "overwhelming force" deterred him. But a future where verification gives less certainty of deterrence, then cheating will call into question both the preservation of our force advantage, as well as the ability not to have to employ it. Increased proliferation of other types of WMD is also feared in the absence of America's nuclear deterrent to offset its vast conventional superiority.

(ii) The Adequacy of Verification

Certainty, or absence of risk, remained at the core of any compliance assessment based on verification processes in the Cold War period. The *reduction* of uncertainty in compliance was always an issue in U.S.-Soviet arms-control negotiations and agreements. Over time, the Soviets surprisingly shifted from resisting compliance-related intrusion to actually embracing it, thereby increasing verification certainty. This process started with satellite surveillance, the legality of which was initially contested by the Soviets, but then soon conceded. Monitoring by national technical means for both superpowers from outside their sovereign areas thus became a vehicle permitting entry into early arms-control agreements. The next step was gradual enshrinement of a principle of non-interference with National Technical Means (NTM) of verification. This principle found expression in early bilateral accords, like the two Strategic Arms Limitation (SALT) and Anti-Ballistic Missile (ABM) Treaties. For example, both the SALT I and ABM treaties expressly reference NTMs and utilization of them in a manner consistent with international law to provide assurance of compliance verification. So long as the NTMs are used for treaty purposes and are consistent with international law, each side committed to not interfere with them. Similarly, each side was enjoined against using "deliberate concealment measures" to impede verification by NTMs of compliance.[65]

On-site inspection experienced an East-West breakthrough in the mid-1980s in the so-called Stockholm Document of the Conference on Security and Cooperation in Europe.[66] That agreement regarding on-site inspection occurred within the framework of conventional force

---

65   *See, e.g.*, ABT Treaty at Art. 12 ¶1 and SALT I at Art. V ¶¶1–3.

66   *Accessed at* http://www.OSCE.org/fsc/22154.html.

VERIFICATION IN AN AGE OF INSECURITY

maneuvers. It was part of an effort to reduce the danger of conflict arising out of miscalculations about military activity. As a result, a transparency measure calculated to build confidence in a multinational setting provided the introduction for cooperative intrusion. By the time of the negotiation of the Intermediate-Range Nuclear Force Agreement a year later, in 1987, the Soviets not only accepted on-site inspection, but they were also prepared to exceed the openness of the U.S. in that regard. We actually "blinked" at the time, primarily out of concern over the potential of the Soviets to abuse verification inspections for intelligence-gathering purposes.[67] As a result, we accepted less compliance certainty at the same time that we accepted the agreement. We did so while being uncertain of even the number of SS-20 missiles the Soviets actually had for their nuclear stockpile.[68] The rationale for accepting reduced certainty stemming from verification deficiencies was two-fold: (i) inspection was not likely to turn up violations by the Soviets; and (ii) any cheating would not be "militarily significant" in terms of the strategic parity between the foes.

Still, the *elimination* of verification uncertainty was never embraced as a compliance-related goal by the U.S. throughout the decades of superpower competition. We recognized that the prospects for "absolute" verification were few and far between. If, for example, we agreed with the Russians that a certain number of missiles would be destroyed by each side, that could be monitored with precision; but if the agreement was not to have more than a certain number of launchers, some extras could easily be hidden. So, in most instances, the U.S. was prepared to accept less-than-certain proof regarding the detectability of arms-control agreement violations in its dealings with the Soviet superpower. Testifying at the SALT II Hearings before the Senate Foreign Relations Committee, then Secretary of Defense Harold Brown acknowledged:

> "Our impressive monitoring capability does not mean that we can be certain of detecting every conceivable treaty violation—or every conceivable change in Soviet strategic forces—as soon as it occurs. That is

---

67   *See, e.g.*, Michael R. Gordon, *Negotiating the Arms Treaty: Verification Issue Proved Thorny*, N.Y. TIMES (January 28, 1988) *accessed at* http://query.nytimes.com/gst/fullpage.html?res=94ODE3DE103CF93BA15752COA96E94.

68   Senate CTBT Debate at p. S12543.

an impossible and unnecessary standard to meet, either for verification or for intelligence generally. No arms limitation agreement can ever be absolutely verifiable."[69]

The Senate never sought perfect verification as a requirement of treaty ratification in the superpower era. Rather, in the context of strategic parity, America insisted upon only "adequate verification." We sought to determine how well we could verify, and whether our security would be threatened by undetected cheating. From the late 1970s onward, we simply pursued a practical safeguard. The standard was succinctly framed by Secretary Brown as:

> ". . . whether we can identify attempted evasion if it occurs on a large enough scale to pose a *significant* risk, and whether we can do so in time to mount a sufficient response. . . ."[70]

Thus, verification required a high confidence level at the timely detectability of militarily significant cheating that could threaten our security.

The metric seemingly changed at the century's end with the diminution in operating nuclear weapons systems and the overall number and types of weapons. Coupled with the expected natural degradation in confidence from chemical degeneration of our untested nuclear devices over time, we were left with a need for greater certainty. There was simply less margin for error, for the components of our nuclear weapons systems degrade in unpredictable ways. At the same time, while many saw diminished need for reliance on nuclear weapons, others saw them as even more important, to confront the non-nuclear WMD arsenals of our foes as the post-Cold War era emerged. Moreover, deterrence of rogue states armed with WMD has been, now is, and will be very different than our understanding of it in the Cold War, when deterrence comprised an overwhelming retaliatory capacity with a nuclear response for mutually assured destruction.

---

69 *See* SALT II Hearings, Part 2, 96th Congress, 1st Session, Washington D.C. (U.S. Gov't. P.O.) at p. 241.

70 *Ibid.* at 244 (emphasis added). *See also* Senate CTBT Debate at p. S12546 ("'effective verification' is an intentionally vague political term of art, but as the old saying goes, we all 'know it when we see it,' for the CTBT, it should mean we have confidence that we can detect within hours or days any clandestine nuclear test that would provide a disaster with militarily significant weapons information.").

In between the establishment of adequate verification as the standard by which to judge the superpower competition, and its apparent refinement after the U.S. came to dominate (with parity maintenance no longer a principle of action), there were years of rhetorical challenge to the standard. As a result, more of a political component became ingrained in the content of the basic verification debate. "Trust but verify" became the mantra. During the Reagan presidency, the administration pushed further in seeking "effective" verification. The administration stated:

> "In order for arms control to have meaning and credibly contribute to national security and to global or regional stability, it is essential that all parties to agreements fully comply with them. Strict compliance with all provisions of arms control agreements is fundamental, and this Administration will not accept anything less."[71]

In doing so, it maintained that treaty violations are "significant" even when not a threat to national security. Yet, the Reagan administration never actually shifted during the 1980s from a "military significance" test of treaty evasion to a more exacting standard of violation alone to seek to trigger material breach and termination,[72] or to use it as a ratification test. In reacting to violations, the balance was ultimately struck in favor of an arms control process that continued to seek only the ability to detect significant departures in a timely enough manner to permit countermeasures. This approach denied the cheater a meaningful military edge. Other retaliatory options were raised and sometimes considered, however, such as the suspension of treaties or selective provisions of them. But there was a clear political component to the "effective verification" equation because it shifted attention from the question— whether the Soviets cheat enough for it to matter—to the more basic issue of whether they were in fact cheating. However, even the more

---

71 See U.S. Department of State Bulletin, "President Reagan's Report on Soviet Noncompliance with Arms' Control Agreements," (unclassified version) at p. 2 (June 1987) (quoting December 23, 1985 report), *accessed at* http://findarticles.com/p/articles/mi_M1079/is_v87/ai_5107237.

72 For example, Richard Perle, then Assistant Secretary of Defense for International Security, in his response at the Kennedy School of Government in 1986 to a question by the author concerning the standard by which we gauge materiality of treaty violations by the Soviets for termination purposes, identified "military significance" as the appropriate standard in a National Public Radio broadcast.

basic question was not maintained in a ratification context. The difference between "adequate" and "effective" verification in the INF Treaty ratification context became a meaningless difference. The chief negotiator of that treaty, when asked to explain any real distinction to the standards, admitted that " . . . the definitions are not that different."[73] To some extent, the distinction lay not in the requisite certainty of violations or their detectability, but rather in the methodology, for the effectiveness tended to focus on the particular arms control regime itself, rather than the threats to strategic security arising from the overall military balance.[74] While there were overlapping circles in terms of military significance, there were also times where they did not necessarily coincide. The significance of the difference manifested itself in the CTBT ratification debate in the late 1990s.

C. THE POST-COLD WAR PERIOD

(i) Enhanced Certainty

With the Soviet Union's demise, the maintenance of strategic parity soon followed as an organizing principle of action. From a verification standpoint, the "military significance" component of the adequate verification standard morphed as well: the risk associated with altering the strategic balance yielded to the less rigorous demand of the "military utility" consideration within a particular weapons system or arms control regime. Mere treaty violations, regardless of significance, retained continuing importance following America's ascent to dominance after the dissolution of the Soviet Union. This was particularly evident during the CTBT Senatorial ratification debate. Treaty opponents attached political significance to any low-level cheating without ever really addressing its military significance, at least in the way that the concept had previously been employed in the context of *strategic* military threat. Through much of the debate, the measurement of the *effectiveness* of verification seems to evolve to the ability to detect violations, regardless of their ultimate military significance. This shift in

---

73   See Testimony of Ambassador Gilmore in response to questioning by Senator Nunn, Senate Armed Services Committee (25 February, 1988).

74   *Cf.* Chevrier, *Verifying the Unverifiable: Lessons from the Biological Weapons Convention*, 9 POLITICS AND THE LIFE SCIENCES, 93, 96 (1990) ("The difference is in the *process* by which the verification judgment is made.")

measurement recognized that the ability to detect was militarily useful because mere violation may still erode the U.S. military advantage.[75] Hence, utility replaced significance as the *de facto* measure, essentially at the tactical rather than strategic level, despite ostensible homage to the traditional rubric employed throughout the debate.

Within the CTBT context, a core opposition argument was that a strict zero-yield agreement would be unverifiable. Because of limits on technical monitoring, there could be inconsistent observance below the detectability threshold.[76] This difficulty created the specter of adversarial development of low-yield weapons for possible tactical use on a country's *own* soil.[77] CTBT opponents generally contended that the CBCT permitted greater certainty by our adversaries in further developing their operating nuclear systems. This created additional risk for us because it left us with greater uncertainty in regards to our tactical advantage through conventional superiority; at the same time, it portended no shift in the strategic balance.[78]

However, a telling aspect of "militarily significance" of the verification factor in the CTBT debate was that America would be left with uncertainty in the efficacy of its *own* operating systems. This ambiguity, rather than the possibility of cheating by an adversary, potentially compromised America's strategic advantage. For example, expert testimony by a director of one of the U.S. nuclear laboratories, stated:

> "I and others who are, or have been, responsible for the safety and reliability of the U.S. stockpile of nuclear weapons have testified to this obvious conclusion [that testing is the preferred methodology] many times in the past. *To forego that validation through testing is, in short, to live with uncertainty.*"[79]

---

75   *Cf., e.g.*, Senate CTBT Debate at pp. S12261; S12279; S12340; S12389; S12393; S12402–03; S12536 and S12546 *with* S12376 and S12543 (Senate Intelligence Committee formulation in the INF ratification debate).

76   *See* Testimony of C. Paul Robanson, then director of Sandia National Laboratory, before the Senate Armed Services Committee, quoted in CTBT Treaty Debate at p. S12529.

77   *See, e.g.*, CTBT Senate Debate at p. S12349–50.

78   *Ibid.*

79   *Ibid.* at p. S12529 (emphasis added).

The fear was that the U.S. advantage of strategic nuclear dominance could be eroded gradually if America did not engage in physical testing. There was an element of continuity in this position. A decade earlier, President Reagan had rejected a nuclear test ban or limitations beyond those that had been agreed upon then. In a 1988 report, nuclear testing was characterized as "*indispensable* to maintaining the credible nuclear deterrent. . . . As long as we must depend on nuclear weapons for our fundamental security, nuclear testing will be *necessary*."[80] For decades, it is only through testing that reliability and assurance of improved safety, and effectiveness in modifications to meet evolving threats and technological surprise could be achieved. Given the prospect of deep reductions in nuclear weapons with the Soviets and later the Russians, testing was perceived to be even more important for certainty about reliability. The reluctance to embrace a test moratorium carried through the early 1990s until legislative restrictions on testing were imposed. The nuclear test cutoff blocked implementation of a planned test ban readiness program, which contemplated a number of yearly tests to try to prove whether or not computer calculation programs and simulation would reliably replace testing. In other words, the U.S. had planned on verifying its own verification of operating systems, but instead opted for a moratorium.

The Stockpile Stewardship Program,[81] which was initiated without testing for verification, uses simulations and computer modeling to replace physical measurements in testing nuclear weapons. Doing so is critical to retain certainty that those weapons will function as designed. We know from open sources that approximately one third of weapons introduced into the U.S. stockpile between 1985 and the moratorium needed post-deployment tests for troubleshooting purposes.

80　*See* Report to Congress entitled "The Relationship between Progress in Other Areas of Arms Control and More Stringent Limitations on Nuclear Testing" (quoted in CTBT Senate debate at p. S12385 (emphasis added).

81　According to the U.S. Department of Energy, the program essentially involves the maintenance of nuclear weapons without physical testing. It was established pursuant to Public Law 103-160 (the Fiscal Year 1994 National Defense Authorization Act). In the absence of physical testing the program seeks to understand the stockpile; assess issues relating to its aging; maintain weapons as required; and assure an enduring infrastructure for the nuclear deterrent. *See* http://www.nv.doe.gov/nationalsecurity/stewardship/default.htm.

　　　　　　　　　　　　　　　VERIFICATION IN AN AGE OF INSECURITY

Although the U.S. weapons were tested and believed to be reliable, an overwhelming 75 percent of the problems that were discovered in that time period were only learned through actual nuclear tests.[82] As a result, CTBT opponents noted that in 1992, a series of tests were proposed to devise methodologies and to create databases in order to verify stockpile stewardship once actual tests were banned.[83] However, these tests never took place, thereby precluding the most certain way to proving simulated accuracy. Compounding this gap in verifying America's substitute system was the fact that the data from past tests did not address all of the concerns arising from an aging arsenal. Finally, the security of past data was less than certain in a new age of computer espionage. To illustrate, even the legacy codes of the U.S. test program were thought to have been stolen by China prior to the Senate consideration of the CTBT. Thus, the future specter of an adversary re-writing U.S. data in real-time simulated testing raises doubt about the accuracy of the predictions of the viability of the arsenal.

The verification of reliability merely through scientific computer testing, simulation, and noncritical explosions, carried a continuous risk. At the same time, other nations are similarly constrained; this also compromises adversaries' certainty in their stockpiles in the absence of clandestine testing. The simulation method has now been employed for nearly two decades, and the question continues to be whether it is an acceptable way to verify an arsenal, and if so, for how long.[84] The means to verify America's arsenal had only progressed from embryonic development into its adolescence at the time of ratification consideration in 1999. Still, in 1996, a B-61–7 nuclear bomb was successfully modified into a B-61-Mod V earth-penetrating weapon without physical testing. While the modification only involved a hardening of the device's outer casing, it provided greater ability to strike hardened targets or underground biological weapons facilities.[85] This demonstrated some

---

82   *Ibid.* at p. S12518.

83   *See* the Signing Statement of President for the Fiscal Year 1993 Energy and Water Development Appropriations Act on October 2, 1992 (seeking new legislation permitting modest testing for strict purposes) (*reprinted at Ibid.* p. S12514).

84   Secretary Gates publicly recognized the dilemma at the end of the Bush Administration. *See* Gates Speech, *supra* note 15 at p. 6.

85   *Ibid.* at p. S12532.

ability to adapt U.S. weapons to evolving challenges without physical testing. The anticipated difficulty though is trying to keep pace with the challenges opponents would present in the future.[86] For example, the Russians were known to have created a new center in the Ural Mountains under 1,000 feet of granite that could not be held at risk. Thus, while the proposed development and deployment of a replacement warhead based on pre-1992 testing[87] would meet the concern of reliability, it would not necessarily meet the challenge of changing threats. Among those threats could be utilizing undetected low-yield tests. Although they might be of only tactical concern and not suffice for perfecting warhead miniaturization technology, if *decoupled*[88] then the magnitude of cheating could have militarily significant implications potentially, particularly as nuclear arsenals are further reduced. For this reason, in all likelihood, Secretary Gates' endorsement of CTBT ratification was expressly tied to the "adequate verification" standard.[89]

Nevertheless, the verification challenge then and now actually has two distinct components: (i) the ability to detect violations by cheaters and the states remaining outside the controlling regimes[90]; *and* (ii) the ability to verify the reliability and safety of America's nuclear deterrent. During the CTBT ratification debate, there was some focus on erosion of the U.S. strategic advantage in terms of an ability to detect cheating. As the then secretary of defense stated:

> "Is it possible for states to cheat on the Treaty without being detected? The answer is yes. We would not be able to detect every evasively

---

86   *Ibid.* at p. S12535.

87   The Bush plan for warhead modernization was based on a previously tested design. *See generally*, Pincus, *Gates Suggests New Arms Deal With Russia*, Wash. Post at p. A9 (10/29/08).

88   Decoupling basically involves muffling seismic shocks either through natural conditions (*e.g.*, caves) or mining technology. Such techniques, if exploited, allow a nation to increase the yield without getting caught doing so. The United States proved this in a 1960 experiment. *See* Frank J. Gaffney Jr., *The Flawed Test Ban Treaty*, The New Republic (October 25, 1999).

89   *See* Gates Speech, *supra* note 15 at p. 8 (answer to audience question).

90   The prospect of military significance attaching to a nation remaining outside the regime was relatively low. That is because the treaty would not come into force by its express terms without all nuclear capable countries—44 then in number— joining the regime.

conducted nuclear test. And from a national security perspective, we do not need to. But I believe that the United States will be able to detect a level of testing, the yield and number of tests, by which a state could undermine the U.S. nuclear deterrent."

In framing the answer in that manner, the secretary of defense essentially invoked the "military significance" standard of the superpower era. While President Clinton maintained that the treaty was also "effectively verifiable," a majority of the Senate rejected his view. They were unwilling to live with uncertainty from potential cheating, as well as the inability to verify the continuing viability of our nuclear deterrent and position of relative dominance.

Opposition concerns over the detectability of low-yield test evasion was raised throughout the CTBT debate. By the close of the debate at century's end, the politicization of verification in the 1980s ultimately lead to shifting the focus of certainty on to the fact of violation in various tactical applications. The military "utility" of cheating thereby became an element of the verification ratification standard. Yet, a decade earlier, at the outset of the standard's "re-interpretation" in the mid 1980s, the initial shift was confined merely to compliance assessment of actual arms-control treaty implementation. The impact of the shift was only indirectly felt on disarmament considerations. The record of Soviet violations and patterns of compliance merely provided context for the Senate ratification assessment with respect to the elimination of a ban of a class of weapons through the proposed INF Treaty. Prior violations did not serve to change the substance of the verification standard as a criterion for ratification where strategic parity was still the controlling principle, nor did the inability to verify the number of SS-20 missiles with certainty derail treaty ratification. While it was recognized that there were ways to elude the confines of the INF treaty, none were deemed "militarily significant," and they did not block the limited disarmament contemplated by the INF treaty. Hence, the "adequate verification" standard for treaty purposes involving partial disarmament of nuclear forces remained tied to "military significance" in a strategic context of relative parity at that time.

A little over ten years later, however, the politicized restrictive standard of "effective verification" resurfaced in the CTBT context. The heightened verification requirement, as originally articulated and linked to the fact of violations, intruded into the ratification judgment itself this time. While not expressly limiting the standard to consideration of the treaty, the substance of this approach substantially influenced the Senate's expedited consideration and rejection of the CTBT in 1999. In the very limited Senate debate on ratification, as in the fleeting hearings that preceded it,[91] the central focus of treaty opponents was also framed in terms of the lack of *complete* verifiability. This represented not only the application of the "effective" verification standard, but also the threat to establish a ratification requirement that approached in effect "absolute" rather than "high" certainty.

Reduced to essentials, the attack on verification of the complete test ban itself was directed primarily at (i) clandestine low-yield testing below a kiloton; and (ii) masked testing through decoupling techniques. To a much lesser degree, there was also a separate concern over "unattended" high-yield tests in the deep ocean where no nation was visibly involved. In the ratification debate, the political price demanded for approval was essentially the *elimination* of uncertainty. Opponents argued they were without confidence that in the foreseeable future, *any and all* nuclear explosions proliferated under the treaty could be detected. Neither America's NTMs nor the international monitoring regime established by the treaty could eliminate all uncertainty. The consequence was two-fold. First, it would potentially allow new weapons states to emerge. Second, existing weapons states could covertly improve the development of their tactical weapons, with some risk of strategic enhancement through testing at sufficient levels masked by decoupling so that they would be at unavailable identification levels.

There was no dispute that U.S. national technical means were incapable of verifying very low yield testing at the time of the CTBT ratification debate. Exact thresholds were classified then and remain so, but public

---

91   For example, in comparison to the 14 hours of general debate on the CTBT following one (long) hearing day by the Foreign Relations Committee, three in Government Affairs and three in Armed Services, there were 38 days of debate on the Panama Canal Treaty, and a total of 55 days on the Treaty of Versailles. See CTBT Senate Debate at p. S12533. The INF Treaty took 23 days of hearings and 9 days of floor consideration. The START I Treaty took 5 days of debate after 19 days of hearings. The 1972 ABM Treaty took 8 days of hearings and 18 days of debate. The 1997 Chemical Weapon Convention took three days of debate after 14 days of hearings. *Ibid.* at p. S12508 (collecting additional treaty consideration periods). *Cf., e.g., ibid.* at p. S12509 (Senator Helms).

sources reflected an inability to detect nuclear explosions at a level of anywhere from one to a few kilotons or below in yield.[92] On the open source record before the Senate, decoupled tests were also beyond monitoring by a factor as high as seventy.[93] That much was certain, but we could not be assured that such testing was, in fact, occurring. Testing of this nature by the Russians on Novaya Zemlya Island in the Arctic had been suspected since the early 1990s.[94]

However, largely missing in the debate was an analysis of the "military significance" of low-yield test activity. By being almost *silent* on this aspect of their argument for much of the debate, treaty opponents successfully shifted the focus to the mere ability to violate the treaty, leaving us in uncertainty and, therefore, at some unstated risk. Meanwhile, an adversary would have greater certainty through surreptitious testing which, in some unspecified way, could improve their nuclear arsenal. This conferred an advantage on the cheater, even if the nature of such advantage was less than certain.[95] The crux of the argument was essentially: "We can't verify what they do, and if our stockpile is not reliable because we don't test, they gain on us."[96] By failing to address with particularity the "military significance" of possible cheating by our adversaries, the treaty opponents' vagary effectively veiled a *de facto* shift to the restrictive "effective" verification standard of treaty violation.[97] As the then chairman of the Senate Intelligence Committee

---

92   CTBT Senate Debate at pp. S12312 and S12382.

93   *Ibid.* at p. 12536. An unclassified CIA paper quantified this ability to mitigate sound and the resulting seismic signal. Thus, for example, a one-kiloton explosion could manifest itself as only 14 tons, and as such would be well below the threshold of the international monitoring system. *Ibid.* at p. S12384.

94   *Ibid.* at p. S12546.

95   *See, e.g., ibid.* at pp. S12387–88 ("Our experience with the W80 [air launched crux missile] illustrates the inadequacy of non-nuclear and low-yield [less than 1 kiloton] testing; and the need for a full-scale nuclear test to judge the effects of small changes. A final deployment proof test at an extreme low temperature produced the surprise that the primary yield was only a small fraction of what was expected; it was insufficient to ignite the secondary.").

96   *Ibid.* at p. S12395 (remarks of Senator Smith).

97   *See, e.g., ibid.* at p. S12515 (Senator Craig) (defining "effective verification" as the ability to detect *a breach*—as opposed to a militarily significant one—in time to respond).

argued in opposition of the treaty: "I'm not confident that we can now or can in the foreseeable future detect *any* and *all* nuclear explosions prohibited under the treaty."[98] At the same time, employment of that higher standard tied to the fact of violation, was now expanded into the ratification context, rather than limited to just a compliance analysis with respect to implementation. This expansion represented a substantial departure from the INF ratification process a dozen years before. The verifiability standard used in it shifted from adequacy toward that of effectiveness, and for some almost to the point of absoluteness. But in the INF ratification debate, only a class of weapons was being eliminated; in the CTBT debate, the fear articulated by opponents was that the treaty amounted to slow-motion nuclear disarmament by the gradual erosion of certainty in the reliability of our deterrent and possibly that of others.[99]

In that regard, the one argument advanced in the Senate that specifically countered the military significance standard in the compliance context was that cheating through a low-yield test would only enhance the development of small devices. Because of the small yield, treaty proponents contended that covert testing could not be "significant." They argued that such cheating would facilitate development of tactical weapons, but they would be used on an adversary's home soil with the goal of offsetting our unstoppable conventional advantage.[100] Additionally, they argued that without the type of testing that the CTBT prohibits, "it will be extremely difficult to build nuclear weapons small enough to be mounted on delivery vehicles."[101] While there could be no guarantees, there was confidence that the treaty would make it "significantly harder" for potential cheaters to test.[102]

With this consideration in mind, the position implicitly evoked the "buffer" approach of the ABM Treaty; that is, creating barriers to achieving the prohibited capability, which would create additional cost and uncertainty for the evader as well as more opportunities to catch

---

98   *Ibid.* at p. S12383 (remarks of Senator Shelby) (emphasis added).

99   *See, e.g., ibid.* at pp. S12391–93.

100   *See, e.g., ibid.* at p. S12349. (Senator Biden).

101   *Ibid.* at p. S12522 (Senators Leahy and Stevens).

102   *Ibid.*

them in time to permit countering action. However, these arguments did not meaningfully impact the verification test advanced by treaty opponents. Rather, the focus was on the threshold of *usefulness*, which was set at five hundred tons of yield. While it was acknowledged that testing at that level "would not be sufficient to gain full confidence in all aspects of our existing weapon's performance or to develop sophisticated new nuclear weapons[,] tests this low *may* be militarily significant."[103] It was acknowledged that in order to serve those goals, tests in the range of one to ten kilotons were needed for most designs. The recognized magnitude of the decoupling factor could shield these larger tests from detection. But this was not how treaty adversaries made their point. Rather, the admitted inability to monitor clandestine low yield tests[104] was nowhere measured against the historic measure of "significance" in terms of the impact on the *strategic* relationship with a cheating adversary. The certainty that there could be violation (at least as America interpreted the treaty), coupled with uncertain risk to reliability and safety, added up to employing a strict "effective" verification standard of violation that was not met when newly applied in the ratification context.

While advancing a stricter standard in reality, lip service was paid to the notion of "military significance" by the Senate debate's end. But the opponents of ratification infused new meaning into the standard and measure. By effectively redefining it as "military utility," a test meeting this measure would simply be a useful development either in proof of reliability, or an advancement in nuclear weaponization.[105]

---

103   *Ibid.* at p. S12393.

104   According to the testimony before the Senate Armed Services Committee of Dr. Kathleen Bailey, former Associate Director of the Arms Control and Disarmament Agency: "The international monitoring system of the CTBT is designed or is capable of detecting greater than one kiloton of nuclear yield for a non-evasively conducted test. So if Russia or someone else decides to conduct a test evasively, the IMS system will probably not be able to detect it." (Quoted at p. S12384.)

105   *See, e.g.*, CTBT Senate Debate at p. S12536 ("What is militarily significant nuclear testing? Our definitions of the term might vary, but I think we'd all agree that any nuclear test that gives a nation information to develop newer, more effective weaponry is militarily significant. In the case of the United States, nuclear test yield's between 1,000 tons and 10,000 tons are generally large

Masking through decoupling, for example, clearly would permit unde-tected, useful tests. Open sources reported at the time that Russia was undertaking low-yield tests to develop a new weapon that would be the lynchpin of a new military doctrine."[106] In any event, while such developments would potentially represent some unquantified diminu-tion in the U.S. advantage, there was no suggestion then that it could be regarded as "significant," either to our deterrent or strategic force projection capabilities against an adversarial nation state—the historic measure in the Cold War. Yet the basic fact that the U.S. deterrent's capability could be negatively affected helped change the balance between adherence and violation in measuring acceptable risk of rati-fying increased arms control to eliminate underground nuclear tests.

Treaty proponents essentially countered by arguing that the U.S. would not miss tests of *strategic significance*. Reliance on the planned multi-lateral monitoring program combined with NTMs would be sufficient to meet a verification standard so defined.[107] They likewise argued that low-yield tests are of questionable value in designing new weapons or that the new design will work as intended.[108] What they failed to recognize was that the standard was shifting politically with the change in threat definition and context. A new weapon state—especially a rogue—armed with nuclear devices would have much different leverage, even if of limited utility, in a conflict. It would constrain our

---

enough to provide "proof" data on new weaponry designs.") (Remarks of Senator Kyl.) *See also ibid.* at p. S12389: "Tests with yields below 1 kiloton can go both undetected and be militarily *useful* to the testing state." (Letter of James R. Schlesinger and others urging rejection of the CTBT.) (Emphasis added.)

106   *See, e.g., ibid.* at p. S12398.

107   Then and in ensuing years, seismanic professionals have continued to maintain that the technological gulf in identifying small yield tests would be increasingly solved to make them detectable. *See, e.g.,* CTBT Senate Debate at p. S12528 (Position of the American Geophysical Union and the Seismological Society of American) (No nation will be able to elude the fully operationally international monitoring system even with a small-yield test.) *See also* R. Plenteda (CTBTO), Ad hoc algorithms and methodologies for radionuclide CTBT Treaty Verification, Geophysical Research Abstracts, Vol. 9, 06134, 2007 Sref-ID:1607 7962/gra/EGU2007-A-06134 ("A total new approach of gamma peak finding that enhances drastically the capability to detect very small signals.").

108   *Ibid.* at p. S12528.

tactical options, if not strategic ones. The latter consideration, based on adversary cheating through decoupling, was in fact potentially "significant." Equally, while the limits of arms control had in the past sometimes outstripped our capacity to verify compliance, this would be the first time we would consider doing it in a way that placed our own deterrent itself at some self-imposed risk, given the failure to vet simulations through baseline physical testing to gauge the ability to monitor chemical deterioration accurately.

Another way in which enhanced certainty was required in the CTBT debate was with respect to our ability to verify the continuing vitality of our nuclear deterrent. The natural degradation of nuclear weapons, coupled with the inability to test them through nuclear explosions—as we had done literally a thousand times before the CTBT—would eventually lead the country into uncharted technical territory. The original limited shelf life of our weapons was expected to be 20 years, and was on average 14 at the time of the ratification debate.[109] In the past, new designs were constantly replaced and tested over time. Prior to America's institution of a test moratorium in 1992, the U.S. encountered defects in the arsenal, and tested whether the "fixes" worked.[110] None of our weapons at the time of the CTBT debate had been designed to remain viable in a no-test status quo. The record before the Senate in 1999 regarding each of the Stockpile Stewardship Program components did not inspire full confidence in its likelihood of success at the time. The answer was simply unknown then with respect to whether computer modeling would suffice to leave our nuclear weapons capacity in the same position of *known* effectiveness. A prolonged period without testing, especially without testing in advance to validate the modeling, left treaty opponents with "reasonable doubt." As one Senator put it as his reason for voting to reject ratification: "We simply *do not know*."[111] Yet, knowledge that nuclear weapons will work—by friend and foe alike—was at the heart of the deterrent function, alliance security and the basis for nonproliferation. To change policy in that regard is a step toward eventual disarmament, rather than control, and therefore it deserved a more transparent debate than the one that

---

109   *Ibid.* at p. S12394.

110   *See, e.g., ibid.* at pp. S12388.

111   *Ibid.* at p. S12532 (Remarks of Senator Warner) (emphasis added).

CTBT produced a decade ago. Since nuclear policy experts have recommended reconsideration of the treaty's ratification,[112] and the ratification is expected to be resurrected by the Obama administration, there will be a need to sort through these considerations this time.

An additional aspect of uncertainty in the CTBT context was that of legacy test data. In previous analyses, some aspects had not been successfully predicted by our models at the time of the Senate debate. As the testimony on the Stockpile Stewardship Program status reflected:

> "We have gaps in our understanding. As we improve the codes, as we add the third dimension . . . a key test of the success of the simulation codes will be how well does it predict those things we could not understand in the past. So that is a very key part of the science-based Stockpile Stewardship Program."[113]

Historically, the U.S. had simply been surprised when systems failed to function properly in actual nuclear tests despite performing well in non-nuclear simulations of nuclear effects.[114]

(ii) The Cost of Uncertainty

Going forward, there were still many things we will not "know in reconsidering the CTBT." But we may be technically more certain in the near future, while we also could be less so in the long term, as information grows stale or inapposite in new conditions.[115] Still, even an "excellent bet" is not a sure thing, to paraphrase the then Director of Lawrence Livermore Labs' testimony before the Senate at the time of the CTBT ratification debate.[116] At that time, some argued we must

---

112   Seeking to ratify the CTBT is among the recommendations of CFR Task Force Study No. 62, *supra* note 32.

113   *Ibid.* at p. S12533 (quoting testimony of Dr. Robinson, then director of Sandia).

114   *Ibid.* at p. S12516 (Senator Grams). *See also* footnote 95, *supra.*

115   While our non-physical testing has improved in the decade since ratification of the CTBT was rejected, Secretary Gates contends that the information on which we base our annual stockpile certifications grows increasingly dated and incomplete. *See* Gates Speech, *supra* note 15 at p. 6.

116   *Ibid.* at pp. S12532 and S12386–87 (quoting General Colin Powell in 1991: "As long as one has nuclear weapons, you have to *know* what it is they will do, and so I would recommend continued testing.").

have *complete faith* in its efficacy.[117] In short, they contended that we must "know," rather than merely believe, no matter the level of confidence, for the latter introduces dangerous elements of uncertainty. Whether any decline in confidence in the reliability of our stockpile without testing is an acceptable risk is ultimately a policy judgment influenced by circumstance, technology, and fiscal sustainability. It is a judgment the U.S. made for decades by no longer testing its weapons in the atmosphere where they would actually be detonated. In that limited sense, America had some uncertainty about function for years in the actual operational environment. But living for so long with even that bit of uncertainty renders illusory the completely risk-free knowledge standard demanded by some CTBT opponents in verifying the continued functionality of the nuclear deterrent.

Similarly, the reliability of both our nuclear infrastructure and the expertise of those continuing to service it were likewise challenged in the CTBT debate. The challenge continues now and will in the future. Even a decade ago an aging expert pool of scientific talent, coupled with piecemeal dismantlement of select manufacturing capabilities, did not inspire confidence in our technical ability to create or refurbish weapons systems.[118] While it was clear that America would have to replace nearly all of the non-nuclear components in its weapons, the designs would be new and problematic. First, "[d]ocumentation has never been sufficiently exact to ensure replication."[119] Second, obsolescence overtook the original technology. An evolving industrial base with new personnel would have to provide the replacements without the preferred methodology of testing.[120] In each of these instances, the

---

117   *Ibid.* at p. S12382.

118   The expertise erosion process has continued for a decade since the CTBT debate. Secretary Gates most recently quantified the "brain drain" in a speech in October 2008. He noted estimates that three-quarters of our veteran nuclear weapons designers and workforce in atom labs will reach retirement age in the next several years. *See* Gates Speech, *supra* note 15 at p. 5.

119   *Ibid.* at p. S12388.

120   *Ibid.* p. S12383. (See quoted testimony of former Commander-in-Chief of U.S. Strategic Forces Command and that of the then director of Sandia National Laboratory.) *See also, e.g., ibid.* at p. S12388 ("Just about all the parts of our present nuclear weapons are going to have to be remade.") (quoting then Assistant Secretary of Energy for Defense Programs, Victor Reis).

verification standard to which the proof of continuing viability was held in the CTBT debate was one of "reasonable doubt."[121]

Likewise, the permanence of the test ban was thought to effectively freeze the ability to enhance or preserve the safety of our weapons. Compliance with the CTBT would erode certainty by not permitting physical testing to validate the scientific promise of reliability. Treaty opponents would not accept a lesser standard than complete certainty that *each weapon* was as safe as we know how to make it.[122] In 1999 a majority of Congress found the level of safety risk perpetuated by the test ban unacceptable and voted against ratifying the CTBT. A decade later, sensitivity remains, as America's secretary of defense maintains there is "no margin of error" in the stewardship of our nuclear arsenal.[123] Still, despite the passage of ten more years without testing, President Obama's secretary of defense confirmed to Congress his belief that "the U.S. nuclear deterrent remains safe, secure, and reliable."[124] At the same time, Secretary Gates maintained the prospect of maintaining a safe, secure, and reliable nuclear deterrent over the long-term is "bleak" without testing or modernization. He stated: "There is absolutely no way we can maintain a credible deterrent and reduce the number of weapons in our stockpile without either resorting to testing or pursuing a modernization program."[125] Still, Secretary Gates acknowledged it is possible in pursuing the latter course to do so without testing.[126]

A further source of uncertainty with respect to verifying the CTBT stemmed from the ambiguity arising from the basic agreement itself. While the CTBT prohibited any "nuclear explosion," it did not define

---

121   *See, e.g.*, CTBT Senate Debate at p. S12532.

122   *Ibid.* at p. S12539. *See also* S12383 ("There are nine weapons in the continuing inventory; only three of those weapons have the three modern safety features of enhanced nuclear detonation safety, the fire resistant pit and insensitive high explosive. Three of the systems in the continuing inventory have only one of those features. . . . [T]o freeze an inventory in place in which every weapon is not as safe as it could be is unconscionable." (Testimony of Dr. Robert Baker, former Assistant for Atomic Energy to the Secretary of Defense).

123   *See* Gates, *supra* note 11, p. 8.

124   *Ibid.*

125   Gates Speech, *supra* note 15 at p. 5.

126   *Ibid.* at p. 8 (answer to audience question).

that term. Nowhere in the language of the treaty could one find an express "zero-yield" ban. The United States certainly interpreted it that way, but this interpretation was not necessarily a universal, binding understanding. What would constitute a technical violation of the treaty at the low end of testing was not perfectly clear. Russia maintained that both hydro-nuclear actions[127] and subcritical[128] experiments comply with the test ban, whereas the U.S. limited its compliance position to subcritical tests alone.[129] Some nations viewed both to be illegal,[130] while others (e.g., China) simply did not provide their interpretation.[131] Article 15 of the Treaty, which bars reservation, added to the lack of predictability. This prevents the U.S. from legally restricting the scope of the treaty by tying it to the U.S.' understanding. As a result, verifying compliance was potentially complicated by the lack of definitional certainty. Clarification of the fundamental

---

127 Hydronuclear testing basically involves the implosion of fissile material, but timed so that the device does not deliver full nuclear yield. In fact the yield could be less than that released by conventional high explosives. At the time of the CTBT debate these tests were regarded as "very useful" to weapons programs, particularly in ascertaining reliability and safety, understanding the physics and in developing new concepts. *See, e.g.,* Senate CTBT Debate at pp. S12261 and S12289. Indeed, during the U.S. adherence to the nuclear test moratorium in the Eisenhower administration, America conducted such tests. *Ibid.* at p. S12292. As such the American position at the time of the ratification debate contravened its own past practice, which was more consistent with the Russian CTBT position.

128 A subcritical test, as the name implies, essentially means setting off an explosion with nuclear materials, but stopping it before it becomes critical. Then, through computer simulation, the effects are determined as if the test had gone critical. *See ibid.* at pp. S12230 and S12362. "Subcritical experiments ("SCEs") . . . involve chemical high explosives and fissile materials in configurations and quantities such that no self-sustaining nuclear fission chain reaction can result. In these experiments, the chemical high explosives are used to generate high pressures that are applied to the fissile materials . . . SCEs try to determine if radioactive decay of aged plutonium would degrade weapon performance." Medalia, "CTBT: Background and CRS Report to Congress" (September 18, 2008) at pp. 28–29.

129 From 1997 through September 2008 the U.S. conducted 23 SCEs. *Ibid.* at p. 29.

130 *Ibid.* at pp. S12381 and S12390.

131 *Ibid.* at p. S12517.

understanding, is therefore on the agenda for any new consideration of the treaty since compliance will have to be verified.

At the same time, there was at least the appearance of certainty that the U.S. would withdraw from the treaty in proscribed circumstances. If the president determined that the certification in the safety and ability of the U.S. nuclear stockpile would not be maintained with a high degree of confidence without testing, then the President was legally obligated to consult with the Senate promptly and to withdraw from the treaty.[132] The delay between discovery of a problem in the annual certification process and treaty withdrawal was thought at the time of the debate to roughly coincide with the time period most likely needed to restore the capacity to test.[133] While adversaries of the process contended that the political process of withdrawal was so rigorous as to virtually eliminate the utility of the withdrawal measure, their reliance on the ABM treaty has since been eroded by history. The U.S. did act to withdraw in that context. There is a precedent for the treaty withdrawal determination, which increases confidence in the process. The political argument advanced by CTBT treaty opponents is no longer viable, and should not be a factor in a renewed ratification debate, as the uncertainty dissipated.

Ultimately, the price of uncertainty over two functions of verification—compliance and reliability—was the death knell of the CTBT, for at least some time. The integrity of the verification process was doubted. The "military significance" of violations was largely assumed or ignored in the Senate debate regarding the arms control measure in terms of its compliance impact. There was no measure taken in a broader context of overall force projection advantages and strategic impact, if any, of low yield noncompliance. The notion that the treaty froze American nuclear superiority into place by forbidding meaningful strategic nuclear testing was simply dismissed as insufficient, for there is no surety in the capacity to modify its systems to meet technological improvements by adversaries. Likewise, the fact that the treaty would

---

132   Article IX of the CTBT governing withdrawal provided for a six month notice period.

133   Senate CTBT Debate at p. S12543. The actual time period is longer. *See* Medalia, *supra* note 128 at pp. 30–32.

not come into force[134] until all 44 nuclear capable nations[135]—that is, those capable of developing weapons—ratified it, was accorded little weight. Rather, it was the verification problems once in force of our own nuclear arms that proved telling, for the absence of physical testing had become the highest risk to our ability to sustain deterrence, rather than the vulnerability of our deterrent to repel attack. Most of the elements of risk associated with verification were subjected to a strict standard. Uncertain judgments about weapons *reliability* took on the same kind of significance as compliance judgments did in the past about the *survivability* of our deterrent in the face of significant treaty violations. Reliability, in turn, would now have a threefold measure in terms of safety, utility, and the ability of our deterrent to keep pace with the type of threats it was required to deter. After all, a stockpile designed for mutually assured destruction and for the purpose of striking urban and industrial targets, would not necessarily be suitable for striking hardened, deeply buried targets, such as deeply buried underground biological weapons labs, without unacceptable collateral damage. Whereas in the past weapons development through testing gave assurance of the ability to conform our arsenal through new designs to emerging new threats and hurdles, the future under the CTBT was thought to be unacceptably uncertain without testing validation. This is another element of the policy analysis that should inform any revisitation of ratification as a part of a shifting nuclear posture.

The U.S. may soon face resumed consideration of the CTBT—to leave it as it is, to seek to amend it, or to augment the monitoring system— after more than a decade of technological development and simulated experience. The uncertainty associated with verification of both compliance and continuing reliability of the stockpile remain legitimate issues. If a comprehensive test ban is coupled with further deep cuts in

---

134   While there would be no formal relinquishment of the testing option, Article 18 of the Vienna Convention on Treaties would legally impede the ability to act in a manner inconsistent with the Treaty during the interim following our signature of the treaty—just as for the other 150 plus nations which signed it. Only the president clarifying our intent not to become a party would relieve us from that commitment. *Ibid.* at p. S12508.

135   *Ibid.* at p. S12390 (quoting Richard Perle).

our nuclear arsenal, what will be the impact on America's national security if other nations cheat or opt out? What signal do we send if detected flaws in our stockpile eventually compel a choice between resumed testing or weapons retirement? What level of intrusion will suffice to verify compliance? These and other verification issues will inform the content of one of the next great arms control debate America undertakes.

D. THE NEW INSECURITY

Deterrence strategy prevailed for decades in the prior superpower threat context, and likely will continue to do so with rogue states. But the same result cannot be assumed with respect to use of nuclear devices in the possession of sub-state actors, particularly if acquired through bribery, theft due to control failures, or by similar means. The U.S. typically will have no territory to hold hostage through its retaliatory capacity with them. Hence, even "marginal" deviation from accepted norms of control can lead to "militarily significant" weapons possession by those who will not be deterred, and who cannot be because of the inability to retaliate in kind. In contrast, a rogue state, to the extent it unlawfully maintains possession of WMD, faces the increasing likelihood of retaliation, particularly as the forensics of tracing weapons continue to improve. So detection prospects must be factored into the rogue state's force employment calculus.

In contrast, the new elements introduced by sophisticated sub-state actors suggest the proprietary of revisiting the prior logic with respect to verification standards and roles. With "parity" a non-issue in this context, there can be no "substantial equivalence" with terrorist enemies, as there was with the Soviets. A zero option actually prevails as the strategic imperative in countering these actors. One suitcase nuclear bomb or mine, or other small WMD device, is all that it takes to be "militarily significant" in any urban center around the globe. That is a certainty in today's new Age of Insecurity. The military utility of the WMD weapons to such actors resides in part in the asymmetry resulting from the very lack of massive deployments of nuclear weapons and relative imbalance in forces with America and its allies. This is precisely the opposite state of affairs that existed in the superpower confrontation, or which continues with today's other nuclear weapons states.

In those circumstances, numerous issues arise as a framework for verification policy analysis. What verification standard follows in nuclear arms control or disarmament given the nature of the threats? Will there be differences depending upon whether control, or limitation or disarmament is involved? How do the standards in other WMD contexts relate to it? Should there be any accompanying evolution in the need for certainty with arms control or disarmament agreements? What will be the future of compliance if there is a failure which may well be militarily insignificant, and even lack utility with respect to the balance of forces as between the parties to an arms-control agreement, but which is "significant" when control of the nuclear/WMD device can devolve to sub-state actors willing to use it? In other words, does the United States have to revisit the need for a more exacting verification standard in its dealings with other nation states to minimize further the devolving risk emanating potentially from non-state actors? Should military requirements for verification shift toward stricter compliance that emphasizes the prohibition of any violation, if not broadly, then at least selectively when a "rogue" regime gains control of an existing WMD arsenal, or succeeds in creating one? How would that be accomplished within a treaty or other legal framework? While these and other issues will command our attention in a nuclear context, the greater practical threat may well emerge from fissile material used in a dirty bomb, or pathogens obtained from peaceful or defensive use in research in friendly, developed states. After all, the know-how that gave birth to the greatest nuclear proliferation to date arose in the peaceful training of an individual named A.Q. Khan, in Europe. Likewise, the only anthrax attack in the United States seemingly emanated from one of its own biodefense lab scientists.

The keys to the compliance and punitive processes are the verification standards employed, which lead to certainty in any compliance judgment. Historically, that range was impacted by the WMD weapons systems' characteristics, deployment, and employment practices. Today, in the face of 21st century threats, the substance of arms control limits is equally impacted, for the types, qualitative and quantitative limits of weapons, and related delivery systems all need to be monitored. For example, mobile missiles with warheads could carry conventional, nuclear, chemical or even biological payloads; each presents substantial verification challenges. The concealable nature of mobile weapon systems is also purposefully calculated to impede detection. While chemical or biological weapons of this sort are illegal, legitimate nuclear payloads are concealed purely for military purposes. Distinguishing such systems from those of a conventional nature likewise increases the complexity of the monitoring and judgmental elements of any verification process, particularly in the absence of functionally related observable differences. Introducing and preserving uncertainty into the military calculus is actually the intentional result of such deployed nuclear or conventional weapons delivery systems, as with Pakistani efforts to deter India.

The characteristics of a weapon also have triggered uncertainty in the verification process. In the past, the size and signature of chemical weapons and precursors rendered detection of undeclared stock quite difficult. Similar difficulties pertained to small nuclear artillery, projectiles, mines, and bombs. While the infrastructure to manufacture such weapons systems may be relatively identifiable, significant covert programs have certainly escaped detection over the years. One need not look any further for a demonstration than the nuclear experience with South Africa, Iraq, Iran, India, Pakistan, North Korea, Libya, and Syria. As a result, the effectiveness and adequacy of disarmament necessarily becomes more closely tied to increasing thresholds of both cooperation and intrusive techniques.

Within the context of bilateral superpower nuclear parity, uncertainty always existed with other WMD, particularly chemical weapons, as well as conventional forces, in assessing the overall military balance. With respect to the latter, comparatively low levels of cheating—even involving hundreds of tanks—were deemed militarily insignificant. The calculation then was far more complicated with respect to chemical weapons. While it was recognized that utilization of even limited stocks of banned chemical weapons could alter military scenarios in a European conflict, the broader deterrence context was thought to provide an acceptable buffer against the uncertainty of that risk. Today, however, developing countries' adherence to the Chemical Weapons Convention[136] cannot necessarily be measured in a broad alliance-based

---

136   United Nations Convention on the Prohibition of the Development, Production, Stockpiling and the Use of Chemical Weapons and on Their Destruction, 32 I.L.M. 800 (January 13, 1993).

context, but rather a regional one. Hence, the calculus of cheating involves a different risk assessment than that existing previously for verification purposes.

So long as the risk of an enemy's surprise attack based on conventional force advantages exists, the temptation will arise to use a WMD equalizer. That capacity may be maintained clandestinely at home, or emerge through precursor transfers provided by a third party (such as from China to Pakistan) in a moment of crisis. The capacity to shift on short notice from legitimate civilian chemical facilities to weaponization uses also always provided a hedge against both noncompliance and asymmetric advantage. This breakout capacity would likely be detected in a time of mobilization, so that the process itself provides some opportunity for verification and warning, even in the chemical context. How will it be deterred in a nuclear free world, or will pre-emptive strikes become the military necessity? In that sense, verification may well help inform the content of tomorrow's force employment doctrines.

In the future, there will be certainty with respect to nuclear devices whether there is a comprehensive test ban or not. Rogue states or terrorists alike will have sufficient assurance that rudimentary nuclear weapons will work without testing. U.S. intelligence previously acknowledged that nuclear testing by adversaries is not a requirement in acquiring a basic weapons capacity. We have long known from the U.S. experience in World War II, when the "little boy" device was dropped on Japan, that rudimentary weapons can work without testing.[137] South Africa created and deployed a small stockpile of six functional nuclear weapons without testing.[138] Pakistan maintained an untested arsenal for years, and only tested for political purposes to counteract Indian testing. Iran, for example, would have equal confidence in the functionality of first generation weapons based on Pakistani designs without ever testing.[139] This will be broadly true

---

137   *See* CTBT Senate Debate at p. S12535.

138   *Ibid.* at p. S12526.

139   *Ibid.* at p. S12545. As of the time of the CTBT debate, the fact was that "the countries of most concern to us—North Korea, Iran and Iraq—can develop and deploy nuclear weapons without any nuclear tests whatsoever." *Ibid.* at p. S12384 (quoting Intelligence Committee Chairman Shelby).

because to the extent that such weapons are acquired through design proliferation from states which tested; there is added certainty in their effectiveness without the new weapons possessor testing on its own.[140]

Thus, if the future nuclear threat comes from a terrorist, the existence of a test ban is largely irrelevant. Verifiable control over fissile material would be a far more significant restraint. If the future threat is from a rogue nation, even a verifiable CTBT has limited value added. After all, how does one deter by agreement a rogue from testing a weapon it bound itself under the Non-Proliferation Treaty not to develop? The fact that sanctions may be available or invoked pursuant to the test ban treaty regime is a specious argument. We would have the capacity to seek such a sanction already on the argument that the testing constitutes a threat to peace and security under the U.N. Charter. Our North Korean experience well illustrates the point—both in terms of the availability of the remedial process and difficulty in implementing it.[141] North Korea now has a verified nuclear capability because of its repeated testing of a rudimentary device. The point of a verifiable test ban would be to limit North Korea's confidence in developing more sophisticated, miniaturized weapons for delivery by long-range missile, unless it was aided by technology transfer from another state which had tested. But if it just wanted to try to deter America, then a slow boat carrying an undetected device parked off U.S. shores could be as effective to achieve that goal, as would a truck bomb driven into Seoul.

The new threats posed by rogue states and sophisticated non-state actors call for renewed consideration for applying an "effective"

---

140   *Ibid.* at p. S12536.

141   To explain, while Security Council Resolution 1718 imposed sanctions for North Korea's nuclear test, they were not actually implemented then in order to entice North Korean participation in the Six Nations Talks. Not until the April 2009 missile test in contravention of that resolution did the political will to implement them finally become manifest. At that time a "Presidential Statement" issued by the Security Council renewed the sanctions imposed by Resolution 1718, which had been suspended after North Korea resumed participation in The Six Nation talks in 2006. *See* Security Council Document SC19634, 6106th meeting (April 13, 2009) *accessed at* http://www.un.org/News/Press/docs/2009/SC9634.doc.htm.

verification standard in certain circumstances. The violations that may have no real "military significance" as between the U.S. and Russia, for example, and thus pass the "adequate" verification test, would become militarily "significant" if a nuclear weapon becomes accessible to a terrorist. While there may be "fairly high confidence" that Russian strategic and tactical nuclear weapons are under adequate control, nuclear artillery shells and mines seemingly are not.[142] What level of certainty should be required in assuring they do come under control and don't leak in a verifiable arms control regime? How do we verify uncertainty about them from an earlier, more chaotic period in the transition from Soviet rule where baseline data may not be available? In the face of today's threats, the more rigorous standard of "effective" verification should be applied, not because of the military significance of potential Russian cheating, but rather because of the third party threat. In that sense, the Reagan-era standard has renewed vitality and legitimacy when applied to controlling weapons or material. At the same time, where we are dealing essentially with the limitation of surrogates, such as a test ban, "adequate" verification may well be equal to the task. A circumstantially impelled sliding standard of verification, then, could be applied in the future. But unlike the past where meaningful differences in the standards were not always recognized (e.g., INF), they should be going forward, for they will differ functionally. This, in turn, will impact our certainty about acceptable risk.

Lastly, the change in the purpose of nuclear capability has changed the need for verifying with certainty. In the CTBT context, the purpose of the U.S. stockpile is deterrence, so the continuing viability of that nuclear arsenal requires high certainty. Yet the broadening of verification missions is evident in other respects too. This expansion is perhaps best illustrated in the safeguards[143] context of the IAEA. That verification process was originally tasked with preventing diversion of nuclear

---

142 Gates Speech, *supra* note 15 at p. 12 ("what worries me are the tens of thousands of old nuclear mines, nuclear artillery shells and so on, because the reality is the Russians themselves probably don't have any idea how many of those they have or, potentially, where they are.") (Answer to question).

143 The structure and content of these agreements between the IAEA and non-weapon members states in the NPT are found in IAEA document INFC/RC/153.

material from peaceful use to weaponization; it was tied to declared sites. Thus, the revelation of undeclared sites and activities—whether in the aftermath of the Iraq war, or through non-governmental organizations about Iran—came as a shock to the system. The systemic vulnerability impelled more intrusion to foster increased confidence that cheating was not occurring at undeclared sites. Safeguards aimed at nondiversion through nuclear "accounting" sought "adequate" verification. Timely detection of "significant" fissile *material* was the measuring standard. Yet the certainty associated with that verification process was not "effective" in the truest sense of the word, for the system was tied only to what was transparent, while the promised compliance was not. The system assumed declaration of sites, but there was no certainty of it, nor ultimately the means to acquire it. Iraq exploited that opening and it took a war to reveal the severity of the problem. One result, of course, was the eventual expansion of the IAEA's inspection mission through the Additional Protocol to seek out undeclared activity, instead of just diversion. Voluntary adherence to the protocol subjects nuclear-related activity, rather than just nuclear materials, to IAEA scrutiny. Confirming the accuracy of the declared activity requires access through onsite inspection, as well as possible environmental monitoring.

In the highly unusual circumstances involving Iraq, the U.N. Security Council created inspectorates, first UNSCOM,[144] and then its successor UNMOVIC,[145] which showed the capacity of the international community to devise verification measures and improvise capacity[146] in the face of a need-driven change in mission. Today, preserving that know-how with requisite certainty carries with it a price. Just as the U.S. faces an expertise loss with its deterrent capacity, so too the international community faces erosion of its verification capacity in the

---

144   The United Nations Special Commission was specially created to verify Iraqi disarmament with respect to chemical and biological weapons, as well as missiles over a certain range, after the first Gulf War.

145   The United Nations Monitoring, Verification and Inspection Commission replaced UNSCOM after it was compromised by use for intelligence collection.

146   The innovations included the first time that high-altitude aerial imagery would be available and placed under full-time U.N. control through dedicated U-2 aircraft from the U.S. as well as helicopter imagery from craft provided by Germany. See Verification Report of the Secretary General, *supra* note 3 at p. 22 ¶45.

wake of the Iraqi mission. In each instance, the ability to continue to rely on the capacity is in jeopardy. Rather than face the loss of confidence associated with diminished expertise and inadequate knowledge management, the international community should pay the costs of verifying so that it will continue to possess the ability to perform such missions.

CHAPTER III

THE PRICE OF INTRUSION

A. INTRODUCTION

The principle of intrusion to verify commitments of agreements arose in the post-World War II nuclear context. The fear of unfettered international nuclear trade raised the specter of weapons proliferation. Despite the almost immediate failure of the Baruch Plan's embrace of U.N. control over nuclear energy, the desire to constrain peaceful use to prevent weaponization ultimately resulted in the creation of the International Atomic Energy Agency ("IAEA"). This agency, born of President Eisenhower's "Atoms for Peace" proposal,[147] serves a dual mandate: international oversight of the peaceful use of nuclear energy, and preventing diversion of fissile material for military use. The functional underpinnings for the IAEA reflect the crux of the American proposal—international verification of the commitment to peaceful use by member states.

Central to this international verification regime is an inspection process to monitor compliance, with Safeguards Agreements between the IAEA and member states calculated to help assure peaceful use. The political process through which the intrusion principle has been accepted reflects a compromise of sovereignty. The process also balances a tension between the needs to verify and to preserve confidentiality, so as not to threaten either security or proprietary information. At the same time, that process is calculated to serve a deterrence function by creating the risk of detecting cheating through diversion. The increased chance of being detected constrains incentives to pursue the prohibited activity.

Through the years, intrusion has changed with circumstance. From the time of initial compromises, which permitted very limited inspection

---

147 Address by Mr. Dwight D. Eisenhower, President of the United States of America, to the 470th Plenary Meeting of the United Nations General Assembly (December 8, 1953) *accessed at* http://www.iaea.org/About/history_speech.html.

on certain reactors and constrained inspector activity, the rights and obligations associated with international inspection have evolved. The key to the expansion of intrusion came as an adjunct to the establishment of the NPT. That treaty's commitment to the renunciation of nuclear weapons tasked the IAEA with policing adherence to treaty obligations through bilateral control between the agency and member state of the regime. A more intrusive inspection regime only evolved after the Gulf War in an effort to address covert weapons programs at undeclared sites.

In the bioweapons context, the notion of augmenting arms limitation with confidence-building measures ("CBMs") surfaced, including a declaratory process that would increase transparency. This development was largely event driven, arising from the perceived proliferation of weapons capability, followed by evidence of actual offensive developmental activity. The anthrax outbreak in 1979 contributed to the process. An aerosol release of the pathogen, presumably by a military microbiology facility in Sverdlovsk, Siberia, killed both cattle and humans.[148] The CBM effort was furthered in the aftermath of the first Gulf War, which eventually produced evidence of long-term developmental activity over nearly a 20-year period by Iraq according to the U.N. Special Commission on Iraq (UNSCOM).[149] While these episodes with state actors impelled efforts to develop a verification process, the development was not successful. Nor have the actions of non-state actors, before and after 9/11, pushed nations toward consensus levels of intrusion. In that regard, U.S. opposition to the compromise BioWeapons Convention ("BWC") measures has derailed the verification process. Yet the underpinnings for that position, as

---

148   In the spring of 1979, an anthrax epidemic broke out which Soviet officials blamed on contaminated meat, and which the U.S. attributed to a release from a military facility. The zone of death and prevailing winds, among other physical manifestations, corroborated the conclusion of an aerolized military source. *See, e.g.*, Meselson, et al., *The Sverdlovsk Anthrax Outbreak of 1979*, 266 SCIENCE 1202–08 (1994).

149   Despite inspector presence in Iraq from 1992 to 1995, disclosure of Iraq's offensive BW capabilities came to light through the defection of Sadaam Hussein's son-in-law, Hussein Kamal. By 1998, UNSCOM inspections produced Iraqi declarations of 8,500 liters of anthrax.

developed below, are logically extended by consistent adherence to prices for intrusion the U.S. simply won't pay.

B. THE TRADITIONAL CALCULUS

As long ago as the 1930s Naval Limitation treaties,[150] the role of voluntary data exchange was recognized as an essential aspect of assuring the limitations of treaty-constrained weapons systems. Over time, numerical thresholds triggering notification requirements became the standard confidence building techniques with respect to activities, such as conventional military force exercises. In any agreed-upon mechanism for constraining military endeavor, the establishment of baseline data became a critical monitoring metric. While such disclosures were voluntary in early arms-control agreements, they were always subject to compliance assessment through human intelligence or national technical means (NTMs). Indeed, for many years, NTMs were a substitute for the absence of on-site inspection. They allowed expansion of the scope of military means that might be constrained by agreement.

Eventually there was even cooperation in enhancing verification through NTMs. For example, both the Anti-Ballistic Missile Treaty and the initial Strategic Arms Limitation Treaty precluded the parties from NTM interference, so long as they were used "in a manner consistent with generally recognized principles of international law." Additionally, these treaties forbade the use of "deliberate concealment measures" to interfere with verification. This approach eventually became standard, with the same language replicated in subsequent bilateral arms control agreements.

Over time, on-site monitoring and inspections were finally introduced into the superpower relationship. This was done initially to help establish baseline data where items were limited by treaty. Thereafter, other forms of on-site inspection were introduced into the arms control process. They ranged from inspections to monitor treaty-permitted residual behavior, to verifying elimination of certain military activity or weapons, systems. Eventually they embraced short-notice or challenge

---

150   *See* TREATY FOR THE LIMITATION AND REDUCTION OF NAVAL ARMAMENT, April 22, 1930, 46 STAT. 2858, 112 L.N.T.S. 65; and TREATY FOR THE LIMITATION OF NAVAL ARMAMENT, 25 March, 1936.

of declared or undeclared sites of prohibited or otherwise constrained activity. Even within the on-site inspection process, the type of verification activity ranged from an episodic hands-on approach to a continuous presence for monitoring the destruction of some categories of weapons, such as intermediate nuclear forces (INF) with the Soviets in the 1980's. Verification technology evolved too, ranging from identification tags, to seals, to open surveillance techniques like utilization of instruments or streaming video to monitor facilities. Today this process extends to the ability to measure residual biological activity, with increasingly remarkable precision.[151]

The ability to verify compliance with arms-control treaties was a cornerstone of the bilateral limitation regimes established between the U.S. and USSR. Early in the process, when President Kennedy ended a three-year test moratorium, he stated: "[w]e know enough now about broken negotiations, secret preparations and the advantages gained from a long test series never to offer again an *uninspected* moratorium."[152] Further arms limitation progress necessitated intrusion. For example, the Threshold Test Ban Treaty ("TTBT")[153] between the superpowers limited the yield of tests, but the yield could not then be verified by NTMs. Verification was necessarily tied to cooperation, which was then absent, so implementation was held in abeyance for years. Underground tests were limited to designated sites where each side deployed sensors in proximity. Only in this way could tests be monitored with sufficient reliability to verify compliance. Although the treaty was signed in 1974, it was not until late 1990 that the treaty entered into force. That only occurred after agreement on new verification protocols were substituted for the originals,[154] which is a precedent that may be necessary to follow in the future—for example, with the location of CTBT monitoring stations in Russia and China.

---

151   *See, e.g.*, Dr. Kay Mereish, *Technical Advances and Field Experiences for Use in Biological Verification*, Presentation at the United Nations Monitoring and Inspection Commission (April 19, 2007).

152   CTBT Senate Debate at p. S12385 (quoting President Kennedy) (emphasis added).

153   *See* TTBT summary *accessed at* http://www.atomicarchive.com/Treaties/Treaty10.shtml.

154   *Ibid.*

Extensive verification measures also enabled the superpowers gradually (i) to limit conventional weaponry, such as tanks and armored personnel carriers in Europe; (ii) to cut the strategic nuclear arsenals through the START Treaties; and (iii) to ban chemical weapons.

By the late 1980s, the Soviet Union's embrace of unprecedented on-site inspection gave rise to a series of choices for the U.S. Then as now, there is a need to balance the security risks from intrusive verification, with the potential benefits and actual costs. America will continue to face these choices in myriad WMD verification contexts in the future of arms control limitation, and even more so as the U.S. moves eventually toward nuclear disarmament.

All of this intrusion comes at a price. For those who would cheat or engage in suspect actions, even inspection limited to agreed-upon locations increases the cost of their covert action. Creating hidden sites necessitates extraordinary behavior, which may well attract attention through NTMs or human intelligence, but not always. For example, the Krasnayarsk radar in Siberia was a huge structure built in violation of the ABM treaty that escaped detection in the initial years of its construction.[155] Even in this century, a closely watched adversary like Iran was able, for a time, to build underground an undeclared uranium enrichment facility at Natanz. In any event, when there is intrusion to monitor compliance, there is greater difficulty and cost associated with either cheating or creating a "breakout" potential.

Yet, for those policing the compliance of others, there is a substantial monetary price tag that every inspection carries with it. Both the cost of building and preserving an inspection capability can be daunting. Cost is particularly problematic if reinvented multilaterally in each new field of regulated behavior involving WMD weapons. Competing concerns over inspection mechanism costs and NTM intelligence sharing thus rise to the forefront of verification process considerations. While the creation of new inspection agencies, such as for the Chemical Weapons Convention,[156] could draw upon earlier multinational models (e.g., the IAEA) for operation lessons, the financial starting costs are

---

155   *See* Adelman, *Why Verification Is More Difficult (and Less Important)*, 14 Int'l Security 141, 145 (1990).

156   *See supra* note 136.

still sobering. The prospect of creating them for other elements of the WMD control chain verification process (e.g., technology exports) will be a hurdle, unless some degree of replication can be introduced.

Another practical cost disability is the non-discriminatory framework for verification. Other than through challenge inspections, every arms-control regime member typically receives at least relatively equal verification attention. In a multilateral context the political price of intrusion is often equality. Hence, search resources can be dissipated in pursuit of the equality principle in verification. Rogue nations and good sovereign citizens alike receive equal attention in the ordinary course. No one would be singled out for verification attention, except by particular triggering criteria. Thus, the factor of verification equality—also enshrined in U.N. verification principles[157]—compromises the ability to ferret out suspect behavior in the ordinary course by targeted attention. This actually enhances the risk that a nation bent on masking its activity is more likely to progress further in the quest for weapons capability before discovery. Therefore, the unqualified application of the principle of equality potentially and needlessly compromises one element of the verification process—that of timely detection. At the same time, non-rogue nations are capable of mistakes which can be exploited. Normal monitoring can help avoid such scenarios. The issue is really one of balancing the process so that limited resources are *effectively* utilized, rather than squandered by implementation of a principle in a politically driven process.

There is also the price of uncertainty, for even short-notice inspections of undeclared activities seldom seem destined to detect a violation, particularly in the absence of mistakes by the inspected party.[158] But there are episodes where suspect activity is revealed through such a process. For example, Iran's voluntary adherence for a time to the Additional Protocol produced evidence through inspection at an undeclared technical university site,[159] which remains an unresolved issue.

---

157   U.N. Verification Principles, *supra* note 4 at Principle 10.

158   *See* Lewis A. Dunn, *Arms Control Verification*, 14 INT'L SECURITY 165, 168–69 (1990).

159   *See* Response of the Islamic Republic of Iran to the IAEA, No. 083/2007 (27 August, 2007) *accessed at* http://www.iaea.org/publications/Documents/infcircs/2007/infcir711.pdf.

Still, the U.S. recognized in the INF talks that there is also the possibility that inspections will be used abusively for intelligence gathering, rather than for monitoring and related compliance judgments. In the Soviet context, the decision to add a right of refusal for challenge inspection was viewed at once as both a cost and information protection measure. Our operating verification assumption was that "the odds are very low that inspectors would ever be permitted to detect a violation."[160] As a result, the cost to actual verification uncertainty and the potential compliance judgment was viewed as low. At the same time, America minimized the prospect[161] of a "militarily significant" loss of its information through the inspection process. Today, resisting such intrusion serves at once that goal, as well as diminishing the prospects in the U.S. of Fourth Amendment challenges to the extent private industry might be a target for such searches, as in the biological and chemical contexts. Yet when an adversary like North Korea balks at the prospect of such intrusion, we are quick to label it as pure evasion, rather than recognize any security-driven need.

In each instance where the costs of intrusiveness need be measured, the equation includes not just a monetary element, but also a national security and sometimes a proprietary component as well. These historic and continuing concerns are to some extent legacy issues of bilateral American and Soviet dealings. But they are also a continuing legitimate security concern, even for rogue states. There are precedents for dealing with such concerns. For example, there have been repeated episodes where "trial" inspections were utilized to build confidence in the broader regime. That experience ranges from chemical to nuclear weapons in the American/Soviet and Russian bilateral experience.[162] Additionally, some experience with information-sharing in compliance

---

160   *See* Dunn, *supra* note 158 at p. 169.

161   *Ibid.*

162   *See, e.g.,* Agreement Between the Government of the United States of America and Union of Soviet Socialist Republics on Principles of Implementing Trial Verification Stability Measures that would be Carried Out Pending the Conclusion of the U.S.-Soviet Treaty on the Reduction and Limitation of Strategic Offensive Arms, 28 I.L.M. 1424. Another example would be the "Bilateral Verification Experiment and Data Exchange Related to Prohibition of Chemical Weapons" (a/k/a the Wyoming Memorandum of Understanding), a two phase agreement involving capabilities data, visits to civilian and military

assessments was gained previously within alliance decisional structures. This occurred primarily in the conventional force and chemical arms control contexts. Increasingly these concerns play out today in the multilateral arms control context. The likelihood is that a balancing of all these factors will continue to be sought, particularly in the chemical and biological sectors. Still, these legitimate security concerns contravene in certain circumstances the *unqualified* U.N. verification principle from the late 1980s that "arms limitation and [the] disarmament process will benefit from greater openness."[163] Yet there is insufficient recognition of the legitimacy of exceptions, even while at the same time parties attempt to "manage access" in a practical way that can serve either a legitimate security need, or improperly abet an illegitimate concealment effort.

C. THE POLITICAL PRICE

The detection of a seismic event is not the same as identifying it. Yet, it is the identification judgment which provides the underpinning for verification of a nuclear weapons test.[164] Armed with the knowledge that a seismic event was a nuclear test of a particular yield in a certain place, a monitoring station can calibrate its systems accordingly. Uncertainty arises where variants are introduced, such as in magnitude or locale. These elements produce a subjective element to identifying the seismic event. At the time of the CTBT ratification hearings, it was unknown what size a nuclear test had to be before it could be surely identified as one by the International Monitoring System ("IMS"). The global verification regime, once that treaty enters into force, will include 321 monitoring stations and 16 radio nuclide laboratories worldwide. There will also be an International Data Center.[165] Even with such an array of international monitoring supplementing NTMs, it seems there would still be no certainty today that a seismic event was nuclear, rather than natural, with decoupled tests in uncalibrated areas.

---

facilities, leading subsequently to intrusive on-site inspections. See Verification Report of the Secretary General, *supra* note 3 at p. 31 ¶86.

163   U.N. Verification Principles, *supra* note 4 at Principle 5.

164   CTBT Senate Debate at p. S12537.

165   CTBTO Preparatory Commission *accessed at* http://www.CTbto.org/faqs/?uid=62&cHash+7feB235717.

Unless there is physical inspection, or expansion of agreed upon sites for calibrated monitoring through a new or modified protocol (as with the Threshold Test Ban Treaty), then these legacy issues remain.

In an effort to reduce uncertainty about treaty violations, utilization of on-site inspections (OSI) are provided for as a matter of right in some arms-control regimes. Yet how that right is implemented is what really matters. In the nuclear context, OSI on underground testing may become a practical issue if the CTBT is resuscitated, ratified by the U.S., and eventually comes into force. In that treaty regime, OSI is not guaranteed. Rather, a gatekeeper function is to be exercised by 51 nations serving as an Executive Council. The ability to secure a majority vote in favor of OSI introduces an element of risk into a key component of the verification process. The political reality of approving OSI will certainly involve gauging the targeted state's likely reaction. After all, those states voting in favor will have to be willing to pay the price of political hostility their vote will engender. China is already on record from the CTBT negotiating period as viewing such a request as a hostile act.[166] Apart from this obstacle, another hurdle for risk assessment is satisfying the necessary level of confidence about a suspect event to satisfy the voting countries. This recognition will complicate the ability to secure approval. Thus, the burden of proof creates the risk that OSI will not be approved, or may compromise our intelligence sources and NTM capability. In stark contrast, the Chemical Weapons Convention required a vote to *stop* an inspection. This variation in process impacts both the burden of proof for political action, as well as the likelihood of intrusion in suspect circumstances.

Efforts to extract a political price for inspection concessions are also found in other WMD regime negotiations. A prime example is the attempt to craft a verification protocol for the 1972 Biological Weapons Convention. In the post-Cold War negotiations beginning in 1995, a North-South divide was evident. Developing nations, including India, Pakistan, China, and Iran, sought from the U.S. the relinquishment of some export controls as a price for admission. Foreshadowing what it would do with the CTBT, Russia sought a narrow definition for certain key BWC provisions. Since Russia—like the Soviets before it—was suspected then of both a covert offensive program for biological

---

166   *See, e.g.,* CTBT Senate Debate at pp. S12380 and S12537.

weapons and low yield nuclear testing, it took an interpretative approach to lessen constraints on military activity that would be subject to inspection. In contrast, European nations and some others sought even more intrusion than America contemplated, raising the specter that verification would compromise potentially both U.S. national (and economic) security, as in the INF negotiations.

The U.S. eventually rejected the verification protocol on the BWC as the price of intrusion was simply too high.[167] The policy judgment that verification would be illusory, coupled with America's own vulnerability to transparency and counter-proliferation considerations, added up to an inspection cost that exceeded the benefits in the political calculation. Instead of the path toward enhanced verification, America pursued an alternative path to higher confidence in treaty adherence. The result is an approach focused on strengthening vulnerable points in the spectrum of activity covered by the treaty, ranging from national implementing legislation, to lab and pathogen security, as well as enhanced investigatory capacity.

To explain, the BWC verification protocol was directed at limited elements of a *transparency* regime. As the chairman of the ad hoc group of states parties to the convention admitted in written testimony to a Congressional committee:

> "[T]he ultimate aim of the Protocol can not be and is not verification of the BWC, certainly not in terms of how verification is understood in the United States. Instead the Protocol will create enhanced transparency of relevant areas of dual-use civilian and military activities."[168]

The key BWC provisions consisted of declarations and related triggers, classification procedures, and investigations. By the time of its rejection—both substantively and processwise—a multiyear negotiation of a "rolling text" had been supplanted by a proposed 200 plus page "composite" document ostensibly reflecting a politically saleable

---

167   *See* WORLD AT RISK REPORT, *supra* note 14 at p. 35.

168   Ambassador Tibor Tóth, written testimony to the Subcommittee on National Security, Veterans Affairs, and International Relations of the Committee of Government Reform, U.S. House of Representatives (July 10, 2001).

compromise.[169] But the U.S. found the price of intrusion too high when it would not verify the convention "effectively" or "adequately."[170]

The cost of intrusion was not worth the goals of increased transparency to the U.S. The perceived flaws flowed from a number of considerations. First, the dual use permitted under the treaty differs from that of other arms control regimes in that intent alone is largely the arbiter of permitted activity. Peaceful versus hostile purpose divides legitimate from unlawful use. That fundamental evaluation turns on a judgment of compliance that selective transparency alone will not unveil. Rather, as with the self-policing approach that has always existed under the convention, NTMs provide the essential investigative tool. In turn, they are typically dependent upon human intelligence, at least in the absence of circumstantial physical signatures, as existed in the Sverdlovsk anthrax incident of 1979 in Siberia.

Hence, a central tenet of traditional verification measures—that of fixing the size of controlled activity—cannot be measured as the typical starting point. Yet, the quest to fix the size of a biological weapon program in Iraq was a central issue at the same time as the Protocol's development. It remained so even in the aftermath of the collapse of the Protocol's negotiation. The difference in biological weapons verification approaches well illustrates the U.S. interest in the high price for actual disarmament, as opposed to mere support of regime transparency.

Even with the practical impossibility of measurement in the broad biological realm, the declaratory process to establish baseline activity utilized a *surrogate* approach. This approach is akin to strategic nuclear weapons regimes in the past. Quantitative thresholds intertwined with particular activities and facilities became the "substitute" for comprehensiveness, just as means of delivery did for the weapon in the nuclear context. The quantities did *not* serve to distinguish presumptive

---

169   *See, e.g., ibid.*

170   *See* Testimony of Dr. Edward J. Lacey, Principal Deputy Assistant Secretary of State for Verification and Compliance, before the Subcommittee on National Security, Veterans Affairs, and International relations Committee on Government Reform, U.S. House of Representatives, July 10, 2001 at pp. 1–2 of 4 *accessed at* http://www.laws.gov/reform/us/107th_testimony/testimony_of_dr_lacey.htm at p. 1 of 4. ("Lacey Testimony").

permissible peaceful use from illegitimate weaponization programs. Additionally, activities outside of the categories identified in the protocol need not be declared nor subjected to the associated clarification process. Thus, even though an approach calculated to promote transparency rather than verification actually reflected an American suggested path,[171] the resulting "composite" package was politically unacceptable given the limited goal to be served.

In examining the categories and related declaratory criteria, the price of certainty with respect to the declarations was judged not to be worth the risks flowing from the transparency. The increased certainty that other member states would have with respect to the accuracy of declared programs did not promote sufficient confidence in the U.S. in a militarily significant manner so as to justify the openness demanded about its activity in return. The shortfall is derived from the definition of what need be declared, as determined by "triggers." They may be categorized as: (i) "defensive" programs; (ii) "contained" research, where the agents in use were prevented from entry into the environment; (iii) "identified" agents involving work with especially dangerous pathogens and production of them above certain levels; and (iv) certain types of "production" facilities, gauged more by know-how than size. Each of these four baskets would not catch all such related activity, but only that within particular criteria and parameters, which even when defined could be subject to differing interpretations. This, in turn, would result in uncertain adherence, just as with the CTBT, although the problem with that regime arose from the lack of definitions.

Apart from interpretative ambiguity, there were other gaps in the declaratory process with the BWC inspection protocol that potentially created unacceptable risk. To illustrate, the registration process with respect to national defense programs, whose dual use potential created both the greatest risk of breakout from the weapons proliferation and a necessary pre-requisite to use, would not be entirely visible in the composite approach. Rather, the BWC regime embraced another proxy approach, whereby the regime would capture those likely to be relevant. This alternative approach was again based on an earlier

---

171   *See, e.g.*, Garamone, *Iraq and Biological Warfare Agents*, AMERICAN FORCES PRESS SERVICE, January 27, 2003.

American proposal.[172] The details of the web designed to capture declarations in this regard had multiple threads. Among them were a size category tied to employment of 15 or more professionals. Smaller facilities were not ensnared. The role of consultants and "independent contractors" was a loophole. The size category constituted a potential circumvention device to the alternate snare for countries with less than ten such facilities, which required declaration of most (80%) of its R&D facilities on a particular activity, such as toxinology. Smaller programs were also targeted for visibility by yet other criteria. The approach, in general, was to carve out as exceptions small scale activities in countries with large programs, while netting such activity in countries which did not have large programs. Although the compartmentalization of data through this approach capped costs for an anticipated intermediary organization to manage, it left the declaratory process open to manipulation. Since the clarification process posited as an adjunct was tied to that which was declared, only the challenge investigatory process could serve as a regime check to deter undeclared areas of activity where there was cheating potential.

As a result, improvement in the availability of select information was perceived merely as a transparency measure focused on essential components necessary for offensive programs. Identifying such facilities, along with other triggers tied not to pathogen possession alone (but the type, level, and associated know-how of work done with them, along with microbiological production capability), together served as "filters" to focus the objects of transparency and thereby make inspections more precise. But the highly selective nature of the criteria resulted in undeclared dual-capable facilities from which militarily significant offensive weapons activity could be conducted. It was simply impractical to include all dual-use facilities.[173] As such, the transparency measure promoted illusory confidence by the lack of both "effective" and "adequate" verification of compliance. Accordingly, the verifiability of the BW convention could not be sufficiently tied, as in other arms control or

---

172   *See* Proposed Text for Article III: Declarations, Current Biologic Defense Declaration," Working Paper of the U.S.A., BWC/Ad Hoc Group/WP 319 (10/2/98).

173   For example, illicit activity could occur in beer breweries, academic labs, or even yogurt manufacturers.

disarmament regimes, to the provision of detailed data exchange. As a result, the price of intrusion for transparency did not meet security needs. Verification in such circumstances would not build sufficient confidence to justify the process.

In rejecting not only the substantive content of the "composite" document, but the entire approach as well, the U.S. paid a price in relinquishing some credibility in the arms control process. This was especially true since there were manifestly many accommodations to U.S. initiatives in principle and in practice found in the proposal. As a result, the necessity of utilizing surrogates in devising verification regimes will not only be a technical device, it will likely be a political necessity as well, if the proposals reflecting our preferences are to be accommodated in future negotiations in pursuit of a more acceptable biologically-related verification process.

In other circumstances, the United States has willingly paid a price for intrusion where there was thought to be adequate access to verify actual disarmament compliance. For example, in verifying Libya's WMD disarmament, the U.S. was satisfied with the adequacy of access provided. Indeed, Libya has been characterized as a "positive model of transparency" with respect to both the nuclear and chemical inspectorates of the IAEA and OPCW.[174] The price paid to gain this level of transparency is known to have ranged from facilitating admission to Western universities in previously restricted areas, to greater economic aid, the lifting of sanctions, technical assistance, and cooperation.[175] The gap between expectation and performance with respect to the incentives to cooperate has resulted in reported Libyan dissatisfaction, but Libya lost leverage through the sequencing of its disarmament activities preceding rewards. Neither Iran nor North Korea are making the same mistake. Indeed, North Korea seems to have learned both from the Libyan experience and its own repeated encounters.[176]

---

174   *See* B. Andemicael, *Challenges for Effective WMD Verification*, 48IAEA Bulletin *accessed at* http://www.iaea.org/Publications/Magazines/Bulletin/Bull481/htmls/wmd_verification.html.

175   *See* Boureston and Feldman, *Verifying Libya's Nuclear Disarmament*, Chapter 5 *in* Verification Yearbook (2004) at p. 100.

176   North Korea, for example, never received from the West the promised light water nuclear reactors under the 1994 Framework Agreement.

D. MANAGED ACCESS

One key principle of intrusion is that of "managed access." The principle provides for "adequate access" through a degree of host country control, the confines of which are often negotiated. It is manifest in the CTBT verification process, and in that of certain other arms control regimes. Yet there are a number of unsettled issues associated with its procedural implementation. The CTBT treaty provisions, for example, address possible denial of entry to an inspection team.[177] They include refusal to allow a representative of the challenging state (e.g., U.S.A.) to accompany the inspectors.[178] Even the entry into the challenged state's jurisdiction can be delayed for up to 72 hours,[179] and cannot exceed 25 days in duration. There is a power to exclude permanent entry for a particular individual from an inspection. Challenges can also extend to equipment.[180] Other powers of restriction extend to access to buildings by inspectors.[181] The ability to ban inspector access by a challenged state extends up to multiple four square kilometer sites that can total 50 square kilometers as off limits,[182] and ranges down to a level of minutia that includes particular displays or equipment.[183] At an even more tangible level, the challenged state is empowered to disallow collection or analysis of samples to identify the existence of radioactive material.[184] Any collection of radioactive samples must be accompanied by approval of a majority of the Executive Council. Again, the degree of intrusion is tied to a political process, which may be calibrated in its response to circumstance, rather than embraced fully.

There are other technical aspects to the OSI regime that also compromise the right and degree of intrusion permitted. A key one relates to

---

177   *See* CTBT ¶88(c).

178   *Ibid.* at ¶61(a). Compare the U.S. rejection of Iraqi efforts to exclude inspector participants based on national origin.

179   *Ibid.* at ¶57.

180   *Ibid.* at ¶22.

181   *Ibid.* at ¶51.

182   *Ibid.* at ¶¶88(a) and 89(d).

183   *Ibid.* at ¶¶89(e), 92 and 96.

184   *Ibid.* at ¶89(c).

the ability to satisfy the burden of proof. While there are going to be monitoring facilities globally, their location was an object of protracted negotiation. Despite the fact that the CTBT requires installation of over 30 monitoring stations in Russia and 11 in China as part of the IMS,[185] both Russia and China were successful in blocking installation of monitoring stations in proximity to particularly sensitive areas where low yield or decoupled testing was suspected. As a result, seismic events in these areas cannot be calibrated precisely even if detected. This would render uncertain the precise location of the event. In those circumstances, the area to be inspected would be larger than desirable, and the results could become somewhat marginalized. Coupled with the "managed aspects" of the OSI regime (i.e., an exclusionary zone from which a target state could legally block inspector access), a cheating state could potentially evade verification. In this respect, the exclusionary right echoed the experience of the UNSCOM when Saddam Hussein blocked inspection of his presidential palaces. While America and its allies rejected those types of conditions with respect to UNSCOM in Iraq, there the dealings were with a vanquished foe. Since every country that concerns the U.S. could decouple at least its small nuclear explosions, the pervasiveness of this technical capacity coupled with access restrictions left OSI possibly compromised in its ability to provide evidence of low-yield noncompliance.[186] An event may not be identified clearly and convincingly to meet the judgment requirement;[187] so suspicion would not yield to verified noncompliance under the OSI regime in this regard. It is a fair point to target for a supplemental accord in any resumed consideration of CTBT ratification if a "high level" of certainty is to be required, as expected.

Despite its limitation, managed access also has been suggested as an innovative mechanism to instill confidence and to enhance certainty with respect to transparency measures in arms control regimes. For example, in the negotiation of a protocol to the Bioweapons Convention, a mechanism provided for mandatory, random visits to assist, clarify, and check the accuracy and reliability of national declarations. As noted above, while aimed at promoting compliance with declaratory

---

185   *Ibid.* at p. S12516.

186   CTBT Senate Debate at p. S12380.

187   *See* U.N. Verification Principles, *supra* note 4 at Principle 11.

obligations, the inspection was not designed to assure adherence to the substantive elements of the convention itself.[188] The inspection process was posited simply to serve a deterrence function. In this way, a reporting function would supposedly build confidence in a state's transparency, but would not rise to the level of a verification process. The idea actually had its inception in a U.S. proposal,[189] although America subsequently rejected the composite approach in which it was contained as part of a political package deal.

Given the limited purposes of the inspection mechanism in this context, there was some common sense exhibited in the resulting limits on its composition and functionality. The size, amount of equipment, and range of on-site inspection were all constrained, consistent with the function of merely assuring consistency in the declaration, as opposed to verification of compliance with the convention's prohibitions. Access would have been managed in that process with respect not only to the building in a complex, but also even down to the specific room(s). The use of a definition sought to provide access focus, because the definition would have tied inspections to a "facility," that is, "any room or suite of rooms, laborator(ies), building(s), structure(s) or parts of a building(s) or other structure(s) which is or are used to conduct activity(ies) as specified in Article 4."

As such, access was supposed to be limited to the room where the declared activity actually takes place. So, for example, the area where fermentation occurs would be the industrial target. Even so, the nature and extent of that access would fall within the vested state's discretion. Moreover, the fact that information requests might be made and denied could not even be commented upon in the inspection report. In this way, access would not only be managed, it would be *controlled*, despite the random and "mandatory" attributes built into the OSI system. The proposed scope of access was simply left to the discretion of the host party. In this sense, the approach may be contrasted with the Chemical Weapons Convention and CTBT regimes in which access is negotiated, but for verification purposes rather than for transparency per se to build confidence in declarations.

---

188   CTBT Senate Debate at p. S12380.

189   *See* Tóth testimony, *supra* note 168.

The added value of the proposed mandatory mechanism was nevertheless thought to be worthwhile by many. The possibility of detection was perceived as a deterrent to embedding illicit activity under cover of legitimate, declared facilities. The argument in favor was that:

"The openness that is created through the declaration obligation, the declaration clarification procedures addressing any anomalies, uncertainties, ambiguities or omissions which can be initiated directly by a state party as well as by the future organization, and the possibility of randomly selected transparency and clarification visits may well influence the decision-making process of the would-be violator. He will at least have to live with the unquantifiable risk of exposing the hidden program, having the visiting team ask questions, and risking that his employees say the wrong thing in the wrong place at the wrong time."[190]

The possibility of a mistake is offered as a justification for intrusion. Yet, there is so little certainty associated with such constrained inspection that American arms-control policy makers at the time discounted its importance. Given that in this context, verification is not even the goal of the inspection, the notion that a contingent, incidental benefit can possibly justify the risks of intrusion was simply unacceptable. Whatever the transparency value of a reporting process reinforced by visits, "managed access" rights could also serve as a mechanism to deny access to evidence that would incriminate the visitor party. As one American official put it at the time:

"[o]nly a small fraction of the facilities declared as potentially relevant to conducting offensive biological warfare activities would be subject to visits on a random basis. Even at visited facilities, illicit biological warfare work could easily be concealed or cleaned up, rendering it highly improbable that international inspectors would detect evidence of noncompliance. Moreover, violators could remove any risk associated with such visits by engaging in illicit biological warfare activities at non-declared facilities."

Equally, the process could serve to facilitate inadvertent disclosure of confidential information, or could harm U.S. commercial interests.

There were only two counter arguments proffered. The first was that cheating through secret facilities has to be "leak proof." Hence,

---

190   Lacey Testimony, *supra* note 170.

a declaratory regime reinforced by visits to check and clarify serve deterrence by increasing the price of circumvention: conducting secret activities is more expensive and prone to exposure. The other counter argument was that the process of clarification offered a beneficial methodology for resolving problems associated with declarations without raising such matters to challenge levels of a politically problematic accusation. It was conceived as a means by which to eliminate suspicions in a more palatable diplomatic manner.

In other arms-control contexts, the counter argument is more persuasive, particularly if "managed access" aspects associated with challenge inspections are relatively constrained. However, most biologic activities do not leave the same kind of "telling" physical signatures as do nuclear and chemical weapons. Although there are forensic technical improvements, the adequacy of restricted on-site inspection in the bioweapon context is far less certain than for other WMD. Accordingly, the techniques devised in the failed biological protocol negotiations may nevertheless provide useful precedents in future WMD negotiations, as well as a roadmap to shortcomings.

For example, with pathogens, there can be a temporal component that impacts detection. Clean up or concealment can occur in the time delay encountered to get an investigative team on the ground. The dual use nature of the material and equipment also facilitates explanation of a reasonable non-military purpose. As a result, even the less constrained operational aspects of a challenge investigation inspection under the proposed biological protocol did not necessarily compensate in certainty of detection because of these inherent limits. The protocol contemplated separate "green" and "red" light approaches depending upon the trigger-outbreak investigation or challenge inspection of a facility. The fact that dozens of investigators can spend days on site for a facility investigation, and as much for a field investigation, conducting comparatively unfettered inspection, does not necessarily overcome those limitations. Plus, the need for a "green light" for certain investigations under the composite text triggers associated process uncertainty in the availability of the OSI. Yet, introduction of this political approval risk came at U.S. policy insistence, driven in part to protect America's pharmaceutical industry.

The composite protocol approach eliminated the need for U.N. Security Council approval—and risk of a veto. There is another instructive political component built into the voting process associated with on-site challenge inspections for offensive bioweapons. Basically, the vote requirements tied to the filtering criteria varied. This served as a check on retaliatory challenges being initiated by visited states. The criteria were linked to both the target of the investigation (field vs. facility) and two types of triggers: (i) alleged use vs. the outbreak of disease; and (ii) the place (sovereign territory or that of another country). Thus, at one end of the intrusion spectrum tied to allegations of use by a state in its territory (or that under its control), it took a three-quarter super majority vote *against* proceeding by an Executive Council to *halt* the inspection. If such alleged use occurred in another country, then the tally needed to halt the investigation was a two-thirds majority. The "red" vs. "green" light process required only a simple majority where there was a suspect disease outbreak: a majority vote of a "red" light to stop the inspection on the suspect's home or controlled territory, and a majority authorizing vote to proceed in another country. Similarly, a positive majority vote would be required to authorize a facility investigation. The more sophisticated breakout of filters and triggers of the proposed protocols stood in stark contrast to the CTBT's simple super majority authorization mechanism. At the same time, the fact that both verification regimes required political approval weakens potentially the potency of the OSI measure. It also renders the challenge invocation process a political decision, with a price to be paid; yet, it is a flexible one which can be responsive to circumstance.

Likewise, the "managed" aspects of the activity of the inspectors reflected the difference in purpose from declaratory monitoring to verifying compliance with the convention. The ability to interview, observe, review records, to sample and to identify were all attributes of the process. However, the manner of application in particular circumstances was still a matter of negotiation between investigators and the host state. Restrictions in the name of national security or preservation of proprietary or confidential information would at once be countenanced and noted. However, a burden of poof is also imposed on the host state to show that the alternatives to denial of requested measures still provide sufficient access.

The "managed access" attributes of the composite text for the proposed BWC protocol ultimately reflected a rejection of the positions advanced by many nations that America suspects. They had advocated minimal intrusion, especially in disease outbreak scenarios. Most U.S. allies on the other hand, advocated a greater intrusion than did America. In fact, the proposed super majority of red light filters through the spectrums of triggers stood as a concession to America, through a more politically nuanced process that was ultimately proposed. Yet, the U.S. found itself positioned somewhat in between the camps of its allies who could be commercial competitors, and its potential military adversaries. As a result, it sought declaratory diminution, while embracing challenge inspections. Accordingly, the U.S. sought to "manage access" in the biological context by downplaying the role of confidence-building measures to seek less transparency, while increasing it in cause-based challenges. That seems a likely path to be followed in the future, as the Obama Administration has already emphasized in declaratory policy its general interest in strengthening inspection regimes, at least in the verification context.[191]

E. DISARMAMENT

In the immediate aftermath of the Cold War, momentum for arms reduction supplanted that of limitation. In some instances, such as with chemical weapons, the effort for arms control extended as far as elimi-nation. But the paths for verifying the regimes diverged, and verification in the nuclear arena revolved around preventing diversion of material and proliferation of know-how in the process. While international inspectorates were crafted both through multilateral inspection organi-zations and ad hoc approaches with respect to chemical and biological weapons, as well as their means of delivery, the more enduring verifica-tion contribution from this period will have been made in the nuclear context. Trilateral efforts by the United States, Russia, and IAEA cre-ated a potential model for selected aspects of the verification process. While the focus was on elimination of excess weapons, they began to chart the course on how to move from reduction to eventual disarma-ment. These efforts remain largely veiled as classified information. The secretive initiative belied the unqualified U.N. verification principle that the ". . . disarmament process will benefit from greater openness."[192]

---

191   See, e.g., Prague Speech, supra note 13.

192   U.N. Verification Principles, supra note 4 at Principle 5.

Yet, as the exception to the rule, the trilateral approach created a potential model that may be employed in technique if not principle with others in the future, including North Korea. At the same time, the magnitude of the effort actually required to move toward complete nuclear disarmament revealed costs and other practical impediments that will be significant hurdles in the future.

(i) The Trilateral Initiative

The prospect of future nuclear disarmament pursuant to the treaty on the Non-Proliferation of Nuclear Weapons ("NPT") has always been tied to verification. There can be no doubt the path will be intrusive. Just as with less ambitious arms-control limitation, the ability to monitor for compliance is at the heart of the ability to agree to disarm, whether wholly or in part. The U.S. and USSR initially tested verification processes through protocols to arm control regimes. Together with the International Atomic Energy Agency, Russia and America subsequently explored that path in the nuclear context. Their Trilateral Initiative ("TI") was a cooperative venture to develop processes and equipment to verify myriad issues associated with the disposition of excess weapons originated fissile material resulting from arms reduction or obsolescence. With reduction of nuclear arsenals and deeper cuts contemplated, the need for enhanced verification became manifest. Since the forms of the material themselves were classified, new approaches had to be developed for IAEA verification. The teams worked toward developing techniques that would allow the IAEA to ascertain whether declared weapons components contained weapons grade plutonium. At the same time, the process was calculated to prevent access to design data.

The elements of the initiative touched upon three basic categories: (i) technical; (ii) financial; and (iii) legal. The result of the effort between 1996–2002 was development of a Model Verification Agreement for IAEA use with weapons-origin materials released from the defense program of the participating nations. Since the U.S. and Russia possess 95 percent of the weapons-grade nuclear material in the world, their ability to agree on appropriate verification for disposition of such materials should provide the necessary underpinnings for a future model bilateral agreement between the IAEA and other weapons states. While Russia and the U.S. concluded their working group activity in

2002, the resulting agreement with Russia remains classified.[193] It still has not been submitted for approval to the IAEA Board of Governors.

The disposition of weapons-originated nuclear material by the U.S. and Russia will not occur in bilateral isolation. The multinational legal process seeks to cap production of fissile material for weapons as well. The proposed treaty has languished for some years, but a fresh initiative may be expected from the new U.S. administration. Whether such production is capped or not, the gradual reduction in weapons is expected eventually to move beyond removal from deployment to actual retirement of weapons.[194] Verifications of the arrangements by which weapons-grade nuclear material will be removed and processed will be a central underpinning for a cascade of future disarmament, as well as materially impacting confidence in that process.[195]

There are two conditions in which the fissile material is inspected, one of which raises the need for significant constraints on the process. If the nuclear material is already processed at the time of inspection to the point that no military secrets will be revealed, then the process and composition of the inspection team requires no distinction based on whether its members come from weapons states or not. In contrast, if the inspection process occurs at an earlier point, then classified properties will remain and the secrets will be potentially accessible during the inspection. As a legal matter, this likely precludes participation by non-weapons state inspectors because of the danger of passing on military information in contravention of the NPT's nonproliferation mandate, unless sufficient protection from disclosure can be built into the monitoring system. At the same time, if the verification process is triggered

---

193   The author's request for declassification and release pursuant to the Freedom of Information Act had not been acted upon at the time of manuscript submission.

194   *See, e.g.*, Prague Speech, *supra* note 13 ("To reduce our warheads and stockpiles, we will negotiate a new Strategic Arms Reduction Treaty with the Russians this year . . . And this will set the stage for further cuts, and we will seek to include all nuclear weapon States in the endeavor.").

195   The orchestration of all this activity occurs in the legal context of the NPT Article VI obligation to disarm. Although the NPT conference in 2000 agreed upon 13 practical steps to implement it, the Bush administration withdrew its support for some of them.

at the juncture where a warhead is actually separated from the delivery vehicle, then it could also serve to validate an arms-reduction agreement. Hence, the functionality of the international verification process is tied to the condition of the fissile material and function; disarmament by removing fissile material from serving a military function, or more simply, diminishing the military function by removing it from operational status. Since the reprocessing of fissile material from weaponized form is such a lengthy process, the pace of prospective arms reduction and disarmament is directly impacted by the ability to inspect material at the classified stage. Equally, the role of the IAEA would be to provide an independent and credible verification of the nuclear component, without at the same time compromising weapon design secrets.

(ii) North Korea: A Future Test Case?

The future of verification may be more intrusive, for in a situation like that of North Korea, where at least some of its plutonium has been weaponized, the path to promised disarmament requires baseline inspection to avoid cheating or proliferation risks. The degree of certainty required of the process with a rogue adversary is necessarily heightened. Given the particular proliferation concerns associated with North Korea, it is also not a given that the level of verification currently contemplated by the TI would suffice. There, the agreed-upon metric for "effective verification" was posited as a "one percent solution." While never formally agreeing to it, the TI working group reportedly proceeded on the basis that "breakout potential" from monitored inventory involving a quantitative factor of one percent could be a militarily significant strategic change.[196] That understanding, in turn, provided the basis for the verification plans embraced. But there is a difference between meeting the verification needs of long-time rational adversaries, and a rogue with a history of proliferation, where that one percent differential of nuclear material could go to the highest bidder.

---

196 Thomas E. Shea, The Trilateral Initiative: A Model for the Future?, *accessed at* http://www.armscontrol.org/act/2008_05/PersboShea.

Despite the ebb and flow of the Six Nations Talks,[197] North Korea may eventually provide a test case for some of the technical verification methods developed under the TI. The fissile material submitted by North Korea, as envisioned in the TI process, would include secret characteristics as the parties examine components from nuclear warheads, assuming North Korea in fact progressed that far in its weaponization program. However, in other respects, the work of the TI does not rise to the full North Korean challenge. Russia, the U.S., and IAEA had all agreed that the TI would not address the verification requirements to confirm that an item is really a nuclear warhead or specific components of it, or even to identify a model. The associated security challenges were regarded as too daunting.[198] Likewise, the IAEA verification role was not contemplated to include dismantlement of a weapons system, including monitoring the removal of a warhead from a delivery system. Thus, depending upon the developmental and deployment stages of North Korea's nuclear arsenal,[199] the TI verification processes, painstakingly created over a six-year period, fall short of certain possible tasks associated with any future North Korean disarmament. A helpful precedent in this context from the 1990s may be the veiled monitoring by Russian and U.S. experts, which facilitated verification of excess warhead dismantlement

---

197   The six nations are the U.S., Russia, China, North Korea, South Korea, and Japan. As of the time of writing, North Korea had withdrawn from the talks, expelled IAEA inspectors and announced it was reconstituting its weapons program. The U.N. condemned the resumption of the nuclear weaponization program. *See, e.g.*, Statement by the President of the Security Council, S/PRST/2009/7 (April 13, 2009) *accessed at* www.un.org/docs/sc/unsc_pres_statements09.htm (condemning missile test). The U.N. Security Council also condemned North Korea's nuclear test on May 26, 2009 as a "clear violation of the Council's resolution." *Accessed at* http://www.unmultimedia.org/radio/english/detail/75308.html. The Security Council imposed additional sanctions and ordered North Korea unconditional return to the Six-Nation Talks on June 12, 2009 pursuant to Resolution 1874.

198   *See* SHEA, *supra* note 196.

199   Open sources indicate North Korea declared a plutonium inventory of 37 kg- within the range of prior estimates. *See, e.g.*, INTERNATIONAL PANEL ON FISSILE MATERIALS, GLÓBAL FISSILE MATERIAL REPORT 2008: SCOPE AND VERIFICATION OF A FISSILE MATERIAL (CUT-OFF) TREATY at p. 1, *accessed at* www.fissilematerials.org ("IPFM Verification Report").

without betraying design.[200] If needed, perhaps that bilateral experience can inform the crafting of procedures with North Korea for its verifiable nuclear disarmament if or when the opportunity arises.

Still, the TI process had moved beyond "the development and testing of concepts to the construction of specific systems intended for use in specified facilities," before the political relationship between the U.S. and Russia changed during the Bush administration. That shift resulted in slowing the pace and eventually freezing the developmental stage of the program. Whether elements of the technological developments associated with the TI process can be utilized in connection with the eventual verification process in North Korea, if there is one, remains to be seen.

Another area in which North Korea could set a precedent would be in the use of U.N. verification expertise from the Iraq wars. Over an extended period in the 1990s, and for a brief time before the second Gulf War, expertise was developed both with respect to missile technology and control over the sales of dual-use technology in hostile circumstances through the UNSOM and UNMOVIC organizations. Today, North Korea is similarly compelled by the Security Council Resolution to abandon its WMD and missile program "in a complete, verifiable and irreversible manner."[201] While implementation of many aspects of the related sanctions were held in abeyance for a time, resumed North Korean missile testing in the spring of 2009 resulted in a political decision to proceed with those sanctions. Apart from monitoring compliance, the U.N. could be tasked in the future with verifying North Korea's abandonment of its missile program as well as dual-use control. The U.N. experience in doing the same in Iraq proved to be a success, albeit at the cost of a war triggered by an erroneous noncompliance judgment.[202] Nevertheless, that experience and similar mechanisms

---

200   *Ibid.* at p. 33. Dismantlement of the Libyan nuclear program did not involve warheads as the program was not as advanced. Libya reportedly had neither a working centrifuge system nor uranium enrichment beyond "cold tests," but had obtained weapons designs. *See generally* Boureston and Feldman, *supra* note 175.

201   Security Council Resolution 1718, the Sanctions Against the People's Republic of North Korea (October 16, 2006) at operative paragraph 7.

202   *See generally*, Brian Jones, INTELLIGENCE, VERIFICATION AND IRAQ's WMD, Chapter 10 *in* Verification Yearbook (2004).

could be employed eventually with North Korea, or even Iran's missile program.[203]

(a) "Attribute" Verification

From a technical standpoint, it is known from open source material that the contemplated TI processes—even at the limited levels agreed upon—could reveal weapons secrets in circumstances where inspectors were allowed access to new measurement data. As a result, there is a recognized need to depart from typical safeguard measurement practices. Yet a state like North Korea, which has past IAEA experience, would be skeptical of a verification process proposal that deviates from the normal IAEA practice. Hence, any proposal in this regard would best be channeled with credibility purposes in mind. In such circumstances, the technique of utilizing "trial verification measures" seems likely to be a necessary step in what will be a highly problematic confidence-building process.

Whether in a trial scenario or otherwise, the technical process likely to be employed is that settled upon in the TI. Denominated "attribute verification with information barriers,"[204] direct qualitative measures were shielded from the inspectors. Instead, the measurements relied upon a comparison of them with unclassified reference points, "with

---

203　*See* Cleminson, *International Verification of WMD Proliferation: Applying UNMOVIC's Legacy,* 9 Journal of Military and Strategic Studies at pp. 15–96 (2006/07). By 2009, Iran successfully developed solid fuel, mobile missiles with a range of approximately 1,200 miles. *See, e.g.,* Thomas Erdbrink, *Iranian Missile Launch Confirmed,* Wash. Post, May 21, 2009 *accessed at* http://www.washingtonpost.com/wp-dyn/content/article/2009/05/20/AR2009052000523.html/?sid=2009052001769.

204　The former head of the TI, Thomas Shea, defined "attribute verification" as involving the comparison of:

> "an object to a set of reference characteristics. For example, the presence of a militarily significant quantity of weapons grade plutonium would be assessed by measures that first determine the presence of plutonium, then assessed that the isotopic composition of the plutonium was such that it was weapons grade material rather than reactor-grade, and finally calculated that the mass of plutonium fell above an agreed minimum defined in relation to each facility."

Shea, *supra* note 196 at p. 5.

the outcomes showing that the actual results are either greater than or less than the reference values, thus verifying a defined 'attribute.'"[205] The verification process for material being converted to peaceful use in nuclear fuel was a relatively straightforward monitoring scheme. The former head of the TI described it as follows:

> "[S]ealed containers would be transported to facilities where the material would be converted and shorn of classified isotopics and chemical properties. IAEA monitoring would begin with the arrival of the classified material at the entry point to the conversion facility. A perimeter monitoring system would assure that only monitored containers, plus other nonweapons materials needed in the peaceful fuel, would be allowed in. All fissile material containers exiting the conversion facility would be measured using normal IAEA safeguards methods, and then seals would be applied to the containers for storage or transport to processing facilities where they would be converted to fuel for nuclear reactors. Managed access would be allowed into the conversion facility annually to ensure that no warhead components accumulated and that no undeclared penetrations occurred that could have resulted in undeclared additions or removals of fissile material. IAEA inspectors could witness containers entering the measuring system, identify tag measurements, confirm seal data, and observe the attribute measurement results on a pass-fail basis."[206]

In this manner, secrets are preserved while, at the same time, the IAEA can offer independent and credible verification, albeit at information levels below that obtained under normal IAEA plutonium safeguards. Technology enables the process in sensitive circumstances at sufficient levels to serve as a basis for independent monitoring. But the scheme is ultimately dependent upon an agreement about the conversion facilities, an agreement currently precluded by North Korea's open hostility.[207]

Any measurement system in such a regime necessarily requires tamperproof certification and authentication. It also will often necessitate use of specifically constructed facilities. As is easily imagined, the security system is what assures the integrity of the process to prevent both

---

205   *Ibid.* at p. 51.

206   *Ibid.* at p. 5.

207   *Ibid.*

cheating or leakage of military secrets. Authenticating the security system is a challenging task. Technology challenges do not end there for the verification process. After all, inspection is just one component. The system must also be able to monitor the weapons origin fissile material that is inventoried. However, this aspect of the process is seemingly much more easily embraced within the framework of traditional IAEA safeguards relating to surveillance and containment, with which North Korea is familiar.

(b) Disposition

At some juncture in the disarmament process with North Korea or any weapons state, the fissile material shifts from classified to unclassified form. At that point, disposition activity is possible. To that end, the U.S. and Russia have already developed a form of "Plutonium Management and Disposition Agreement" ("PMDA"). The agreement contemplates the possibility of the IAEA performing the necessary verification to implement irradiation over a time period that is expected to last about 20 years. In many respects, the process is likely to mirror normal safeguard measures for nonweapons states,[208] but the verification measures were not finalized.[209] Yet the extended responsibilities on the IAEA resulting from the shifting nuclear material under its watch will be demanding in terms of increased personnel and costs: one open source estimate made by a former nuclear weapons state gauged the impact at a factor of a two or three fold increase.[210]

At bottom, though, the PMDA focused mechanically on the elements of disposition. Therefore, verification was more of a secondary consideration. The monitoring arrangements remain an unfulfilled promise, as the contemplated consultation with the IAEA failed to materialize. As such, they are part of the verification agenda going forward. The monitoring arrangements are another area in which North Korea may prove to be a test case. The lack of a sufficiently developed bilateral

---

208   *Ibid.*

209   *Ibid.* at p. 6 n.4.

210   South African working paper The possible scope and requirements of the fissile material treaty, U.N. Conference on Disarmament (CD/1671)(25/05/02).

U.S.-Russian precedent will require the U.S. to explore these issues in hostile circumstances, rather than merely competitive ones.

(iii) Future Problems

(a) Legal Responsibility: Who Pays?

Apart from technical concerns about the verification process, there are also legal considerations. The TI process only contemplated voluntary submission to IAEA verification with respect to excess weapons-origin fissile material. In a North Korean disarmament scenario, the submission to IAEA auspices would no doubt be compulsory. The availability of the TI process in either instance is also dependent upon whether resources for it are equal to the task. In the present environment of fiscal constraint, the IAEA is not in a financial position to play a meaningful role absent further contributions, as it simply cannot afford the price of participation. Obligatory verification measures for weapons-origin material will come with a hefty price tag. Financing that process will be a subject of future negotiation. In a very real sense, the integrity and credibility of any future international verification process for nuclear disarmament will only be as good as the dollars reliably funding it; the cost for putting the weapons genie back into the bottle will be very pricey. The circumstantial dependency of available funding is not an adequate legal basis for an obligatory arms reduction or disarmament regime with a formal international verification process. One of the other unanswered elements of the TI and future disarmament implementation of NPT Article VI, then, is who shall pay for verification related to its implementation?

There is no agreement yet among the member states of the NPT. Under existing international law, there is no definite answer. Perhaps the closest principle by analogy would be that of the "polluter pays"[211] from an environmental context. There is certainly precedent for this approach in the WMD context. Article IV(16) of the Chemical Weapons Convention provides that:

> "Each state party shall meet the costs of destruction of chemical weapons it is obligated to destroy. It should also meet the costs of verification

---

211 See, e.g., *The Trail Smelter Arbitration*, 3 U.N. Rep. Int'l. Arb. Awards, 1911, 1938 (1941) (Ad Hoc Int'l. Arb. Tribunal).

of storage and destruction of these weapons unless the Executive Council deems otherwise."

In such circumstances, the cost-shifting approach would probably follow the U.N. scale of assessment, per the convention.

Resistance to the cost-shifting approach is expected by at least some of the weapons states, such as Russia. In contrast, when the U.S. placed excess weapons materials in unclassified form under IAEA safeguards in the mid-1990s, the U.S. paid for the inspections.[212] The IAEA staff, apparently willing to recognize that disarmament benefits all, suggested establishment of a dedicated disarmament verification fund based on allocation principles like those of its safeguards inspection program for future mandatory disarmament obligations.[213] Payment responsibility could mirror the U.N.'s contribution allocations tied to gross domestic product. The payment issue remains open at this time. Apparently, it is one thing to be willing to compromise one's sovereignty in the name of collective security; it is quite another to pay the costs associated with the process. The costs in the nuclear context will dwarf those experienced, for example, under the Chemical Weapons Convention, where the main cost "has been that of destroying huge stockpiles."[214]

Finally, cost-driven verification issues are arising in the Fissile Material Cut-Off Treaty negotiations. For example, to the extent that a future treaty only bans new production, monitoring is more limited. The principal budgets would be for inspecting reprocessing as well as enrichment facilities. With respect to the latter, it is essentially a "pass-fail" oversight system; that is, either HEU is being produced or not. Otherwise, there would be a need to safeguard the spectrum of storage through processing activity. However, critics maintain that the cost savings from such a "focused" approach are frequently exaggerated.[215]

---

212   IPFM Verification Report, *supra* note 199 at p. 63.

213   *See* SECURING THE BOMB: IAEA MONITORING OF EXCESS NUCLEAR MATERIAL, at p. 3 *accessed at* http://www.nti.org/e_research/cnwm/monitoring/trilateral.asp.

214   Remarks of Amb. John Holum on *Consolidating the BWC Compliance Regime* at the Carnegie Moscow Center Seminar, 24 February, 1999.

215   *See* A. MEERBURG AND F. VON HIPPEL, COMPLETE CUTOFF: DESIGNING A COMPREHENSIVE FISSILE MATERIAL TREATY, ARMS CONTROL ASSOCIATION, *accessed at* http://www.armscontrol.org/act/2009_03/meerburg_VonHippel.

They argue that cost considerations should be accorded less emphasis in deciding upon the scope of disarmament related agreements. With the "who pays?" question still unanswered, the problem now becomes whether or how much the cost should influence the substance of future negotiation.

Verification of compliance with a cut-off treaty will be expensive. The IAEA already recognizes that the magnitude of the endeavor could cost as much as its current annual safeguards budget.[216] The agency may also be asked to monitor and assist other aspects of nonproliferation and disarmament. It is well positioned, through the Trilateral Initiative for example, to implement monitoring as excess military material is converted to unclassified forms.[217] The agency also could become involved in key aspects of future expansion of fuel cycle safeguarding, whether in an international, regional, or national context. Of course, if there is a shift to a multilateral fuel cycle infrastructure, then the opportunity to design new production facilities with safeguarding built in will diminish monitoring costs thereafter. But the system's cost will be "front-end loaded."

The IAEA is equally apt to be involved in the future, as it has in the past, with extraordinary monitoring activities such as nations decommissioning clandestine or illegal weapons programs. The verification efforts of the IAEA in the South African, Iraq, and Libyan matters were all funded by voluntary contributions, as there is no contingency fund to support that work. Contributions can be conditioned though, a practice that can influence the process or even diminish the perceived credibility of the IAEA's independence. While the ability to exercise some control is a systemic temptation and vulnerability, the resulting diminution in confidence of other parties does not ultimately serve

---

216   *See* 20/20 VISION FOR THE FUTURE: BACKGROUND REPORT OF THE DIRECTOR GENERAL FOR THE COMMISSION OF EMINENT PERSONS, at p. 25 ("20/20 Director General Report"), Annex to the Report of the Commission of Eminent Persons on the Future of the Agency, GOV/2008/22-GC(52)INF14(23May2008) ("Report of the Commission").

217   *See* Report on the Trilateral Initiative. IAEA Verification of Weapon-Origin Material in the Russian Federation & United States, IAEA Bulletin 433 (2001) at p. 49.

U.S. interests.[218] Yet, as more nations agree to the Additional Protocol and the agency augments its safeguarding practices with investigation measures, as with Iran and North Korea, then unanticipated non-routine costs only will increase. For example, IAEA involvement in verifying and monitoring the shutdown and sealing of the Yongbyon nuclear facility beginning in July 2007, including containment and surveillance of nuclear material, were all voluntarily funded by two member nations for a one-year period.[219] Since the need was not foreseen in the Agency budget, the IAEA Secretary General characterized it as ". . . a clear example of the need for an Agency contingency fund to allow us to respond effectively in such critical unforeseen situations."[220]

These verification costs are the equivalent of the part of the iceberg beneath the surface. Yet even the portion that has been visible is a looming menace too. The IAEA is transparent in revealing the deficiencies in resourcing its existing operations. The agency struggles to keep up with its basic safeguarding, while the "significant quantity" of material it polices has increased a thousand times in less than a quarter century.[221] From a "looming infrastructure deficit" to unfunded liabilities for retiree insurance and other benefits, the picture of even the current financial situation is that of a highly stressed verification system. Continuing reliance on voluntary contributions for a third of budgeted operations,[222] and on ad hoc fund raising for extraordinary but increasingly foreseeable activities, is no way to run a risky business—much less one tasked with safeguarding nuclear safety and

---

218   For example, the close interaction of UNSCOM with Western intelligence agencies eventually necessitated its replacement. *See generally*, Jones, *supra* note 202 at pp. 202–205.

219   IAEA Director General Dr. ElBaradei, Introductory Statement to The Board of Governors, 3 March, 2008, *accessed at* http://www.iaea.org/NewsCenter/Statements/2008/ebsp2008n003.html.

220   *Ibid.*

221   Report of the Commission, *supra* note 216 at p. 28. The IAEA defines "significant quantities" as 8 kilograms of plutonium (and 25 kilograms of contained uranium 235 for HEU—enough to mark a bomb.

222   *Ibid.* at p. 27.

core nonproliferation duties.[223] Equally, the approach makes it largely impossible for the IAEA to drive through procurement or investment the technological development necessary to meet anticipated verification needs—either to promote greater efficiency or effectiveness.

The IAEA and other regimes should shift toward a "user fee" approach. Nations that present no oversight problems and which can be so certified, can then be subjected to less routine oversight. The cost savings of untying such expense from the "equality" verification principle will be a common sense recognition born out by decades of experience that risks simply aren't equal. Scarce resources should be spent where needed. The equality principle can be served and efficiently funded by subjecting each certified facility to the same chance of a random inspection regime reasonably calculated to ferret out in timely fashion if an entity is slipping.

Similarly, in the future, if America and Russia as possessors of 95 percent of the nuclear global arsenal involve the IAEA in the effort to dispose of excess weapon origin material, then both are going to have to pay. The U.S. has done so thus far, while the Russians have been remiss. A proportionate contribution from others deriving a direct or indirect benefit from it should be part of the calculus. For example, many nations have enjoyed security benefits from the U.S. and Soviet nuclear deterrents. There is no reason why those benefited nations shouldn't share proportionately in the verification costs of downsizing that nuclear arsenal. Similarly, other nations will benefit from the expertise and technologies being created that will have application in other contexts; those nations ought to contribute too. That contribution dialogue ought to be a meaningful part of other multilateral negotiations involving new nonproliferation or disarmament measures. In some instances, the best system will resemble the contribution regime to the U.N. or NATO, but that model will not be ideal in other situations, as when the embrace of principle properly reflects the price of yesterday's inequities under the NPT.

---

223 *Ibid.* at p. 31 ("The statutory functions of the Agency—including in nuclear energy, nuclear applications, development, safety, security and safeguards—should be fully funded from assessed contributions.").

The financing approach derived from the Polluter Pays Principle, as modified to reflect security realities, can also be applied in the civilian commercial sector. In the future, as nations consider whether to have unilateral or multilateral approaches to the nuclear fuel cycle, they ought to be factoring the price of intrusion into that calculation as well. The true financial cost ought not to be just that of infrastructure. The cost of verification should be included. And there will have to be recognition that the price will be set by others for inspection and monitoring, as they are going to have to live with the risks. Countries vulnerable to attack will want those risks to be acceptable, rather than uncertain. At the same time, there will be economies and efficiencies promoted through standardization and regionalization. In other words, future verification procedures will carry a truer price for intrusion, one that should more directly reflect the real cost of the services, as well as the imprimatur of international inspectorates like the IAEA.

This approach, in turn, will permit the IAEA and similar entities to fully fund agency activities from assessed contributions. The IAEA has identified this need as "critical,"[224] and assuring it in this manner will help insulate verification regimes in the future from the pressures that reliance on conditional contribution carries with it. This will be particularly important as new ground is broken in a nonproliferation and disarmament "renaissance" that gives confidence, and not just hope, in reducing WMD threats.

(b) Practical Concerns

Completely apart from monetary cost considerations, there are many other practical concerns. Among them are adjustments in the declaratory submission process at the IAEA that would be needed if it is to intrude into oversight of fissile material in classified form. The normal process simply would not work, for it would result in the dissemination of weapons-related knowledge that is expressly prohibited by the NPT. The usual precise measuring process undertaken in the safeguards context would also be problematic with respect to classified forms of weapons origin material. Hence, an international verification process required for nuclear arms reduction and eventual disarmament is

---

224   20/20 Director's General's Report, *supra* note 216 at p. 27.

incompatible in substantial part with the nonproliferation verification measures developed over decades to date. Customizing existing agreements with weapons states requires special treatment, which at once is necessary as well as somewhat inconsistent with the equality of treatment verification principles the U.N. embraced in the nonproliferation context. Thus, while the U.S. and Russia may have contributed through the TI to creating a model form of verification that will be useful for other weapons states in the future, progress from that foundation toward implementation will carry a heavy intrusion price. It seems likely, as a result, that actual future submission of material to such IAEA inspection will be done through a phased approach. Confidence in the scheme will have to be built experimentally. There will be a need to provide a "test laboratory" for the approach.[225]

Moreover, it is a difficult enough challenge to balance security modification and reduction/disarmament considerations among the long-time weapons states, without the added complications of being in a quasi state of war with one of the participants. The more viable path with North Korea, therefore, is to devise first a verification scheme focused on our best calculus of the number of warheads they made, or which they agree they made, and to then verify their dismantlement. The inspection parameters for such an approach would be less expansive than needed to provide high certainty that we have eliminated their weapons program completely, so it will only be part of the process. A phased approach to verifying other facilities, personnel, and documentation might follow in implementing the "action for action" principle that enabled the limited disarmament progress that was made prior to the April 2009 breakdown in the Six Nations Talks. In that way, the declared activity is first verifiably dismantled, and then suspect challenges follow. Historically, that has been the model for numerous arms control regimes. That same framework can be utilized to structure the disarmament approach with North Korea. Each side will have more invested in success through a stepped approach, and progressively more in jeopardy with any detection of cheating. While risk is built

---

225   In the broader context of confidence-building among nuclear weapons states, former and then current high-ranking officials of Great Britain's defense establishment proposed using their country as a "disarmament laboratory." *See* Persbo and Bjørningstad, VERIFYING NUCLEAR DISARMAMENT: THE INSPECTOR'S AGENCY, *accessed at* http://www.armscontrol.org/act/2008_05/PersboShea.

into the disarmament approach, intrusion can help build the credibility of verification. Likewise, the benefits flowing from the process are calibrated to create confidence in each level of verified disarmament. However, as the effectiveness of North Korea's conventional forces erodes, intrusion requires the country to lay bare its last effective protection against outside attack. Access will be a precious commodity, not lightly traded, for the intelligence-gathering risk from their standpoint is as much a pathway to vulnerability as it is to possible rapprochement. At the same time, incentives to relinquish a weapons program should only be paid once, even if on the installment plan.

As the U.S. considers the practical issues likely to arise from the North Korean disarmament process, we will do well to be mindful of our own similar precedential concerns in the broader arms reduction context, as well as differences. The risk of the proliferation of knowledge is present in both settings. If actual warhead dismantlement is to be verified, it will likely follow declaration and initial containment monitoring. In effect, we will know what to target in North Korea and where if the process breaks down to the point of considering a surgical military strike. That is not a shared vulnerability that we recognize with respect to our own stockpile, for the number of North Korean existing nuclear weapons are barely a fraction of our own. Even if U.S. inspectors are frozen out of participation on aspects of the verification process—probably much like we would want to restrict inspector access to our more advanced weapon designs—we may need to recognize a similar concern by our North Korean adversary. Thus, the price of intrusion sought, for example, might be restriction by nationality to the Chinese and Russians. But the U.S. trusting verification of a rogue largely or at all to its own competitors is not a proposed concession likely to be entertained for long. Even if it were, in very limited respects, there could be no such grant without somehow exacting in return concessions that provide America and its allies with enough certainty. Would a verification metric, such as the 1 percent solution in the TI,[226] be enough when dealing with a rogue that is known to have proliferated in the past? If the U.S. is to seek greater certainty in defining

---

226 ". . . The 1 percent figure served as the defacto reference for determining the sample-plan sizes for verification and reverification." Thomas E. Shea, *supra* note 196.

a verification scheme around less acceptable risk, then America must be sure to have defined what is "militarily significant" in these unique circumstances to its own satisfaction. This approach suggests a departure from uniformity in verification standards and approaches in "special" cases. The notion that existing U.N. verification principles, such as equality, will be one size fits all, is again belied by circumstance; customization will be needed to decide what is appropriate in each unique circumstance presented. The potential tradeoffs in linking all such choices to exact the requisite "high level" of confidence necessary for verification will be an extraordinarily delicate balance to strike.

One path to such certainty, as in the TI initiative, will probably be the creation of disarmament facilities in each country. To the extent the planned facilities are subject to full six-country participation and approval, confidence increases among all concerned. The challenge is more likely a practical one—empowering inspectors during the construction process to assure that there are no secret deviations that could compromise the integrity of the process. If the facilities reflect some uniformity, it will serve multiple purposes: from building confidence with the North Koreans, to enhancing cost reduction, to promoting the economy. But such consideration alone should not drive the verification process in the most challenging reduction/disarmament cases, as North Korea will no doubt continue to prove.

F. THE LIMITS OF COOPERATIVE INTRUSION

The ability of verification processes to provide compliance certainty will always encounter inherent limits. But in some WMD contexts those impediments are more problematic than others. In assessing compliance with the Biological Weapons Convention, for example, one verification problem stems from the very nature of the prohibition, which simply bans activity for hostile, offensive weapons purposes. The very same activity, if conducted for peaceful purposes, is perfectly legitimate. Hence, at the heart of any BWC-related verification process is the quest to ascertain intent. That exercise necessarily involves a judgment call as to the legitimacy or illicitness of dual-use activity, with little (if anything) objectively differentiating the two. As a result, increased transparency to build confidence in BWC adherence became, for a time, the political goal, rather than verification of treaty compliance. In this sense, compliance became both diluted and elusive.

Certainty became illusory for the buffers to breakout were as thin as veneer in both the public and private sectors. It came as no great surprise then when the Bush administration found that transparency regimes are *ineffective* for verification purposes, and that the work necessary to establish transparency wasn't worth the cost of doing so. At the same time, NTMs and human intelligence was elevated in the spectrum of national technical means for monitoring compliance, albeit sometimes with misplaced reliance, as in Iraq.

While annual national declarations and related visits contemplated in the protocol to the BWC were judged inadequate, the surprising assessment was that challenge investigations would not improve the verifiability of the BWC.[227] Although the deterrence value against cheating was recognized with respect to such inspections, again inherent limits were thought to devalue them. The first assumption was that the delay between securing approval for any investigation request and deploying inspectors would be adequate to permit clean up or concealment. This assumption too had a premise; namely, the absence of a physical signature. The other assumptions were the potential small scale and unremarkable features in relevant facilities.[228]

However, in the years since this judgment, there have been advances in technical monitoring capability. The "degree of verifiability" has improved. While the threshold assumption has eroded, at least where biological activity is denied, this development still leaves in place the additional argument that even where activity is admitted, it can still be "explained away" as permitted use.

The limits of cooperative intrusion have been recognized apart from the biologic context as well. In the nuclear and chemical contexts, managed access limits information to that provided or available at the particular time and place of inspection. That does not always suffice, as the experience in Iran demonstrates. The simple truth is that location matters. Verification ultimately only can reveal what is actually accessed, whether through a fleeting inspection or through remote monitoring cameras in sealed areas. There are limits then to verification even with cooperative intrusion, for the verification will be constrained by how

---

227   *See* Lacey Testimony, *supra* note 170.

228   *Ibid.*

the parties define the cooperation. Thus, even when a highly intrusive inspection scheme is posited, as with the proposed Fissile Material Cut-Off Treaty, the U.S. may reject it as unverifiable within its own definition of the concept. Cooperative intrusion that was "good enough" for some countries, would produce only "false confidence" in the Bush administration's judgment. Instead, ad hoc investigation was posited as a viable vehicle for verification based upon national technical means and methods ("NTMMs").[229] This principle of action impelled a more balanced approach in allocating verification responsibility as between cooperative and NTMMs. Yet this balance was struck with new ingredients in the sense that NTMs were more pervasively augmented by commercial satellite imagery. Where once NTMs were limited to certain "have" nations such as the U.S. and Russia, increasingly these "methods" became available to others, giving birth to a modification of the acronym NTM to NTMM to reflect adaptation to this new reality. This development held the potential to diminish pressure for international inspectorates in certain arms-control regimes. It also leveled the playing field to some extent, but only in regulatory contexts where the infrastructure needed for activity of concern is manifest.[230]

The second element of the soliloquism was that "effective verification," as we have known it, is not suitable to be tasked to an international organization in the biologic context. The conclusion stemmed from a judgment that "managed access" could be used "as a last resort to deny access to any incriminating evidence."[231] As a corollary, reliance on NTMMs became regarded as the "fundamental reality." The conclusion followed that efforts to strengthen the verifiability of the BWC would necessarily proceed from that direction.

---

229   *See* DeSutter, *supra* note 5.

230   "Both the manufacturing of chemical and . . . biological weapons can take place in small-scale facilities. The plutonium route to nuclear weapons requires reactors and reprocessing facilities that are large and relatively conspicuous, but the uranium route can be pursued in facilities that are modest in size and lack distinctive tell-tale external features." Testimony of Dr. Ashton B. Carter before the U.S. Senate Committee on Foreign Relations, 10 March, 2004, *Overhauling Counterproliferation, accessed at* http://belfercenter.ksg.harvard.edu/publication/3262/overhauling_counterproliferation.html.

231   *Ibid.*

More generally though, the Reagan era concept of "effective verification" was infused with greater clarity by the U.S., as temporal and other differences from the superpower era emerged. Verification would be deemed "effective" when:

> "the degree of verifiability is judged *sufficient* given the compliance history of the parties involved, *the risks associated with noncompliance,* the difficulty of response to deny violators the benefits of their violations, the language and measures incorporated into the agreement and our own national means and methods of verification."[232]

There is "high enough certainty" for application of this standard when the U.S. is able to detect "significant" noncompliance or a pattern of noncompliance in timely fashion to counter the threat and to deny the benefits of the violation.[233] While embracing traditional demands of the historic verification concept, the new assessment approach is compartmentalized. Significance is tied to the cheating associated with a given agreement, rather than to the overall military balance, as during the Soviet era of parity. Relativity is thus measured by particularized obligation, a rather narrow context in the grand military scheme. But the "risks associated with noncompliance" offer an evaluative criterion open to factoring in that the greater threat may involve third parties in some circumstances. The judgmental process is also broadened beyond mere legal and technical assessment to include other factors, which is sensible in both a broad as well as narrower judgmental context, and logically should be extended.

At the same time, the new "gloss" may allow other countries to understand better what level of verifiability will satisfy the U.S. The U.N. verification principles are framed in terms of meeting both "adequate" and "effective" verification.[234] They are conjunctively rather than disjunctively linked as "an essential element" of all arms limitation and disarmament agreements. These two components, facially construed, aspire to meet what for the U.S. has at times been separate standards of strategic or tactical import, and at others as one without meaningful distinction (e.g., the INF treaty ratification). Refinement of the

---

232   DeSutter, *supra* note 5 (emphasis added).

233   *Ibid.*

234   *See* U.N. Principles of Verification, *supra* note 4 at Principle 1.

standards serve at least minimally to produce greater certainty as to American process expectations, albeit in a multilateral environment where those views may not be uniformly shared. At least America would provide a sense to one and all of the basis for its limited embrace of cooperative intrusion in international inspectorate regimes.

However, the notion that an ad hoc, voluntary inspection process is an adequate substitute for a "rights-based" challenge inspection framework is illusory. Whatever the limits of "anywhere, anytime" as a principle of action for a treaty verification regime, there is less risk from others associated with such intrusion, when access is appropriately managed. It appears that the "New U.S. Approach to Verification" was calculated to avoid constraint, in the sense that its freedom of action to verify could be built politically or militarily as circumstance permitted or warranted, rather than through the rule of law. Security policy in the verification context, as elsewhere,[235] became divorced from restriction or limits that might impair or impede U.S. action. In short, verification became unhinged from legal regimes, and grounded upon voluntary cooperative security or NTMMs. The absence of a mechanism would not prevent substantive agreement; rather, it was suggested the omission would facilitate it. As such, it was "back to the future," for the U.S. again urged other nations to agree to bans without verification other than NTMMs and voluntary cooperation, much as we did early in the Cold War. Yet, the U.S. had found such an approach completely unacceptable in the post-Cold War period of the initial CTBT ratification debate. Likewise, by completely foregoing short or no-notice challenge inspections, the U.S. ignored the fact that both the IAEA and UNSCOM found such on-site inspections "to be their single most important verification tool" in the Iraq experience[236] when coupled with other techniques that focused on them.

---

235   For example, under the administration of President George W. Bush, the U.S. decided that it "will oppose the development of new legal regimes or other restrictions that seek or limit U.S. access to or use of space. Proposed arms control agreements or restrictions must yet impair the rights of the United States to conduct research, development, testing and operations or other activities in space for U.S. national interests. . . ." U.S. Space Policy (8/31/06).

236   *See* Verification Report of the Secretary General, *supra* note 3 at p. 54 ¶199.

As a result, in the bioweapons and nuclear contexts alike, verification advocates found themselves arguing that a combination of managed access techniques could be negotiated to allow far-ranging challenge inspections. They contended that the chemical weapons regime could serve as an example, but not necessarily a model for intrusion. That debate continues and awaits resolution in the next round of arms limitation negotiations and ratification. In each instance, there will be careful scrutiny of cooperative intrusion limits in a fact-specific context to settle the matter. The answer may not be the same, or even admit to principled consistency. It is likely to prove an imperative in the Iranian nuclear context, where undeclared sites were at the heart of the problem. To think that national means and human sources could not be aided by a formal right to conduct challenge inspections is to ignore history, for it is the *combination* of all these means that best served to promote higher confidence in the verification process. The propriety of using a combination of verification methods has long been recognized as a key principle of disarmament.[237] Adherence to that principle is both consistent with past practice, as well as present and future needs. But where the cost seems unreasonable, then a basic policy choice has to be made whether to accept a lower probability of detecting noncompliant activity. In other words, are we willing to live with some uncertainty with a rogue, as we did with a hostile superpower?

---

237   *See* Tenth Special Session of the U.N. General Assembly, Resolution S-10/2, U.N. Document A/RBS/S-10/2, June 30, 1978.

CHAPTER IV

THE LEGACY OF UNCERTAINTY

A. PROBLEMS IN PRINCIPLE

The practical objectives and needs of nuclear arms control verification are changing with the emergence of different threats. As a threshold matter, the scope of WMD arms control will have to be enlarged to meet new risks from sophisticated terrorists and rogues. But whereas the inability to verify had served for decades as a limitation on agreement, now enhanced means of verification—particularly cooperative models—could turn it into a facilitating factor. This is most likely in instances where the emerging threats are viewed as a risk held in common, so that multilateral political pressure effectively compels it. Through such cooperation, verification can be or may become *more than adequate*[238] to meet the risks arising from nonparties to arms-control regimes. The challenges will be experienced primarily in the interstices of these intersections. Where security remains dependent on nuclear weapons, for example, then intrusive verification will have two principal limits: (i) the inspection could allow the opposition sufficient insight to learn how to defeat the weapon; and (ii) third parties without existing weapons knowledge could acquire it through the inspection process, thereby proliferating the expertise.[239] This latter consideration also can serve to better inform a nation bent on cheating, like Iraq under Saddam Hussein, on the best method to do so; that is, if the nationals of a cheater acquire expertise about the inspection process, they may be able to help devise better ways to circumvent the procedure.

The U.N.-approved verification principles from late in the last century expressly recognized the need for constraints to protect against proliferation risks of the inspection process. However, the enshrined principles of equality of access and nondiscrimination guaranteed for

---

238   *See* Ivan Oelrich, *The Changing Rules of Arms Control Verification; Confidence is Still Possible*, 14 INT'L. SEC. 176 (1990).

239   *Ibid.* at p. 177.

all parties to the particular arms control regime[240] potentially contravened in some instances, such as proprietary needs of private parties, the legitimate security concerns of member states. Thus, while the U.N. verification principles still stand unqualified, practical considerations served either to limit them in practice, or to drive the arms control and disarmament process necessarily into bilateral contexts between weapons states like the U.S. and Russia to avoid security concerns.[241]

The problem of equality remains exacerbated by the NPT's existing legal apartheid scheme. Security may sometimes be compromised, rather than strengthened, by a stricter verification standard in the nuclear weapons context. Greater intrusion through inspectors, including from a nuclear have-not nation, could create a proliferation risk of disseminating weapon expertise. Hence, the opportunity to expand the scope of regulation of WMD can be limited, unless the verification process is implemented pragmatically, with due regard to such security challenges. While little is publicly known of disarmament practice to date in this regard, it appears the IAEA does acquiesce to compromise on this principle. The practice with the Libyan disarmament apparently restricted access to nuclear weapons related information only to IAEA inspectors from weapons states.[242]

At the same time, where cooperative intrusion actually facilitates control limitation (e.g., on readiness) or even elimination of a particular WMD weapons system, then any resulting vulnerabilities require reasoned articulation of opposition to inspection. The U.S. has not always been prepared to do so, since it can be counterproductive. For example, where identification problems compromised American national technical means of intelligence gathering, the U.S. was not willing to reveal to the Soviets which encrypted missile test data was

---

240   *See* U.N. Principles of Verification, *supra* note 4 at Principles 5, 10, and 15.

241   *See* U.N. Disarmament Commission, "Verification in All its Aspects: Study on the Role of the United Nations in the Field of Verification," U.N. Doc A/45/372, 28 August 1990, Section II.

242   *See* Boureston and Feldman, *supra* note 175 at p. 98 (reporting the IAEA placed weapons related documents under seal, transferred them to the U.S., and by agreement had representatives present when the seals were broken).

problematic in the late 1980s.[243] To identify the areas of concern would reveal the limit of our NTMs used then for verification. The U.S. would, in short, be revealing not only its lack of certainty about risks, but also providing a roadmap to its vulnerability.

Still, once Soviet/Russian acceptance of on-sight inspection was embraced in practice as in principle, then the prior verification inabilities that impelled our disagreement of certain proposals, such as the CTBT, eventually had to be defended on their technical merits. As such, while the political component of the verification standard was diminished in terms of focusing simply on violations, military significance again assumed its rightful place as a legitimate criterion of certainty, at least in the compliance judgment effort with respect to competitive strategic relationships with Russia and China.

The U.N. Principle of nondiscrimination in verification[244] also has inherent limitations yet to be fully, much less formally, recognized. While determinations about the adequacy, effectiveness, and acceptability of verification methodology is recognized to be contextual—tied to the particular agreement—the nondiscrimination principle is not so limited. Rather, equality within a regime is mandated. However, a regime such as the NPT is founded upon a discriminatory organizing principle—compartmentalizing states according to whether they have or do not have nuclear weapons. Thus, where the regime itself is so structured, implementation has been historically tied *in practice* to the distinct categories in which the parties are found. But the discrimination in verification processes—who is subjected and how—in the NPT regime, is and will likely continue to impact the negotiation of ancillary agreements. Those agreements will be calculated to help promote the disarmament goal, so as to eliminate eventually the lack of equality and treaty-recognized discriminatory categories.

This approach is manifested within the scope of the negotiations of a fissile materials ("FMT") versus cut-off ("FMCT") treaty regime. In the FMT approach, the nuclear weapon "have not" nations push toward

---

243   *See* Antonia and Abram Chayes, *From Enforcement to Dispute Settlement: A New Approach to Arms Control Verification and Compliance*, 14 INT'L SEC. 147, 153–54 (1990).

244   U.N. Verification Principle, *supra* note 4 at Principle 15.

a treaty that would place existing stocks within the treaty regime with verification measures, rather than simply cutting off future production. To date, the U.S. as a "have" nation seeks a cut-off regime. If nations push for a fissile material treaty consistent with all of the U.N. verification principles, then they would be seeking removal of existing asymmetries. For example, there would be more equality between weapons and nonweapons states in terms of submitting to safeguards. Enhanced transparency would come with safeguards. At the same time, the open access principle, if applied, would contravene the nonproliferation mandate of the NPT. But such a broad FMT with compliant verification processes, while ostensibly serving the NPT goal of eliminating nuclear weapons, would actually jeopardize that goal by creating proliferation risks through access to information. That could, in turn, facilitate exercise of the "supreme national interest" withdrawal provision and trigger a breakout of new weapons states. Yet, the price of waiving such sovereign rights or risking proliferation to serve verification principles would be an end in itself—in contravention to the Verification Principles, and at odds with serving the NPT mandate. For this reason, there is increasing expert recognition of the need for secrecy within nuclear verification processes. But even within legitimate constraints, there is still a push for measures to be developed that give all states confidence in implementation.[245]

That goal can best be served by the confidence of nations in the inspectorate generally. The credibility of the regulatory regime is tied to expert acceptance of its effective functionality. Hopefully, there will not be a similar blind faith as was experienced with the placement of IRA weapons "beyond use." There, the prominent experts involved with decommissioning IRA weapons were literally blindfolded and sworn to secrecy before the unveiling which served to verify compliance.[246] Such extreme measures ultimately sufficed in that situation because of both the personal credibility of the inspectors and the ensuing events, which offered further circumstantial proof of the actual

---

245   *See* Report of Commission, *supra* note 216 at p. 22.

246   Warren Hoge, Envoys Visit I.R.A. Arms Caches, Advancing Ulster Peace, June 27, 2000 http://www.nytimes.com/2000/06/27/world/envoys-visit-ira-armes-caches-advancing-ulsterpeace.html?n=Top/Reference/Tunes%20Topics/organizations/I/Irish%20Republicanof20 Army Peace.

effectiveness of the process. A secretive verification measure thus served well in a matter of war and peace. If need be, secrecy in the nuclear disarmament verification process may facilitate rather than prevent agreement, which might result if the openness mandated in existing U.N. verification principles controlled entirely. Thus, disarmament may be best served by less rather than more transparency in verification measures with respect to regime parties with no direct need to know.

In contrast, nonproliferation will continue to be better served by even greater transparency under most circumstances. Universal embrace of the IAEA Safeguards with the Additional Protocol, coupled with even more intrusive measures when necessary, will best serve to rule out clandestine activity and to prevent diversion. Hence, an enhanced standard of transparency will better serve to verify compliance with nonproliferation goals.[247] Reduced to essentials, it is one of the incongruities of the verification process that the emerging nuclear-free order may require dual verification standards with more secrecy in disarmament than transparency in order to permit greater intrusion to assure compliance—albeit exacted at a price to confidence in non-weapons states.

This result logically flows from the unequal status enshrined in the NPT. To the extent the acceptance of restricted dissemination represents a departure from the existing U.N. verification principle of equality, it also flows from the fact those principles were largely derived in nonproliferation or arms limitation contexts, and not that of disarmament. Simply stated, the goals being served in each instance require different methodologies and rules. The organizing principle will still be "trust but verify," but the conditional implementation narrows down those who are trusted to share in the information garnered from verification. It may well be that in the future, "constrained transparency" will produce the most "effective" verification of compliance for disarmament purposes.

Equally, U.S. opposition to including verification in the FMCT regime as unachievable stood in stark contrast to the U.N. mandate, both as

---

247   See 20/20 Director's Report, *supra* note 216 at p. 22.

applied to fissile materials, as well as to the U.N. Verification Principles, to which it has historically ascribed. Those principles provide that:

> "[v]erification arrangements should be addressed at the outset and every stage of negotiations on specific arms limitation and disarmament agreements."

Indeed, for decades the U.S. lead the effort to establish that and other principles and to give them their content. To add to the inconsistency, the U.S. would be doing so in circumstances where it had also taken the position there was no need to revise the U.N. verification principles, even when international disarmament professionals were willing to do so.[248]

Still, there are instances where there is recognition that unqualified principle yields in practice to circumstantial need. While transparency is associated with the principles of verification, there should be recognition that non-transparency (the preservation of confidences) also promotes the ends of verification.[249] Proprietary information in the CWC context is often noted to illustrate this point. More significantly, there simply would be no recognition of "managed access" as a valid verification technique but for the need to qualify the openness principle to serve legitimate national security needs. Thus, whether by compartmentalization of how gathered information is disseminated, or simply by shrouding it from view, verification can also be well served even without transparency in appropriate circumstances.

Perhaps the most daunting struggle in pressing for suitable changes in verification principles is that of the burden of proof standard. The challenge of Iraq's clandestine WMD programs and those elsewhere was said to exemplify the need to shift the burden of proof to the suspected party.[250] In cases of uncertain proof coupled with strong grounds for suspicion, the risk was said by the American administration to be too

---

248   *See, e.g.*, Patricia Lewis (Director of U.N. Institute for Disarmament Research), "The Impact of the 1990 and 1995 United Nations Verification Studies on Today's Political Environment," at p. 17 (20 October, 2005). *See* U.N. Verification Principles, *supra* note 4 at Principle 9.

249   *See* U.N. Verification Principles, *supra* note 4 at Principle 5. *See* UNIDIR Verification Handbook, *supra* note 7 at p. 5.

250   *See, e.g.*, A. Carter, *supra* note 230 at p. 90.

great to forego remedial action. But mistakes can and have been made. Iraq is unfortunately the perfect example. As a direct consequence, the political reality for the foreseeable future is that there will be substantial resistance to shifting the burden to the accused. Equally, there will be opposition to lessening the standard to "more likely than not," instead of the present "clear and convincing" showing required. In these circumstances, prudent policy will focus more on making a prima facie showing of illicit conduct. Shaping the expectations of those judging the appropriate evidentiary threshold that triggers intrusion will be the future path to achieving the requisite showing of clarity. Only then will the shift in burden of rebuttal be triggered. That is an evidentiary approach readily understood by international lawyers; it is a basic element of Western jurisprudence. Going forward, then, it will be best to seek to infuse the burden with a satisfactory threshold, than to continue to try to reverse entirely which party carries the burden of proof. This point was well made, albeit lost, in the CTBT ratification debate. Senator Reed pointed out that while monitoring might not suffice to verify that a seismic event was low-yield testing, it would be enough to offer as evidence to trigger an on-site inspection from which clear and convincing evidence could emerge.[251]

Despite the examination of all aspects of verification by U.N. appointed group of experts during and after the Cold War,[252] verification has not yet evolved fully to reflect either custom and practice or present needs. Recognition of the need to harmonize practice with principle and circumstance would be timely. A more refined set of principles would better serve special cases like North Korea or Iran. Otherwise, there will be continued ad hoc improvisation in volatile circumstances, within a negotiating framework of unqualified principles being invoked to justify respective positions. In short, the failure of verification principles to evolve with changed threat assessment risks to meet new compliance needs may cost us more than uncertainty—it may well risk lives.

---

251   CTBT Senate Debate at p. S12344.

252   *See generally,* Verification in all its aspects: Study on the Role of the United Weapons in the Field of Verification CNN Document A/43/372, 28 August, 1990 and U.N. Document A/50/377, 22 September, 1995).

B. METRICS IN CONTEXT

The crucial measures of detectability from future threats will test the metrics of verification. Although numerous weapons could be unaccounted for within the superpower strategic balance, loss of control of a single WMD could be catastrophic today with undeterred enemies. As the IAEA Director warned the U.N. General Assembly in October 2008:

> "The possibility of terrorists obtaining nuclear or other radioactive material remains a grave threat. . . . The number of incidents reported to the Agency involving the theft or loss of nuclear or radioactive material is disturbingly high. . . . Equally troubling is the fact that much of this material is not subsequently recovered. Sometimes material is found which had not been reported missing."[253]

The ability to accurately verify nuclear inventory on a global scale must be a high-priority task, where adequate resources are devoted to the process on a sustainable basis. After all, the most difficult obstacle to terrorist acquisition of a nuclear bomb is obtaining weapons grade nuclear material.[254] For example, it is publicly known that a foreman tasked with management at a Russian nuclear facility exploited the three percent (3%) margin of error in measuring equipment to steal approximately 1,600 grams of ninety percent (90%) enriched uranium. He did so without any discernable deviation in inventory on the books of the facility. If he had not been detected in the attempted sale, he could have stolen enough to make a bomb, without the IAEA ever being able to detect that any nuclear material was diverted and missing from the baseline records.[255] Only the replacement of scales with digital state-of-the-art equipment, with virtually no margin of error, enables a more trustworthy verification process to prevent similar episodes.

Even where safeguards are in place in a less suspicious locale, the potential for diversion is no less a possible threat. For example, the application of mass measurements in large commercial plutonium reprocessing plants can permit militarily significant diversion. One

---

253 World at Risk report, *supra* note 14 at p. 43.

254 *Ibid.* at pp. 43–44.

255 For an open source description, *see ibid.* at p. 16.

VERIFICATION IN AN AGE OF INSECURITY

example provided by analysis in open sources well illustrates the problems that can arise from even acceptable metrics:

> "At Japan's new Roklasbo reprocessing plant . . . the design throughput is 8,000 kilograms of plutonium per year. With measurement errors on the order of 1 percent, which is 80 kilograms per year, the "significant" quantity of plutonium required to make a nuclear weapon being eight kilograms or less, the IAEA cannot certify on the basis of measurements alone that a significant quantity has not been diverted."[256]

The "one percent" IAEA standard at Rohkosbo is the same as the one percent solution in the Trilateral Initiative. Yet the metric alone is no solution to the threat of state diversion or non-state actor acquisition. Metrics limit the verification problem, they do not eliminate the risk. The removal of plutonium at very low rates simply couldn't be confidently detected for years given the uncertainty in measurement.[257] Yet if the IAEA, Japan, Russia, and the U.S. all agree to a one percent metric in these contexts where the goal is to prevent diversion, should we accept the same verification metric in more troubling situations?

At one level, the easy answer to the issue is that verification is a process not wholly dependent upon such monitoring metrics. So with the Japanese example, measurements are supplemented with monitoring calculated to identify anomalies in flow and concentration. Additionally, there is active surveillance of activities that are associated with diversion. Moreover, at new facilities, IAEA verification extends into the plant construction itself to ascertain the accuracy of declared pipe locations, etc., before radiation renders them inaccessible to inspectors. In short, in a new regime verifying, for example, fissile material, there will be a need for a variety of changes to increase certainty of nondiversion of "significant quantities."[258]

While these measures are focused on the regulated activity itself, there is also the prospect that in the future the nature of what is to be

---

256 Meerburg and Von Hippel, *supra* note 215 at p. 6. (Safeguards at Pre-existing Reprocessing Plants).

257 For a description of measurement uncertainty in various contexts, see IPFM Verification Report, *supra* note 199 at pp. 52–56.

258 *See, e.g., ibid.* at pp. 57–58 (description of proposed changes). Other studies assume an average of 4 kilograms of plutonium per warhead (*Cf., e.g.,* IPFM Verification Report at p. 16), despite the IAEA standard. *See supra* note 221.

regulated can be adjusted. Given the nature of the threats and questions as to the adequacy of measures supplementing metrics, part of the solution rests with the targets of constraint. For example, as a near-term shift, there should be an increased impetus to move away from the historical approach of agreeing to arms-control limits of verifiable surrogates, and to focus instead on the nuclear material itself. Specifically, the inherent difficulty in verifying arms-control limits on warheads through the NTMs had previously lead to constraints on launchers. Launchers were a substitute for missiles, which in turn were a substitute for warheads themselves. Going forward, verification challenges presented by threats from sub-state actors, will likely be directly tied to control of warheads and, for example, fissile material.

Hence, while arms control might be "adequately" verifiable through a bilateral agreement (e.g., Pakistan and India) limiting launchers, the security interest of other states will be in command and control over the warheads, and *full accountability* of nuclear material itself. Hence, compliance with numerical launcher limits becomes somewhat meaningless to others if the payload is not verifiably accounted for by the weapons state in a secure command and control environment. The requirements to meet Western security needs in that instance, ultimately requires far more than verification alone can offer in the bilateral arms control context. Moreover, one ready alternative to avoid intrusion—such as centralized repositories susceptible to monitoring and conducive to guarding—can be militarily undesirable from the host countries' point of view. Perfectly valid security concerns dictate dispersion of the weapons or nuclear material. Functional military secrecy sometimes may operate at cross purposes, then, with even nonadversarial verification and related concerns.[259] As such, the historical impetus toward ease of monitoring in delineating the limits of control by agreement surfaces today as a double-edged sword; it prospectively cuts for and against

---

259   The problem is analogous to those encountered with respect to conventional arms as a function of actual operational import. *See* Robert D. Blachwolf, *Conceptual Problems of Conventional Arms Control*, 12 Nat'l. Sec. p. 28 (1988). In the nuclear context, an example is the practice of Pakistan of dispersing its weapons at times of heightened alert with India. The dispersion practices may create a vulnerability to seizure by terrorists. *See, e.g.,* David E. Sanger, *Pakistan Strife Raises U.S. Doubts on Nuclear Arms,* N.Y. Times (5/4/09) *accessed at* http://www.nytimes.com/2009/05/04/world/asia/04nuke.html.

both security and verification considerations, depending upon whose national interest is involved. As a non-party to bilateral accords, the U.S. and its allies will have to rely on NTMMs or alternative techniques other than verification of an accord to serve their security needs in this regard.

C. CHALLENGES ON THE HORIZON

(i) Bio Security

In the aftermath of the 9/11 attacks, a number of nations contended that there was a need to strengthen the multilateral ban on bioweapons.[260] The foundation of multilateral efforts to combat rogue proliferation and possible terrorist use of biological weapons remains the 1972 Convention ("BWC").[261] While banning the development, production, or acquisition of toxin weapons and related delivery systems, there is no traditional verification regime associated with these restraints. Rather, articles V and VI together provide for consultation and cooperation in self-policing to solve problems arising under the convention; failing that, resolution of noncompliance issues may be directed to the U.N. Security Council, which can pursue on-site investigation and remedial measures. From the onset, U.S. intelligence was judged equal to the task of guarding our security interests if another nation developed such weapons. And America always took the position its other weapons systems would neutralize any resulting capability asymmetry.

Today there is a program of cooperative measures in place between the U.S., Russia, and other former Soviet states[262] to reduce the WMD threat. But progress toward establishing transparency to build confidence in compliance within the multilateral BWC has been halting. In fact,

---

260 A compilation of statements may be found in Jenni Rissanen, *Regrets and Uncertainty over Protocol at First Committee*, BWC PROTOCOL BULLETIN, October 25, 2001.

261 The text of the Convention is *available at* http://www.state.gov/www/global/arms/treaties/bwc1.html.

262 This program is administered by the Defense Threat Reduction Agency as the operational leader for the U.S. Department of Defense and U.S. Strategic Command. A description is *accessible at* http://www.dtra.mil/oe/ctr/programs/index.cfm.

cooperation on a multinational verification protocol ended early in this century by the Bush administration.[263] The basic challenge stems from the simple fact that the materials, equipment, and technical know-how associated with biologic weaponization are also legitimately utilized in research and commerce.[264] The magnitude of the dual use threat increases with advances in DNA synthesizing capabilities. Additionally, a number of nations (e.g., Egypt; Syria; Israel) are outside the treaty regime, while some members were or are suspected of cheating.[265] At the same time, national states certainly have no monopoly on this WMD capability, as non-state actors ranging from individuals to organizations have sought and even used such capabilities in the past.[266]

In terms of securing U.S. pathogens and biolabs in a verifiable manner, America turns increasingly to legislatively mandated tracking programs[267] of certain agents, as well as more probing programs for vetting personnel. Yet, the U.S. is not verifying the effectiveness of these approaches on biosecurity through a governmental review process.[268] Biosafety labs at the maximum containment level are also expanding capacity dramatically, nearly tripling in a little more than a decade at the outset of this century,[269] which concomitantly taxes the verification system detecting the risk of security lapses.[270] At the same time, our advances in verification technology are creating a microbial forensic

---

263 Statement by Ambassador Donald A. Makley on 25 July, 2001 to the Ad Hoc Group of BWC State Parties *accessed at* http://www.state.gov/t/ac/rls/.rm/2001/5497.htm ("Amb. Makley Statement").

264 WORD AT RISK REPORT, *supra* note 14 at p. 9.

265 *Ibid.* at p. 10 identifying Russia, China, North Korea, and Iran as possibly pursuing secret offensive programs.

266 *Ibid.* at pp. 10–12.

267 *See, e.g.*, the Select Agent Program established in 1996 which provides through regulations for reporting Transfers, and subsequently expanded in 2002 to include registration requirements.

268 *See* WORLD AT RISK REPORT, *supra* note 14 at p. 28.

269 *Ibid.* at p. 25.

270 *See, e.g.*, Eric Lipton and Scott Shane, *As biodefense field grows, so may risks*, INTERNATIONAL HERALD TRIBUNE, (August 3, 2008) *accessed at* http://www.int.com/bin/printfriendly.php?id=14970686.html.

capacity[271] that will increasingly permit verification of the sources of pathogen strains. Looking forward, there is an obvious need for a verification system built upon a baseline inventory of pathogen reference strains, as well as standard procedures and authentication processes to make sample identification, collection, and analysis meet our security needs.[272] That will include extending the regulatory reach in the U.S. of federal authority over life science companies that neither accept federal funding or work with "select agents" on the list, for those alternative pursuits can just as easily threaten security. In other words, just as the U.S. Energy Department oversees nuclear material, so too there is a legal process need to extend verification oversight to high containment biolabs.

Americans and others should anticipate that future verification systems will include procedures and oversight systems in order to assure biosafety and biosecurity relating to dual uses in the life sciences. Since the traffic in life-science activity knows no boundary, an international regime and associated verification processes may be over the horizon's sight line today, but they will probably be in view tomorrow. We can only hope that the process is created by design to avoid a tragedy, rather than arise in reaction to one.

In stark contrast to the Chemical Weapons Convention, the Biological Weapons Convention contains neither verification mechanisms nor any multilateral oversight or implementing authority. The 1972 regime outlaws member states from not only taking measures to possess an offensive capability through a series of prohibitions, but also precludes assisting others. Enforcement, in turn, was left to the municipal law of member states, bilateral consultation, and U.N. Security Council. That remedial approach remains in place in part as a Cold War vestige of Soviet refusal for many years to permit on-site inspections. At the same time, verification of any event is a challenge given dual uses involving

---

271   *See* WORLD AT RISK REPORT, *supra* note 14 at p. 29 ("Microbial forensics [is] a set of genetic and physical techniques for analyzing a biological or toxin agent that has been acquired by a proliferant state or terrorist group, [which] can clarify where a breach in laboratory security has occurred. It can also help identify the perpetrators of a biological weapons attack and support criminal prosecution.").

272   *Ibid.* at p. 29.

a broad range of life science activity, including pharmaceutical development. In the absence of a disproportionately high inventory of toxins beyond that conceivably needed for defensive research, intent is left as the primary indicator of illicit conduct,[273] which is exceptionally hard to verify and often depends upon human sources. Likewise, the physical structure of facilities devoted to such uses is rather ordinary; a focus on external features in a verification process is not possible.[274] As a consequence of these intelligence challenges, and in the face of the non-state actor threat, the focus shifted to strengthening national implementation of the convention, rather than seeking to rely on an international inspection regime.

To this end, U.N. Security Council Resolution 1540 is a key international legal process tool. States have a legal duty under this mandatory norm to both adopt and implement "effective" measures of control over biological and other WMD, as well as their means of delivery. That obligation extends to "appropriate" controls over related materials, such as pathogens. However, there is no uniformity of content or coverage yet with respect to the standards, much less verified enforcement of them. While steps have been taken toward harmonization of high-level nuclear standards,[275] a similar foundation for a biological best practices to facilitate a national verification process is nowhere to be seen. Yet, from a verification standpoint, whether in a nuclear or biological context, there is a need for specific standards for the physical protection regime to facilitate either NTMMs monitoring compliance or international verification processes, assuming a compromise approach is found in the future.

Today, with the advent of political and technological developments, including portable techniques, it is again becoming increasingly feasible to contemplate a verification regime for bioweapons. Broadly speaking, the underpinnings for the regime would principally be driven by enhanced transparency through some combination of declarations, monitoring visits, classification procedures and challenge investigations.

---

273 *Ibid.* at p. 35.

274 *See* Lacey Testimony, *supra* note 170.

275 *See, e.g.,* Convention on the Physical Protection of Nuclear Material. *See also* IAEA Information Circular 225 on the Physical Protection of Nuclear Material.

However, each of these elements proved problematic for the U.S. in the last ten years. The result was an aborted effort to negotiate a verification protocol for the Biological Weapons Convention in the arms control and nonproliferation framework of this convention. This result ensued, even though the approach mimicked or drew upon verification principles accepted in the Chemical Weapons Convention context, which America both signed and ratified.[276] Differing circumstantial aspects of the regulated weapons of mass destruction accounts for the deviation in the acceptability of the application.

First, the conventions and verification approaches were designed based on very different assumptions. Formulated at the time of superpower competition, the common wisdom underpinning the Biological Convention was that only the U.S. and Soviet Union had the weapons capability at that time. In this sense, the regime assumed a finite existing capacity would be static, much like the limited number of nuclear weapons states recognized within the NPT. As a result, the purpose of the convention was twofold: constraining use in military conflict of bioweapons by either superpower, and stifling proliferation of the capability. In contrast, the approach of the Chemical Weapons Convention (CWC) recognized as an operating assumption the existing pervasiveness among nations of the weapons capability, as well as limited legitimate needs in a law enforcement context. So establishment of a broad verification mandate and international implementation structure was built into the substantive negotiation and resulting legal architecture. Therefore, the belated multilateral verification effort with respect to the BWC, then, is remedial in nature; it is a recognition of failed assumptions—that possession of the capability was and would remain highly limited; voluntary confidence-building measures devised through the convention review conference mechanism would foster compliance;[277] and a default enforcement mechanism through the U.N. Security Council would suffice politically.

---

276 The Chemical Weapons Convention was anticipated to provide practical experience that would contribute to the development of measures in the biological field because of the overlay in the area of toxins between the two conventions. *See* Verification Report of the Secretary General, *supra* note 3 at p. 58 ¶223.

277 Initial efforts began in the mid 1980s at the Second Review Conference when CBMs were adopted including a reporting provision of data relating to

Another basic difference precluding twin verification approaches between the chemical and biologic regimes arises from the nature of the weapons themselves. While chemical weapons are quantifiable, biological weapons are created from living organisms, which tend to quickly self-replicate to weapons production levels. As a result, *every* quantitative toxin measurement is temporal in nature, and it can be outdated rapidly. Moreover, bioweapons are more like nuclear weapons in terms of the destructive potential of even a small amount of material. Hence, the magnitude of the threat binds biological weapons more closely to nuclear than chemical ones. However, from a verification standpoint, a significant difference is that the production of nuclear weapons requires a rather substantial infrastructure, whereas adequate biologic material for weaponization can be produced by any poor nation with a modest pharmaceutical facility and an effective delivery system.

Saddam Hussein's threats to use biological weapons during the first Gulf War removed any remaining veil of illusion over the counter-proliferation failure and inadequacy of the BWC's lack of verification. The result was an effort at the Convention's third review conference[278] in 1991 to promote a new, comprehensive, and effective verification focus. There, pragmatic concerns arose to challenge principle in seeking to devise a remedial scheme. The major concerns included: (i) definitional issues; (ii) triggers for inspection; and (iii) appropriate constraints on technology transfer. Each element presents its own separate challenges to establishing an effective overall verification scheme.

The definitional quandary well illustrates the inherent verification limitations. For example, if inspections are to be tied only to listed, existing biological agents, the continuing transformative potential of the life sciences is ignored. Science and technological development therefore militates in favor of a broader definition, as demonstrated in the CTBT approach, rather than limiting the scope to the currently identified agents. However, doing so will ensnare perfectly legitimate applications in the regulatory web. Unlike nerve agents in chemical

---

bioweapons programs and cooperation in permitted technology; research dissemination related to the convention; and information exchange related to the outbreak of infectious diseases.

278 There are review conferences every five years under the Biological Weapons Convention.

weapons, where there are known precursors, the dual use nature of biological agents for pharmaceutical purposes and related equipment makes general monitoring of them an inadequate focal point at best, and completely unwieldy and unaffordable at worse, for it may well compromise trade secrets and other proprietary information. As a result, there is considerable pressure to avoid over-intrusiveness, even if the competing interest somewhat compromises our certainty over this type of threat.

Triggers for challenge inspections are similarly problematic. First, there is a basis for challenge in most verification protocols where monitoring divines deviation from baseline figures outside of acceptable parameters for error. In the biological context, the dual nature of use impels the effort to devise reporting filters to focus declarations and inspectors alike on "militarily significant" quantities of particular agents. This way, an effort is made to establish an objective indicia of subjective intent about potential military use. But identifying dependable signatures of national intent apart from a quantitative approach for such biological challenges presents ongoing difficulties, both for technical and compliance enforcement aspects of a potential verification process.

In the post-Iraq war environment, the *absence* of plausible reasons other than military purpose is the likely standard of proof that will need to be met in any biological compliance regime. The reasons will have to be behaviorally based. Hence, the range of potential challenge inspection triggers to acquire proof—from allegation based on NTMMs to outbreak of infectious disease—are certainly more compatible with our national and economic security needs than random routine inspections. In short, we are again "back to the future" in verification, in that as with the INF debate about the level of intrusiveness, the judgment is that it is better to compromise our certainty than our security. In both instances, it seems less likely that routine inspection would produce evidence of militarily significant cheating, than that it will create an opportunity for competitor or adversarial intelligence gathering. Hence, one would expect a focus on challenge related inspections as the centerpiece of future negotiations over a verification process. Yet, in the Bush administration their value was demeaned, much as they were in the late 1980's. While acknowledging that such intrusion "generally . . . could help to deter cheating" the combination of delay in securing approval and the dual capability nature of biological agents left officials concerned that there would be time to clean up or conceal evidence, or to explain it away.[279] With respect to the issue of clean-up or concealment, improving biologic forensics technology may offer a basis for reexamination of this conclusion. As to the "explaining away" issue, it is always a potential problem, exacerbated in a biological context. However, the concern alone is not a sufficient basis to drop the pursuit of a challenge regime, especially when some quantum of initial evidence is required to trigger the process or to continue it.

Lastly, the notion of constraints on technology transfer in the biologic context is a concern of the "have-not" nations. As in the NPT nuclear regime, one challenge to verifying nonproliferation is the potential to create "virtual" weapons states, where political will is the lone significant buffer to weaponization breakout given technological transfer entitlement. The resulting North-South split in the negotiation of a biological weapons verification protocol reflected this key element of the price of intrusion. Developing nations argued that if they were in good standing with the Biological Convention, there would be no need to add a layer of buffering restraint through national or multilateral coordinated policies by nations with developed life-science capabilities to restrain technology transfer to them.

The claim to such unfettered entitlement arises from Article X of the convention. That provision reads, in relevant part:

> "(i) the States Parties to this Convention undertake to facilitate . . . the fullest possible exchange of equipment, materials and scientific technological information for the use of . . . agents and toxins for peaceful purposes. . . ."

Determining how to fulfill this mandate at the same time as serving nonproliferation goals remains the source of tension that has been irreconcilable in many aspects to date. Developing nations argue that if they submit to mandatory inspection under a verification regime, there is no need for further constraints. However, as with the problematic monitoring of low-yield nuclear tests under CTBT, verification of a ban is somewhat illusory. With nuclear tests, nature is aided by manmade technologies to yield uncertainty; with biological weapons, the fact that equipment is as easily used for a vaccine as for a weapon is

---

279   Lacey Testimony, *supra* note 170 at p.3.

the source of difficulty. In each instance, a verification regime that adheres to the equality of treatment principle is a double-edged sword that can cut against as well as in favor of security, especially if one accepts the conclusion that even a challenge inspection is unlikely to catch a cheater, unless the cheater makes a mistake. Only future enhancement of verification technologies offers more promise.

In all of these circumstances, a principled verification scheme for bio-weapons is risk-laden if it is based on a mandatory visit to build transparency confidence, even if the visited states were randomly selected; there are also risks if there are unconstrained exports or a difficult political approval process to permit challenge inspections. Rather, an approach of a broad declaratory mandate, targeted inspections activated by triggers, rapid initiation of challenge inspections coupled with coordinated export policies and a notification scheme, all seem like necessary elements of an acceptable regime. At the same time, the pace of technological development largely dictates our ability to engage in biological forensics with sufficient distinctiveness to engender confidence in investigations.[280] That certainty will at once be a necessary element and variable in any future verification regime. It will also be a key to reversing the American judgment that "[t]he traditional approach that has worked well for many other types of weapons is not a workable structure for biological weapons.[281]

(ii) Fissile Material

The path to the future realization of the Non-Proliferation Treaty goal of eliminating nuclear weapons will involve a series of steps over the long term. Apart from political efforts occurring at NPT review conferences,[282] a recognized first step is to stop further production of

---

280　*See, e.g.*, Dr. Kay Mereish, "Technical Advances and Field Experiences for Use in Biological Verification" (April 19, 2007) (Genotyping analysis as a powerful verification technique).

281　*See* Amb. Makley Statement, *supra* note 263.

282　For example, following adoption of principles and objections at the 1995 conference and appointment of a special coordinator, in 2000 nuclear weapon states committed again to eliminating their nuclear arsenals. It was at the latter conference that negotiating efforts to this end were channeled to the Conference on Disarmament, under whose auspices a verifiable treaty banning production would

nuclear material for weaponization. Episodically throughout the Cold War period, this approach was viewed as a mechanism by which to cap the building of nuclear weapons. While this effort is now multilateral in context, as a practical matter it impacts a very limited number of nations.[283] The effort has evolved over time in terms of process, goals, and forum. Beginning at the end of the Cold War, in late 1993 the United Nations General Assembly initiated the process of consideration of such restraint following a shift in position by the Clinton Administration. Through a consensus resolution, it recommended an "internationally" and "effectively" verifiable production ban to cut off the material needed to make nuclear weapons. What constituted "effective" verification was not defined there or under the auspices of the Conference on Disarmament which followed. However, the process arose close in time to the seeming merger of the "adequate" and "effective" verification American standards, as stated during the ratification of the INF treaty.[284]

Explosive nuclear devices can be fashioned at varying levels of uranium enrichment. The prospect that it can be used by non-state actors to build crude weapons has haunted threat assessment in this century. As a result, there is likely to be renewed impetus for agreements to secure and *eliminate* excess stocks of highly enriched uranium (HEU) to preclude terrorist access and proliferation. Many believe a verification mechanism would help assure these goals. Indeed, President Obama promised to "seek a new treaty that *verifiably* ends the production of fissile materials intended for use in state nuclear weapons"[285] in his arms control speech in Prague in April 2009. This cut-off effort (FMCT)

---

be negotiated. Progress has been largely nonexistent, other than informal discussions and the tendering of drafts, including one in 2006 by the U.S. See discussion, infra.

283 Apart from the nuclear weapon states that are parties to the NPT, India, Pakistan, and Israel would be targets of a FMCT regime, as well as non-weapons states producing fissile material for non-military purposes, particularly Japan, but also Canada and Australia.

284 *See* textual discussion at p. 20, *supra*.

285 President Obama's Speech in Prague, as delivered, *accessed at* http://www. marketwatch.com/news/story/story/aspx?guid=%7B6/A/EE9A%2DAA02%2D (emphasis added).

for targeted controls may extend at some point to civilian and research programs, as well as to prior military activity, in order to reduce these threat sources. Aspirants who would preclude future weapons use for such existing material embrace a more expansive approach, which is broadly reflected in proposals for a fissile material treaty ("FMT").[286] The military reach will probably only extend in the near term, if at all, to weapons-grade materials declared to be in excess of reduced weapons needs. There will also be ongoing uses relating to HEU-fueled naval reactors to contend with for years to come. Verifying actual stockpile reduction and security of fissile material will, therefore, reclaim a position on the arms control agenda for the foreseeable future. Political efforts to reduce or eliminate civilian use of HEU also may be embraced.[287]

Threshold problems in verification will likely range from the definitional scope[288] of nuclear material encompassed, to practical problems like use of HEU in naval reactors, to remedial measures in the civilian sector. Each will be challenging. Conceptually, the focus on scope will probably be tied to nuclear materials, which can be induced through chain reaction to produce a weapon. The verification challenge arises where there is a seeming need to exempt "fissile material" to be used as fuel for commercial reactors, despite the fact that the very large plutonium stocks are civilian. Like the recognition under the biological weapons convention, there can be duel use of fissile materials. However, the difference in conventions is that physical signatures (i.e., degree of enrichment) readily distinguish the purposes in the nuclear context, whereas this is not the case with toxins. Nevertheless, quantitative measures can be telling in each instance.

Unlike facilities designed with IAEA safeguarding in mind, research facilities typically have physical security issues, particularly in academic

286 IPFM Verification Report, *supra* note 199 at p. 1.

287 *See, e.g.*, the working papers of Nordic countries at the 2005 NPT Review Conference.

288 *See, e.g.*, IAEA Technical Note (1999). In contrast, one would not expect to include tritium, a non-fissile material with a 12 year half life produced in reactors by irradiating lithium, but one which is nevertheless critical for many types of nuclear weapons, particularly those that are miniaturized, for yield boost or in fusion reactions.

or health care settings. Moreover, verification of fissile material typically operates against baseline data. There is widespread recognition that verification at a standard high-confidence level will not be possible in the civilian sector. Yet the absence of an accurate civilian HEU inventory means that verification will be uncertain at its most basic level. This is a remarkable gap considering it involves probably half of the global stockpile. Still it may be more manageable in other aspects of documenting past nuclear activity. At the same time, embracing a fissile materials treaty will necessarily impel participating states to separate their civilian and military sectors for existing material and safeguarding measures.

A FMT-scope related issue with verification and threat implications arises from the use of HEU in naval reactors to fuel ships, both with respect to possible weapons diversion use, and as a potential source for a terrorist weapon. Theoretically this issue potentially extends to non-nuclear weapons states as well, for Safeguard Agreements have long permitted withdrawal of material to be used in "non-proscribed military activities."[289] As a practical matter, thus far only nuclear weapons states have fueled submarines and aircraft carriers in this manner, although others may very well join the naval fuel club.[290] If a nation does so, then its negotiations with the IAEA could create an opportunity to explore the adequacy of IAEA safeguard measures in this context, where the focus is on nuclear "accountancy."

The degree of intrusiveness and its acceptability with respect to HEU for military naval ships was thought to be at the heart of the nonverifiability conclusion of the Bush administration with respect to a fissile material treaty. Since only the U.S., Russia, and Great Britain, presently, and perhaps India[291] and Brazil in the future, are involved, it

---

289   *See* IAEA INECIRC/153 (1972) at Article 14.

290   *See* IPFM Verification Report, *supra* note 199 at pp. 5 and 35.

291   India on July 27, 2009 initiated trials for its first nuclear powered submarine, which is expected to be ready for operational use in 2011. *See* VISHAL THAPAR, INDIA UNVEILS NUCLEAR SUBMARINE, SPEAKS GENTLE, *accessed at* http://ibnlive. in.com/news/india-unveils-nuclear-submarine-speaks-gentle/97946-3.html.

is a confined issue. But the U.S., at least for a time,[292] concluded the price of intrusion—both monetary and in terms of compromising national security interests—was too high to assure "effective verification" of nondiversion to weapon use with the requisite "high degree" of confidence. Yet what is the confidence to be satisfied? The answer varies. At one level there is a need to know the quantity withdrawn, particularly as the potential military significance of such stockpiles increases with deeper cuts into weapons stockpiles. Second, confirming composition and employment for use as fuel would present the more intrusive aspects of the monitoring challenge. At this point, these issues are negotiable, as is the certainty to be required with respect to nondiversion. But a "shrouding" approach, as in the Trilateral Initiative, offers encouragement that verification is not unsurmountable. While the technology needed differs in the two circumstances, the principle of "information barriers" ought to apply.[293] The verification process here serves goals that need not intrude into design sensitivity.

In contrast, the scope of military fissile material that may fall in the relative near term within an expanded cut-off treaty is that from "excess" weapons. There, the verification goal would be to validate that such nuclear material, and any related facilities, are *irreversibly* de-weaponized. The scope of verification procedures, in turn, will be tied to the process of avoiding the proliferation of weapons knowledge. When no longer in such weaponized form, one would expect extraordinary verification measures tied to military sensitivity to return to the normal IAEA Safeguards process.

At present there is no reported technological solutions to the HEU-fueled naval reactor verification issue. While there is periodic consideration of a shift to LEU fuel for modified reactors, that prospect remains

---

292   Since the Obama administration declared intent to seek a verifiable FMTC, it seems to reject the prior administrative conclusion. That prior view is reflected in a "white paper". *See* "United States of America: White Paper on a Fissile Material Cut-Off Treaty—Conference on Disarmament," May 18, 2006. *See* Geneva.usmission.gov/press2006/0518whitepaper.html (press release).

293   Other analysts also agree the approach is potentially viable. *See* IPFM Verification Report, *supra* note 199 at p. 81.

at the exploratory stage in the U.S.[294] As a start, a declaratory process about HEU stockpiles specifically reserved for naval reactors, coupled with stockpile withdrawal notices and decommissioning, could be explored. However, this type of declaratory process would be little more than an initial confidence-building measure. Whether this traditional transparency approach would be coupled with some form of verification measure in an agreement among the existing nations' fueling ships is another level of policy consideration. Conceptually, the process was posited (and rejected) as a protocol to the Biological Weapons Convention. But there is at least a precedent to be considered in ascertaining whether similar problems prevent embrace of the approach in this context. Conceivably, as in the Trilateral Initiative on excess weapons material, there could also be consideration of IAEA involvement in some monitoring process. IAEA involvement would help build confidence in nonweapons states members of the NPT. As with the TI and in other superpower arms control measures in the past, there would probably be a need to establish a "test" verification protocol.[295] Combining such an established approach with more recent innovations like "managed access" employing "information barriers" may result in innovative hybrid monitoring processes. In this way, a FMT verification process may ultimately yield best practices that would eventually be employed in a future verification system for disarmament tied to fissile material in nuclear weapons states.[296]

Prospects for verifiable fissile material control have been enhanced through technological developments since the superpower era ended. The ability to determine with high certainty the accuracy of a declaration of past or ongoing activity became a central element of the nonproliferation and disarmament process during the ensuing years. In test cases ranging from South Africa's voluntary relinquishment, to

---

294 See, e.g., Senate Committee on Armed Services, National Defense Authorization Act for Fiscal year 2009," 110th Cong. 2d sess., 2008, S. Rep. 355, p. 515, accessed at http://www.fissile material.org/ipfm/site_down/gtmr08.pdf. France is believed to have previously converted its ships from HEU to LEU, so there is precedent for the prospect. See IPFM Verification Report at p. 36.

295 See, e.g., supra note 162.

296 See also IPFM Verification Report, supra note 199 at p. 3.

bilateral accords between the U.S. and Russian, "nuclear archeology"[297] enhanced the prospect of developing forensic tools to test the adequacy of transparency measures. But the monitoring system is comprised of very intrusive measures. The process ranged from an examination of operating and loading records, to related analysis of reactor power coolant flows, temperatures, and energy production. A comparable analysis would also be undertaken with respect to enrichment facilities when they are involved. When combined with physical inspection of the facilities and other types of physical evidence in reactors,[298] the possibility of detecting falsification is increased. This approach worked, for example, in the "completeness investigation" conducted by the IAEA with respect to South Africa's stockpile declaration after it voluntarily gave up its covert weaponization program.[299] However, nuclear accounting materials advanced verification only so far; it was necessary to bridge the gap with an analysis of "operational records, electricity consumption, reports on chemical losses, etc. What made the process manageable and built confidence was the fact that the South African program existed for a limited period and produced a relatively small quantity of HEU."[300] In comparison, a similar task associated with more developed nuclear programs will be dauntingly complex. Likewise, the challenges of dealing with former clandestine programs will also eventually be highly problematic.

Even unique cases can illuminate the sources of the anticipated difficulties. In circumstances like those with North Korea, which has a long history of counterfeiting allegations against it involving everything from dollars to insurance claims, the possibility of falsified declarations,

---

297   Steve Fetter, *Nuclear Archaeology: Verifying Declarations of Fissile-Material Production*, 3 SCIENCE & GLOBAL SECURITY, 237, 238 (1993). *See also* MOHAMED ELBARADEI, NUCLEAR TECHNOLOGY IN A CHANGING WORLD: HAVE WE REACHED A TURNING POINT? (November 3, 2005) *accessed at* http://www.iaea.org/Archive/DgStatements/2005.html (Employment of advanced nuclear forensic techniques to "reconstruct the chronology and nature of past nuclear activity, and to verify the origin of the associated nuclear material.").

298   *Ibid.* The article explores utilization of induced radioactivity in production reactors and isotopic composition of depleted uranium.

299   *See* Verification Report of the Secretary General, *supra* note 3 at p. 25 ¶56.

300   South African working paper, *supra* note 210.

whether in the Six Nations Talks or an eventual new bilateral or multi-lateral forum, is more than a remote contingency. An intrusive verification process with physical access is thus an essential element of testing North Korea's plutonium production declarations that were made prior to the collapse of the negotiations in April 2009. The reports in open sources indicate that internationally recognized processes were being demanded, including taking samples and other recognized forensic activities.[301] This was not precedent-setting. After all, the most recent forensic tests to verify Libya's declaration were part of the IAEA's verification plan. This was the case even in circumstances involving voluntary admissions and a "high degree" of cooperation, in marked contrast to North Korea.[302] Before that, the IAEA had also successfully resolved discrepancies with South Africa in 1993. This initial case of weapons dismantlement occurred with full IAEA access.[303] Indeed, North Korea had, in 1994, been subjected to what were then "new methods, technologies and analytic techniques, particularly environmental monitoring[304] employed to detect undeclared activity."

The proposed forensic activities were "tried and true" scientific procedures that were being sought for verification with North Korea. In this sense there was no visible "exceptionalism" being applied to the current assessment of abandonment of a covert program; nor were there public complaints. But implementation of agreement in principle eventually became mired in detail. The agreement reportedly had included expert inspection, official document review, and scientist interviews.[305] An "iterative process of verification" was expected by the U.S. State Department. The aim was to resolve discrepancies in order to achieve

---

301   *See, e.g.,* Interview of Ambassador Christopher Hill, December 10, 2008, *accessed at* http://www.state.gov/p/eap/rls/rm/2008/113048.htm.

302   *See* Boureston and Feldman, *supra* note 175 at p. 101.

303   Verification Report of the Secretary General, *supra* note 3 at p. 25.

304   North Korea was the second nation (after Iraq) to be subjected to samples swiped from buildings, as well as from surrounding vegetation, soil, and water sources. *Ibid.* at p. 26 and note 25 at pp. 80–81.

305   *See, e.g.,* Edward Cody, *Accord in North Korea Talks,* WASH. POST at p. A12 (July 13, 2008) (Remarks of Chinese Vice Foreign Minister Wu Darvei) *accessed at* http://www.washingtonpost.com/wp-dyn/content/article/2008/07/12/AR2008071200454.html.

a "complete and correct declaration." This process would be facilitated by short-notice access to both declared or suspect sites as well as sampling.[306]

Nonetheless North Korea moved to suspend its dismantlement in a matter of months, ostensibly in response to the delays by the U.S. in removing it from its list of State sponsors of terror.[307] Even while still permitting inspection by IAEA and American inspectors for a time, North Korea threatened reassembly and broke seals at its nuclear plant,[308] before finally expelling the inspectors.[309] While an accord was announced of access based on "mutual consent" to undeclared sites, with sampling and forensic activities, including removal for analysis, North Korea thereafter reportedly moved to block such sampling and to restrict inspections just to the Yongbyon plant.[310] The process seemingly collapsed with a North Korean nuclear test and start up of Yongbyon for further reprocessing activity, despite a U.N. Security Council demand for resumption of the talks without preconditions.[311] Yet, the verification means requested that triggered the breakdown in the Six-Nation talks were neither new, different, nor precedent-setting; only the uncooperative setting was.

---

306   BBC NEWS, N. KOREA HANDS OVER NUCLEAR DATA, (June 26, 2008) *accessed at* http://newsvote.bbc.co.uk/mpapps/pagetools/print/news.bbc.co.uk/2/hi/asia-pacific/747495.html ("BBC News Report").

307   *See* B. Demick, *N. Korea Suspends Dismantlement of its Nuclear Program*, THE BOSTON GLOBE at p. A5 (August 27, 2008).

308   *See* Choe Sang-Hun *N. Korea Threatens to Restore Plutonium Plant*, N.Y. TIMES (August 24, 2008) *accessed at* http://www.nytimes.com/2008/08/27/world/asia/27Korea.html. *See also* BBC News, "North Korea Nuclear Seals Removed," (September 24, 2008) *accessed at* http://www.newsvote.bbc.co.uk/mpapps/pagetools/print/news.bbc.co.uk/2/hi/asia-pacific/7633140.stm. ("BBC News Report").

309   *See* MALCOLM MOORE, NORTH KOREA EXPELS NUCLEAR INSPECTORS, (24 Sept. 2008) *accessed at* http://www.telegraph.co.uk/news/worldnews/asia/northKorea/5155821/North-Korea-expels-UN-nuclear-inspectors.html.

310   *See* Choe Sang-Hun, *North Korea Limits Tests of Nuclear Site*, N.Y. TIMES at p. A8 (November 25, 2008).

311   *See* U.N. Security Council Resolution 1874, 6141st Meeting, Document S/2009/301 (12 June, 2009) *accessed at* http://www.un.org/News/Press/docs/2009/sc9679.doc.htm.

A future question, though, is whether some of the measures will have to be new or different when there is less than full cooperation, if or when a verification agreement is ultimately reached and implemented with North Korea. This issue should arise at the outset of any resumed negotiations because it is the reasonableness of assumptions about the operation of the reactor that will influence findings relating, for example, to neutron absorption in components of a reactor core as one element of the calculus. This introduces an element of uncertainty into the compliance assessment of whether a nation like North Korea gave accurate declarations. So too does the problem of distinguishing between plutonium produced and isotopes ranging from tritium to Po-210.[312] The uncertainty factor has been estimated at about ten percent in plutonium production, a multiple of what would be the ordinary risk of inaccuracy. However, with public sources also indicating that North Korea turned over about 19,000 pages of records of its plutonium programs in the Six-Nations Talks,[313] one would not expect it to maintain consistency throughout if false operating histories were included in activity documented. Any discrepancies would serve as a "red flag", which acts as a potential check on the assumptions in assessing their reasonableness if a verification process eventually triggers compliance suspicions. Still, the residue of uncertainty, while potentially acceptable in many instances in terms of an adequate verifiability criteria, may not be so given North Korea's proliferation history. "Special circumstances" limit the value of prior verification solutions and standards. The question for policy decision is to what extent, and if so, what are the resulting boundaries of intrusion that will reduce the risk of undeclared material potentially becoming available to the highest bidder or reserved for possible use. Hard cases likely make for harder rules; hence the stalemate over verification of North Korea's declaration and resulting collapse of the effort in 2009.

Similar uncertainties may be encountered in future verification of enrichment activity when the IAEA "goes blind" for a period of time in terms of existing means of monitoring. Iran has threatened this in the past. North Korea did so beginning in April 2009, with its expulsion of

---

312   Fetter, *supra* note 295 at pp. 243–44.

313   *See* BBC NEWS REPORT, *supra* note 306.

the IAEA monitoring team[314] and its oversight tools. Transparency has its benefits in eliminating certain types of risk at declared facilities, such as may be associated with multiproduct streams from uranium enrichment cascading.[315] The specter of falsified production records can also arise.

This prospect militates in favor of preserving at least normal safeguards in managing the ongoing enrichment dispute with Iran. However, in the meantime, while safeguards are preserved, there should be enough physical signatures to know that only lowly enriched uranium continues to be produced. This offers no comfort, however, with respect to break-out potential arising from enrichment know-how and infrastructure capacity. Since a facility that is capable of producing LEU is also usually capable of producing HEU at a certain stage of development, it is only a matter of time before the knowledge buffer is eroded to the point of break-out weapons capability. At that point, the weaponization process is reduced to a matter of political will, coupled with the adequacy of the production facility.

Thus, there are some different considerations pertaining to rogue nations as the verification process seeks to meet more mainstream challenges of disarmament and civilian use. Many of them played out in the previous attempted negotiation of a fissile material treaty, which President Obama has pledged to pursue again. Capping the production of such material would certainly limit weapons quantitatively. At the same time, the approach, at least aspirationally, is seen as part of the foundation for their eventual verified elimination.[316]

Much of the focus on ordinary verification issues, as opposed to those in exceptional circumstances, have focused on categories of production associated with fissile material. For example, it is expected that in uranium enrichment facilities, there will be discrete categories of experience

---

314 *See* Kim Sue-Young, *North Korea Expels IAEA Nuclear Inspectors*, THE KOREA TIMES (4/16/09) *accessed at* http://www.koreatimes.co.kr/www/news/nation/2009/04/113_43297.html.

315 For a description of resulting limits on "facts" as a forensic tool, see Fetter, *supra* note 297 at p. 248.

316 Negotiation of the ban was one of the "13 Practical Steps" toward disarmament adopted at the 2000 NPT Review Conference.

that can dictate the level of inspection needed. They range from those facilities where no HEU production was undertaken, to active facilities. In the former situation, verification is expected to be straightforward. While there remain some concerns over undeclared feeds to create excess production of LEU, the problem of covert production of HEU at a declared facility seems unlikely given environmental sampling techniques today.

However, there is a lurking issue about meeting the timely detection criteria. The availability of sampling results and IAEA timing criteria[317] have not been entirely in sync.[318] The perceived risk has thus far been acceptable with respect to a state "breaking out," but it is a known vulnerability. Diversion of a "significant quantity" of nuclear material is tied directly to what is needed to manufacture an explosive device, such as eight kilograms for plutonium. The relevant time period is within a month, or up to a year in a case involving a protracted diversion of small quantities. The probability standard for detection is a "reasonable" one. Thus, while the verification process may be adequate, it is not necessarily effective. If tomorrow's threat is the risk of diversion to terrorists, rather than by the host country, then there is a need to revisit this verification safeguard, as well as to expedite related sample processing.

In contrast, where there has been HEU production,[319] there is likely to be a temporal factor influencing the technologies needed. One approach identified as potentially feasible is tied to "characteristic isotopic signatures." Another proposal for legacy facilities is the use of age-dating of uranium particles, where prior use is more than 20 years in the past.[320] Basically, the verification task will be assuring that production is not renewed without triggering breaches of seals or other monitoring equipment. In this regard, there is prior verification

---

317   *See* IAEA Safeguards Criteria (January 2004). *See also* IAEA Safeguards Glossary *accessed at* www.ipfmlibrary.org/bn196.pdf.

318   *See* IPFM Verification Report, *supra* note 199 at p. 43, n.121.

319   Another basis for distinction among reprocessing facilities arises from new construction. There the IAEA can verify design and install instrumentation in the construction phase.

320   *See generally*, IPFM Verification Report, *supra* note 199 at Chapter 4.

experience to draw upon from a U.S.-Russian bilateral agreement in the 1990s.[321] That precedent includes recognition that related monitoring can be capped and temporal, in that it ends upon a conclusion that the facility is irreversible. There is also the IAEA monitoring experience in North Korea's decommissioning of Yonblong.[322] Of course, with existing facilities there is no such option. Accordingly, other verification options need to be explored, some of which may be susceptible to traditional safeguard approaches.[323] In any event, if there is to be "effective" verification of a fissile material treaty, there will be a need to confirm that there is no undeclared activity beyond acceptable risks at the minimal level. Hence, participating states will have to commit to the Additional Protocol,[324] if they have not already done so, as supplemented by managed access agreements for weapons states.

While disputes over scope, definitions, transparency, and other provisions have raged over the years, it was a breakdown on verifiability that brought the fissile material cut-off process to a halt. The United States applied the brakes at the same time it embraced the objective. Despite endorsing a legally binding ban on the production of new fissile material for weapons, America questioned whether "effective verification" was realizable. Our judgment, publicly announced after a two-year policy review, was that a cut-off treaty would:

> "require an inspection regime so extensive that it could compromise key signatories' core national security interests and so costly that many countries will be hesitant to accept it."

---

321 *See* Agreement between the Government of the United States of America and the Government of the Russian Federation concerning cooperation regarding Plutonium Production reactors (September 23, 1997) *accessed at* ipfmlibrary.org.

322 *See generally,* Application of Safeguards in the Democratic People's Republic of Korea, Report by the Director General (August 2007).

323 *See* IPFM Verification Report, *supra* note 199 at Chapter 5.

324 Merely adhering informally to selected aspects of the Additional Protocol is not enough, as the experience with Iran evidences. *See* Transcript of Q&A with Director General on Activities in Iran, 22 February, 2008, *accessed at* http://www.iaea.org.NewsCenter/Transcripts/2008/transcr220208.html.

Equally significant to the policy assessment was the announced conclusion that:

> "even with extensive verification measures, we will not have high confidence in our ability to monitor compliance with an FMCT."[325]

In this instance, even a highly intrusive inspection regime was viewed as realistically incapable of achieving a verifiable treaty. The lead U.S. State Department compliance officials took the conclusion one step further in disclosing that:

> "We believe that attempts to negotiate 'good enough' cooperative means for verification as some have suggested, are not only futile, but also harmful, delaying completion to the treaty."[326]

This conclusion was advanced in the face of long-established verification principles. For decades they have recognized the need for adequate measures of verification to be included in agreements to ensure both compliance and to build confidence.[327]

Remarkably, the continuing quest for "effective verification" now purportedly stood as an obstacle to treaty completion, whereas before the lack of it provided grounds for refusing treaty ratification with the CTBT. This policy conclusion came within the same nuclear disarmament context, for whether by test or production ban, each approach was a widely recognized step toward the goal of a nuclear weapon-free world. Yet the functional role of verification was transformed from necessity to roadblock in achieving a legally binding agreement; at the same time both approaches left a non-binding moratorium in place with the other NPT weapons states as a voluntary confidence-building measure. As such, the rationale was very similar to the opposition grounds for the verification protocol to the Biological Weapons Convention. Political behavioral constraints thus rested for compliance on national technical means and methods, rather than international intrusion. There would be no verifiable international legally binding

---

325   The text of the U.S. State Department's press guidance statement may be *accessed at* http://www.armscontrolwonk.com/2004/fissile-material-cut-off-treaty-policy.

326   DeSutter, *supra* note 5.

327   *See, e.g.*, Tenth Special Session of the U.N. General Assembly, Resolution S.10/2, U.N. Document A/RES/S-10/2, 30 June, 1978.

obligation, contrary to the manifest political will of the United Nations General Assembly.[328] Less certainty about risk was viewed as more desirable than cooperative measures that reduced the margin for error. But the price was deemed unacceptable at the time, since challenge inspections could theoretically place any type of military secret at some potential risk, not just nuclear ones.

The pragmatism of long-term reliance on NTMMs coupled with voluntary restraints in the form of a production freeze seems destined for political and policy challenge. First, the self-reliant approach contravenes the express mandate of both the U.N. General Assembly and the Conference on Disarmament that the ban be "internationally" verifiable. Not all nations who would be parties to the regime have national technical means. While methods such as commercially available satellite imagery increasingly help to fill the gap in some instances, the confidence derived from it is not as high as comes when coupled with on-site inspection. Also, since commercial companies operate in a market, pricing or exclusive contracts could preclude participation by certain nations, thus running afoul of the U.N.'s verification equality principle.

While the U.N. Security Council might be able to step in to fill these holes, it would be circumstantially dependent, rather than as a matter of right. The U.N. review process would also be subject to a veto,[329] whereas international inspection regimes may be subject to the lesser standards of a majority or supermajority vote. In any event, the availability of the Security Council process in past decades in the biological weapons context does little to inspire confidence in relying upon it for performance in another context. Additionally, as the U.S. and Russia move toward further reduction of nuclear arsenals, the amount of excess

---

328   *See* The Nuclear-Weapon Free World Resolution, *supra* note 20 at operative paragraphs 12 and 20.

329   The CTBT relied in Article V on the Security Council for enforcement. This process, with Russia or China able to wield a veto, was criticized as leaving them as "final courts of appeal for sanctions or other punitive acts." CTBT Senate Debate at p. S12348. Equally though, it left the U.S. in the same position with its veto power.

nuclear material in stockpiles[330] will perpetuate the risk of theft, particularly in the absence of verifiable disposition agreements. Elimination of excess materials will be revisited as a baseline measure, and related verification alternatives with it to assure an irreversible process of deweaponization of such material. Since dedication of some of that excess weapons stockpile can be anticipated for future HEW use in research and naval reactors, intrusion will be necessary to assure nondiversion back to weaponization of it. The requisite inspection constraints will be a function of whether the fissile material is to be verified while still in a classified composition, or need to wait for degradation to the point where it is no longer militarily sensitive. A related challenge will be verification of the inability to re-use facilities for proscribed purposes, as discussed above.

In each instance the verification process will have to serve to promote confidence in compliance, rather than to make transparent the inability to do so. It is this latter concern that has lead many countries seeking disarmament to take a stepped approach. While a starting point of declaring and verifying all past production of weapons-grade material is conceptually desirable, it is impractical. Basically, there is a fundamental problem in accurately accounting for weapons-grade production of nuclear material. The margin of error with plutonium alone is thought to be "enough to manufacture several hundred nuclear weapons."[331]

Hence, if confidence is to be built rather than questioned, the focal point of declarations, and any related verification of them, will be tied to what can be counted with high confidence. Second, if a FMT regime is to be established in the near term, then there will have to be recognition that if naval reactors are the principal present and future challenge to the verification regime, then they need special treatment—at least until such time, if ever, as there is a shift to LEU-fueled reactors. In the

---

330 The U.S. and Russia together have hundreds of tons of HEU that is excess and being blended down to LEU for use in light water reactors. As of 2007 these countries had over 40 tons of excess weapons plutonium, a large percentage of which was committed to disposition by agreement. *See* IPFM Verification Report, *supra* note 199 at p. 8.

331 South African working paper, *supra* note 210 ("For practical and political reasons, the declaration of historically produced stocks of weapons material by all states with nuclear weapons is not believed to be feasible.").

meantime, those few states impacted could be committed to "managed access" in the Treaty, with the details to be worked out later in customized "safeguards" agreements or protocols. In that sense, Article IV and the related protocols of the Chemical Weapons Convention offer ample precedent for such an approach to structuring agreements. As with the Chemical Weapons Convention, context serves to permit site-selected, modified methodology, as an interim measure.[332]

Third, the challenge inspections mechanism, particularly any involving naval reactors, would probably benefit from a "red" and "green" light approval approach. One would generally expect Russia and Great Britain to align with the U.S. on the basic point of a special mechanism for naval reactor-related challenges, if nothing else. Given the differing circumstances, as with the Chemical Weapons Convention, there would be different voting mechanisms. In other respects, the inspection mechanism might well draw from the NPT's Additional Protocol. America already has such an agreement with the IAEA. As a nuclear weapon state, the United States benefits from "unequal" treatment in that U.N. principles also recognize national security-related significance. Specifically, the U.S. is permitted to exclude the IAEA under the Additional Protocol where it:

> "would result in access by the Agency to activities of direct national security significance to the United States or in connection with locations or information associated with such activities."

The scope of application of the exemption remains a work-in-progress for the U.S. However, like the managed access approach of the Chemical Weapons Convention, the expectation should be that even defense-related sites can develop procedures that will permit challenge inspections in the nuclear context. While we may not be willing to allow a rogue state to invoke the same template, we would do well to be mindful of our own concerns when seeking to impose inspection on such adversaries. Armed with that knowledge, we are more likely to be able to draw upon that negotiation experience, as well as from within our own interagency vetting process, to identify concerns of vulnerability—both

---

332 *See generally*, Dr. Peter Bochme, Industry Verification Branch, OPCW, "The Verification Regime of the Chemical Weapons Convention. An Overview" (November 28, 2008) *accessed at* http://www.opcw.or/news/new/article/the-verification regime-of-the-chemical-weapons convention.htm.

legitimate and illegitimate—in mapping out both test and permanent challenge inspection mechanisms.

D. PROCESS CONSIDERATIONS

The mutuality of cooperative monitoring is another assumption that provided a foundation for superpower exchanges, and to some degree multilateral WMD control bargains. Such cooperation ranged from data exchanges, to on-site inspection rights, to over-flight, unmanned sensors and identifying tags, etc.[333] In circumstances where a state opts out of an arms-control regime, as North Korea did with the NPT, substantially equivalent requirements can be imposed by U.N. Security Council mandate and even extend beyond then.[334] In other instances a state may voluntarily agree to do so. The nuclear disarmament of Libya exemplifies this latter approach, for Libya agreed to act as if the Additional Protocol was already in effect.[335] While the voluntary process worked in that instance, it did not with Iran, which never legally perfected its obligation and continually traded limited access for concessions.

Thus, in this multilateral approach, U.N. Security Counsel Resolution 1540 embodies the key legal process tool. But, the assumption of mutuality is not a given element of that equation. More likely, if it is to be achieved in the Korean context, then it will be the product of asymmetric bargaining. An example would be North Korea securing inspection rights in South Korea as part of an "action for action" bargaining process. There, the concern that verification inspection becomes a vehicle for intelligence gathering and prospective targeting is a legitimate problem. So far, existing U.N. verification principles

---

333   *See* Oelrich, *supra* note 238 at p. 181.

334   *See, e.g.,* U.N. Security Council Resolution 1718 at operative paragraph 6 (deciding, inter alia, North Korea "shall act strictly in accordance with the obligations applicable to parties under the Treaty on Nonproliferation of Nuclear Weapons and the terms and conditions of its International Atomic Energy Agency (IAEA) Safeguards Agreements and shall provide the IAEA transparency measures extending beyond those requirements, including such access to individuals, documentation, equipment and facilities as may be required and deemed necessary by the IAEA.").

335   *See generally,* Boureston and Feldman, *supra* note 175.

recognize only equality in that regard, and not exceptional circumstances which compromise entitlement.[336] But there are precedents, at least legally, if not practically. For example, while the NPT provides an "unalienable" right to peaceful nuclear technology, the sanctions process with Iran has sought (unsuccessfully) to block an entitlement to the means to implement the full nuclear cycle.

At the same time, the breakdown in cooperative or intrusive inspection measures for rogue states like Iraq, Iran, and North Korea, can actually provide the timely warning that has always been one aspect of verification's function. The very lack of transparency by resistance to intrusion, such as that of North Korea, reveals the adversary's intent in a sense. It sometimes even does so with a clarity that NTMs or verification measures do not provide. In other instances, as with Iran, inspection becomes the hostage of a calibrated approval process, which is only permissive in return for substantive concessions. Whereas conceptually the desired result in either instance would be a guaranteed or automatic alliance response,[337] that has proved to be a politically elusive component of the process, particularly as a consequence of the Iraqi experience.

There have always been varying degrees of strictness in political emphasis on compliance with WMD arms-control agreements. With respect to the Soviet Union and later on with Iraq, the inference borne of the political divide was that when in doubt, we erred on the side of concluding there was a breach.[338] Yet during the Soviet era, parity in military force impelled restraint given the certain catastrophic consequences of a nuclear exchange. With Iraq, in contrast, the lack of parity coupled with political pressure lead to a worst case scenario from ambiguous evidence.[339] The burden of proof of compliance shifted to the accused and was not met. The intrusiveness of verification shifted accordingly to a more exacting standard, along with the certainty of attendant military consequences.

---

336   U.N. Verification Principles, *supra* note 4 at Principle 10.

337   *Cf.* Oelrich, *supra* note 238 at p. 182 ("conventional arms control context").

338   Adelman, *supra* note 155.

339   *See generally*, Chayes and Chayes, *supra* note 243 at p. 155 (same conclusion in the context of partial and uncertain evidence of Soviet violations.).

Today, we proceed in the aftermath of the Iraq experience. We simply do not know yet whether public perception of a regime as a "rogue" will yield political pressure to be more vigilant about verification than military necessity actually dictates for security. Similarly, the remedy in a multilateral context is another uncertainty, an issue that arises now specifically with respect to both Iran and North Korea. We can expect that what constitutes "clear and convincing" verification evidence—the U.N. Verification Principle standard—will be more rigorously applied in the future in making compliance judgments.[340] In contrast, the military requirement of parity in the superpower strategic force balance was well served by a diminished compliance requirement tied to the "significance" factor. However, parity is not part of the military equation with either Iran or North Korea, or other aspiring rogues. Nuclear and security guaranties certainly are, though, from their national security standpoint, and verification will likely be included only as part of a "package deal."

In the future, as arms control and disarmament moves further into highly sensitive areas, it does so in varied environments. Whether hostile circumstances, such as exist today with North Korea, or the more normal suspicion of potentially adversarial powers, negotiation of verification procedures will always be problematic. The challenges associated with "getting to yes" will require flexible approaches. Certainly in the past, parties decided to forego options that would only limit, rather than ban types of weapons systems, because the resulting verification process would be prohibitive—both as to cost and the degree of intrusion. These verification considerations have long had a direct impact on the scope of agreement and will continue to do so.

Perhaps the best example is found in the INF agreement. In it, the Soviets and Americans decided against only limiting the number of such weapons, or preserving a conventionally armed option, because otherwise verification would have been a nightmare due to the ease of concealment. On the other hand, there have been instances where proof of verification processes made agreement possible, and implementation was easier than feared. The use of confidence-building measures has

---

340   *See* U.N. Verification Principles, *supra* note 4 at Principle 11.

been key. In this regard, employment of test inspection processes proved invaluable. In some instances that methodology made substantive agreement possible; in others it made implementation possible while lessening conflict. The Soviet American experience aptly evidences the possibilities of "pilot trial" processes.[341]

The INF experience at the height of the Cold War reflected the contribution that full-scale trial inspections conducted *in advance* could have as a model for baseline data verification. At that time, "mock" inspections included "the testing of plans, concepts, procedures and equipment, and the training of inspection and escort personnel."[342] There were over 400 on-site inspections by the time the treaty was ever signed[343] in preparation for it and to vet the proposed regime. We know that on the basis of that experience, such inspections were subsequently included in the START I and Conventional Forces in Europe treaties.[344] Similarly, "practice" inspections were also utilized in the biological weapons context to assuage industry concerns about jeopardizing proprietary information.[345] Even in the context of accusation of clandestine biological weapons, voluntary agreement based on reciprocity resulted in on-site inspection of nonmilitary facilities, despite the absence of verification measures in the treaty.[346]

Thus, there is considerable precedent, albeit uneven in terms of its effectiveness, for utilization of trial, test or voluntary measures to build confidence in the verification process itself. This would seem to be an essential element of verification in the future as we face increasingly sensitive intrusion, both in terms of the nature of the compliance agreed

---

341   *See supra* note 162.

342   *See* Verification Report of the Secretary General, *supra* note 3 at p. 27 ¶66.

343   *See* JOHN P. HARAHAN, NEW NATIONAL VERIFICATION AGENCIES, *accessed at* http://www.fas.org/nuke/control/cfe/cfebook/ch2ab.html.

344   *See* UNIDIR Verification Handbook, *supra* note 7 at p. 87.

345   *Ibid.* at p. 76. However, voluntary inspections in the biologic context were less successful in a more accusatory weapons context in the early 1990s, when the U.S. Great Britain and Russia sought to ascertain BWC compliance within the "Trilateral Framework Agreement." *See* Jack M. Beard, *The Shortcomings of Indeterminacy in Arms Control Regimes: The Case of the Biologic Weapons Convention*, 101 AM. J. INT'L. L. 271, 295 n.140, 302 (2007).

346   *Ibid.*

upon, as well as the circumstance. North Korea could very well be another test case of verifying the viability of a verification process itself, ranging from the functioning and calibration of instruments, to the measures to be taken and personnel to be involved. As explored below, the process would also benefit from establishment of a "Special Verification Commission"—as in the INF Treaty—to permit at least initially compliance issues to be addressed among the parties, rather than in the U.N. Security Council.

E. ENFORCEMENT PREDICTABILITY

To the extent that the verification standard in this century continues to shift toward stricter compliance because of threat assessment, the shift will impact the compliance judgment with both existing and new WMD treaties. It will also affect the substance of future terms of control. In the past, greater detail in agreements became necessary, as the evolution in arms-control agreements between the U.S. and U.S.S.R. evidenced. This increased complexity yielded more interpretative disputes arising from the verification process.

Interpretative issues endured in a multilateral context in the post-Cold War period as well. For example, the CTBT's lack of definition of outlawed nuclear testing fueled part of the Senate ratification debate. The prospect of some countries construing the proposed treaty's prohibitions to permit tests with some undetected yield, with others like the United States embracing a "zero-yield" construction, stressed the significance of the verification and enforcement debate.

Then as now, problematic drafting or creative ambiguity alike necessitates increased resort to dispute resolution forums and associated mechanisms within the particular arms control regime.[347] The Standing Consultative Commission of the ARM Treaty was an initial mechanism decades ago. Today the clarification process has evolved mechanistically. One such example is the Industry Verification Branch of the OPCW. There, informal consultations are discussed within that cluster, as consensus is sought with meetings chaired by member state facilitators supported by technological staff.[348]

---

347   *See ibid.*

348   *See generally,* Bochme, *supra* note 332.

Some authorities previously argued during the Cold War that managing the dispute resolution process was the real key to "good faith" treaty adherence. They maintained that it served at once our military and confidence-building needs. As a result, they rejected a "law enforcement" model of vigilance bent on ferreting out violations. However, so far, the key threats of today are less tied to the military balance as between treaty parties, than to controlling proliferation, particularly with rogues and sub-state actors. With that shift there is a renewed need for stricter compliance tied to effectiveness, which may well compel an eventual shift to a law-enforcement model of arms control and disarmament. In President Obama's speech in Prague, he alluded to this point regarding arms control by saying that: "[r]ules must be binding. Violations must be banished. Words must mean something." The president identified a need for a "structure in place that ensures when any nation [breaks rules] they will face consequences."[349]

In a sense then, perhaps the time has come for certain elements of the 1946 Baruch plan's call to treat violations as international crimes, with concomitant penalization essential by the U.N. or its surrogate. The related process question of Security Council punishment and vetoes would be a litmus test for the commitment to strict compliance by friend and foe alike.[350] But predictable consequences known in advance may prove far more attractive than ever before in the post Iraq international legal process, including verification of arms control and eventual disarmament. In contrast, America[351] was previously unwilling to leave to an international organization an open ended process of setting penalties. This hesitancy existed even where it enjoyed the veto power. That same hesitancy lead in part to our initial rejection of such an approach in the CTBT negotiations. Yet, the very lack of certain and meaningful penalization for violation to deter it fueled opposition to the treaty at the time of the ratification consideration.[352] The punitive uncertainty we insisted upon—deferring punishment for violations to Security Council

---

349   *See* Prague Speech, *supra* note 13.

350   The 1946 Plan contemplated "vetoless" Security Counsel consideration, which was rejected. *See supra* note 18.

351   *See, e.g.*, CTBT Senate Debate at p. S12530.

352   *See, e.g.*, CTBT Senate Debate at pp. S12314 (no teeth; almost powerless to respond); S12345 (no teeth; enforcement would be impossible) and S12348

consideration and sanctions—ultimately created an infirmity in the compliance regime that bolstered the argument to reject the CTBT regime.

At one time following World War II, international punitive approaches were the stuff of dreams for liberal internationalists and legal visionaries. Most recently, punitive sanctions became a neocon aspiration with respect to verified Iran and North Korea noncompliance with the NPT. Similarly, during the prior CTBT Senate Debate, China's transfer of M-11 missiles to Pakistan while India futilely awaited imposition of sanctions required by U.S. domestic law was noted.[353] In short, proliferation persists in the absence of punishment. The failure to enforce restrictive norms by exacting real costs for violations continues today, with ad hoc grappling through a highly political process. In the end, as one Bush administration official put it:

> "verification is designed for detection and deterrence of noncompliance. If detection has no consequences for the violator, then verification has no meaning, and deterrence is unachievable."[354]

In the future threat environment, the twin goals of strict compliance and a law enforcement model may well become the pragmatic concern of realists, as part of tomorrow's security agenda. Thus, whereas the parity of superpowers was once thought to eliminate the viability of a "condign punishment" model,[355] the post Cold War era has seen a continuing struggle over what punitive sanctions fit deviations from WMD-related behavioral norms. The political impasse and resulting Security Council paralysis could actually impel renewed impetus toward a more certain arms control regime of appropriate and predictable coercive sanctions for violations. While international legally binding norms, as contemplated, might not be realized, there could be coordinated policies on penalties within cooperative multilateral forums like the nuclear suppliers group, or missile technology control regime,

---

(Russia and China might emerge as the final courts of appeal for sanctions or other punitive acts).

353   *Ibid.* at p. S12510 (Senator Helms).

354   DeSutter, *supra* note 5.

355   Chayes and Chayes, *supra* note 243 at p. 155 (same conclusion in the context of partial and uncertain evidence of Soviet violations.).

coupled with financial measures through sanctions against those supporting proliferation. But without confidence in a verification process, there can be none in a compliance assessment; nor can there be enforcement.

Significantly, it was the very lack of the means "to enhance or punish noncompliance" that lead to the conclusion at the close of the Cold War that verification is "hollow" and "less important than has been generally assumed.[356] The lack of enforcement teeth was used, as noted above, to argue against ratification of the CTBT;[357] possible sanctions for illegal testing was simply viewed as having no compelling impact on the decisional process of nations intent on building nuclear weapons.[358] The political judgment was it simply would not deter violation in the aftermath of the Iraq invasion of Kuwait. The lack of a properly calibrated response eventually resulted in draconian punishment—not for a failure to comply, but for a failure to prove compliance. Then the very lack of certainty in the effectiveness of the verification process impelled coercion.

In the near future, as the Iranian and North Korean compliance processes play out, we have more evidence of the need to establish calibrated responses in advance of the next crisis, or at least parameters for them. Politically improvising responses during a crisis through unilateral or multilateral legal measures has proved to be inadequate. We can also expect that verification processes will be held to a strict standard of proof in the aftermath of erroneous Iraqi assessments. So while we return full circle to the Baruch Plan's vision[359] that a key to precluding use of WMD is to "provide immediate, swift and sure punishment" to violators, "the process of invoking it will no doubt require greater certainty in meeting the "clear and convincing" standard. Prior politicization at the enforcement stage (as in Iraq) coupled with action

---

356   Adelman, *supra* note 155.

357   CTBT Senate Debate, at p. S12530 ("This treaty simply has no teeth.... The CTBT's answer to illegal nuclear testing is the possible implementation of sanctions.") (Senator Luger.) *See also ibid.* at p. S12381 (the perceived benefits in international stature and deterrence "far outweigh" concern over international sanctions).

358   *See, e.g.*, CTBT Senate Debate at p. S12530 (quoting Senator Lugar).

359   "Penalization is essential...." Baruch Plan, *supra* note 18 at p. 1.

in the face of actual uncertainty (or misplaced certainty), will likely drive the verification process when involving other nations toward greater certainty. But if America acquiesces to a shift back toward acceptance of less risk, then the price should be enhanced challenge measures. They will likely have to be somewhere in between managed and unfettered access, for the process will not typically be dealing with a vanquished nation.

In the politically challenging environment of the U.N. Security Council enforcement mechanism, nonproliferation compliance judgments only have a chance to be as effective as the verification processes informing them. The existing matrix of multilateral treaties in most instances has dedicated supporting mechanisms and inspectorates for monitoring the ongoing expert capacity that is a key strength of verification systems. Institutional expertise comes from field expertise, with judgment the enduring product of institutional experience combined with practical lessons.

But nonproliferation and disarmament issues are not always ensnared in the neat confines of treaty mandates or the organizations sustaining them. There have been and will continue to be instances in which WMD threats to international peace and security trigger the creation of innovative inspection regimes under Security Council auspices. The Iraqi WMD and dual-use experience with U.N. created organizations such as UNSCOM in the 1990s, and UNMOVIC briefly thereafter, reflect one verification path to WMD disarmament compliance enforcement. Uniquely, this experience extended to areas like bioweapons and missiles where no international threat verification system otherwise exists. That expertise is worth sustaining; especially where a quick reaction capacity is necessary. The specific methodologies employed in the Iraqi "verification laboratory"[360] have continuing vitality, particularly if shared with other monitoring organizations.[361] Other paths may flow eventually out of either coalition task forces or even nonproliferation

---

360   Report of the Secretary General, "Verification in all its Aspects, Including the Role of the United Nations in the Field of Verification," A/52/269 (6 August, 1997) at p. 3 ¶3h (View of Canada), *accessed at* http://www.un.org/Depts/ddar/Firstcom/SGreport52/a52269.html.

361   *Ibid. See also, e.g.,* UNMOVIC, compendium of Iraq's Proscribed Weapons Programmes in the Chemical, Biological and Missile Areas (June 2007) at

policy coordination groups, such as the nuclear supplier group[362] or multilateral technology control regime.[363] With self-selected organizations, any related verification mechanisms will never be as inclusive as that of multilateral regimes. As a result, there will be limits to their ability to serve broad confidence-building purposes, although detection and deterrence will be well within the gambit of their ability. Verifying member declarations with respect to their implementation of policy coordination would serve to tighten arms-control efforts, even in the voluntary context of policy coordination.[364]

In each instance, the accessibility of the know-how and databanks would need to conform to blended verification principles of openness and secrecy to prevent proliferation. International confidence in inspectorates of this sort will only be built over time. As a result, knowledge management with respect to prior inspection experience will be important to building and maintaining technical expertise in the particular discipline. But perhaps more important than that in building the perception of legitimacy of compliance judgments will be the professionalization of the inspectorate. There must be some space between the institutional mechanisms that trigger inspection and those that carry them out, as well as the means by which they do so. Systems confidence will translate into greater faith in resulting compliance judgments borne of them. This will be particularly important in the near term to enhance the ability of the U.N. Security Council to react to any biological incidents, especially given the continuing dependence on

Chapter VIII (Observations and Lessons Learned) *accessed at* http://www.globalsecurity.org/wmd/library/news/Iraq/un/index/unmovic.htm.

362   This regime is an informal association of countries seeking to coordinate export licensing pertaining to unmanned delivery systems to prevent WMD proliferation, *accessed at* http://www.mtcr.info/english/index.html.

363   The Nuclear Suppliers Group is a group of countries seeking to counter proliferation of nuclear weapons through coordinated implementation of guidelines for exports, enforced according to national laws and practices, *accessed at* http://www.nuclearsuppliersgroup.org.

364   While the MCTR is, for example, a missile technology expert voluntary coordinating mechanism for policy, there can be mandatory elements. In the U.S.-India nuclear accord, the U.S. Congress passed legislation conditioning acceptance of the deal on Indian adherence to MCTR policy coordination. *See* S. 3709, 109th Cong. (2006).

that sole enforcement mechanism in the absence of any verification organization for the regime.[365] In view of the threat forecast for a near-term WMD attack of this nature, the ability of the U.N. to support verification and enforcement will be best served by further commitment to preserving its capacity in this area. The abandonment of it because of the lack of any ongoing Iraq threat, which originally impelled the institutional response and development of the expertise, would ignore the recognized risk. To do so would amount to disarmament of the verification process itself.

Strengthened U.N. competency in the form of a *standby capacity* to respond to biological threats would substantially help fill the gap in nonnational means to verify and inform a compliance judgment. That can only serve to build confidence in an enforcement response in circumstances where the U.S. has diminished verification credibility for NTMMs after the Iraqi post-war findings, and because of American derailment of a verification protocol for the Biological Weapons Convention. Past experience, particularly in the context of peace operations, has demonstrated the viability of U.N. or neutral third-party verification functions in the implementation of agreements in hostile situations. There are likely to be future circumstances where the implementation of disarmament verification measures occurs in similar circumstances. Surely there will be useful applications from the peacekeeping verification role of the U.N. and other neutrals in a WMD enforcement context to establish customized verification procedures and confidence in them. In short, there could be a practical verification role for the U.N. in the future nonproliferation process, particularly with missile or even dual-use items in view of its unique institutional experience in Iraq as well as other nations. However, the role is likely to arise in the extraordinary context of dismantling a clandestine WMD program—sometimes under hostile circumstances.[366] It will be part of a collaborative and coordinated verification effort.

---

365 As discussed earlier, the prior U.N. verification experience with Iraq would also be potentially useful in the context of verifying abandonment of North Korea's missile program and control over dual use items imported/exported.

366 Neutral "third-party" verification, such as through the U.N., "[m]ay be essential . . . particularly when the level of hostility among the parties is high." Verification Report of the Secretary General, *supra* note 3 at p. 61 ¶244.

The Office of the Secretary General of the U.N. plays such a role in peace initiatives and peacekeeping missions. An extension of that role, where experience warrants it, is on the political horizon. Rather than improvising on an ad hoc basis, the nascent efforts to institutionalize that special expertise and role should be embraced as a matter of American nonproliferation and disarmament enforcement policy now and in the future. But there will be a need to craft agreements or guidelines in advance for these arrangements. This will help to avoid potential "turf wars" erupting between national inspectorates of interested states and those of international organizations.[367]

---

367   Reportedly there were disagreements in the Libyan disarmament context. *See* Boureston and Feldman, *supra* note 175 at pp. 90–91. (Bilateral arrangement with the IAEA verifying dismantlement and a U.S.-Great Britain team physically destroying the capabilities.).

CHAPTER V

CONCLUSION: DELIVERANCE FROM INSECURITY

As long as we have lived with the certainty of catastrophic risk from weapons of mass destruction, we have also grappled with the uncertainty of trying to control them to some extent by agreement or otherwise. The prospect of continuing to do so in perpetuity without their further use is belied by past experience. Shared recognition of this simple truth impels many nations toward WMD disarmament. Today the prospects for accelerated movement in that direction are increasing. With the advent of undeterrable risk from terrorist use, and the questionable stability of rogue nations armed with WMD, there is a renewed effort by the international community to bind itself to irreversible elimination of these weapons. The regimes by which nations will do so continue to take shape. Step-by-step arrangements to shift military doctrine, reshape arsenals, and demonstrate appropriate transparency, will also serve to reinvigorate efforts at the bilateral and multilateral levels.

The wealth of practical verification experiences with which we confront tomorrow's challenges, in turn, have contributed to an ongoing evolution in theory, technology, and process. There is now a broader context and range of applicability in which to utilize verification as an element of our layered WMD defenses.[368] While the traditional approach remains tied to legal obligations of nations, there is an increasing role for the process with respect to behavioral constraints, including confidence-building measures in appropriate circumstances. Equally, even the verification process itself can and should be tested as necessary before implementation, and sometimes even before agreement. However, the degree of intrusion in the process must always be carefully calibrated, both with respect to goals and to the host environment— whether that environment is hostile, cooperative, or simply passive.

But as open access to the results of the monitoring and inspection process was once thought to increase confidence in arms control, transparency

---

368   *See* Verification Report of the Secretary General, *supra* note 3 at p. 15.

may sometimes be found counterproductive to building or preserving security, particularly as the actual disarmament proceeds commences in earnest. The "building block" approach to strengthening verification of the Biological Weapons Convention, for example, failed for the very reason that it did not address compliance, but rather only confidence. Voluntary measures did not lead to obligations in that instance. In contrast, a "testing" process for proposed verification measures has served not only to build confidence, but also to facilitate substantive and process-related bilateral agreement in the past, and can do so again in the future. The ability to extend fully that confidence in a multilateral context may well be constrained by the nature of the verification process in the nuclear disarmament context. Similarly, confidence in the process itself, or to a neutral party administering it, or both, may also be compromised where the international organization is politically tainted in the context of challenge assessments. This problem may be unavoidable so long as the verification organ or mechanism is dependent largely upon or triggered by national intelligence.

As the political environment for expanded WMD arms control and disarmament develops, there will be substantially increased costs. The quest for more cost effective measures will promote technological progress in verification techniques. Equally, though, the principles of verification developed in the Cold War period can and should evolve as well to reflect more cost-effective and rational allocation of resources. While existing costs have been multiplying, those anticipated for the future will dwarf them. Although verification in non-WMD situations include "common services" as a potential cost reduction approach, the viability of that option is yet to be fully examined in the WMD context. More often there has been some pooling of resources or attempted coordination instead. Still, cooperation need not be equated with equality of access in the nuclear weapons context if proliferation of know-how is to be avoided. The greatest promise in cooperation is probably in knowledge and data management, rather than in the techniques employed to actually verify. The exception is in the investigative context, where there are some similarities and linkage between the peace-keeping security operations, sanctions validation and disarmament verification experiences.[369]

---

369   *See* Verification Report of the Secretary General, *supra* note 3 at p. 46 ¶159.

The challenges associated with violation-related inspections, particularly short or no notice ones, will continue to be extraordinary. That verification process will always be much more difficult than verifying data or declared operations. Yet both types of verification will remain central components of the process if there is to be adequate verification that is also effective. But the standards by which we will gauge compliance judgments in the future will need to be shaped not only by the strategic or tactical threats from parties within the particular treaty regime, but also threats from actors outside it. Where "military significance" once served as the measure of "adequacy" of verification in the context of superpower parity, there is post-Cold War evolution toward ascertaining "utility" in gauging the *effectiveness* of arms limitation or relinquishment. Although there continues to be homage paid to the prior standard, the threats of this century suggest that what is adequate compliance as between competitors may not be effective with undeterred enemies. As a result, there is an ongoing need to revisit verification standards from a non-party risk perspective. In principle, nations have for decades embraced the need for adequate and effective verification as a necessary element of all arms limitation and disarmament agreements.[370] But that standard must evolve to gauge the effectiveness of verifying compliance against the *full threat spectrum*. That evolution may require variations in how verification is conducted, for different threats may dictate application of different standards.

A quarter of a century ago, movement toward a more restrictive standard focused on mere violation was politically laden with ideological overtones. The potential shift engendered by the debate then acted as "brakes" on the momentum of the arms control effort. Now and in the future, renewed focus on that stricter verification standard should be viewed in a changed threat environment. Doing so will promote confidence that arms limitation and disarmament agreements will, in fact, serve to eliminate or at least minimize the risk of WMD attack from all adversaries. In that sense, the 21st century standard for compliance determinations will have to assess non-party risks as well. We have already witnessed a new form of "dual use" guerilla warfare in which terrorists created missiles in effect by arming themselves with commercial transport. Tomorrow they may arm themselves from

---

370   *See* U.N. Principles of Verification, *supra* note 4 at Principle 1.

nuclear arsenals or dual-use biological/chemical material. Minimizing those opportunities will flow from existing and future arms-control regimes that can be both adequately and effectively verified in practice as in principle.

As we move eventually toward disarmament, the standards by which we will gauge verification of compliance must be equal to that task. While the weight of that demand is heavy on any verification system, the certain consequences of failure require no less. To that end, we will have to close disparities between treaty compliance and the existing verification means available to serve that function. Otherwise, the imbalance will continually jeopardize the shared nonproliferation and disarmament aspirations of this century. Strengthening verification standards and practice will ultimately renew the commitment to compliance. It will then serve not only as a catalyst to future agreement, but also enhance the certainty that those security challenges that nations choose to meet by agreement will not be illusory.

APPENDICES

- Draft Treaty on the Cessation of Production of Fissile Material for Use in Nuclear Weapons or Other Nuclear Explosive Devices (May 18, 2006)

- The Baruch Plan

- Address by Dwight D. Eisenhower (December 1953) ["Atoms for Peace" speech]

- Treaty on the Non-Proliferation of Nuclear Weapons (March 1970)

- Convention on the Prohibition of the Development, Production and Stockpiling of Bacteriological (Biological) and Toxin Weapons and on Their Destruction (March 1975)

- Agreement Between the Government of the United States of America and the USSR on Principles of Implementing Trial Verification of Stability that Would Be Carried Out Pending the Conclusion of the Soviet Treaty on the Reduction and Elimination of Strategic Offensive Arms (September 1989)

- Signing Statement of the President for the Fiscal Year 1993 Energy and Water Development Appropriations Act (October 1992)

- The U.N. Disarmament Commission's Sixteen Principles of Verification (1996)

- U.S. Working Paper on the Convention on Biological Weapons (October 1998)

- United Nations Security Council Resolution 1718 (October 2006)

- United Nations Security Council Resolution 1874 (June 2009)

APPENDIX I

DRAFT TREATY ON THE CESSATION OF PRODUCTION OF FISSILE MATERIAL FOR USE IN NUCLEAR WEAPONS OR OTHER NUCLEAR EXPLOSIVE DEVICES (MAY 18, 2006)

Draft Mandate Text

1. The Conference decides to establish an Ad Hoc Committee on a "Ban on the Production of Fissile Material for Nuclear Weapons or Other Nuclear Explosive Devices."

2. The Conference directs the Ad Hoc Committee to negotiate a nondiscriminatory and multilateral treaty banning the production of fissile material for nuclear weapons or other nuclear explosive devices.

3. The Ad Hoc Committee will report to the Conference on Disarmament on the progress of its work before (DATE).

The States Parties to this Treaty (hereinafter referred to as the "Parties"), have agreed as follows:

Article I

No Party shall, after the entry into force of the Treaty for that Party, produce fissile material for use in nuclear weapons or other nuclear explosive devices, or use any fissile material produced thereafter in nuclear weapons or other nuclear explosive devices.

Article II

For the purposes of this Treaty:

1. "Fissile material" means
    (a) Plutonium except plutonium whose isotopic composition includes 80 percent or greater plutonium-238.
    (b) Uranium containing a 20 percent or greater enrichment in the isotopes uranium-233 or uranium-235, separately or in combination; or
    (c) Any material that contains the material defined in (a) or (b) above.

2. "Produce fissile material" means:

   (a) To separate any fissile material from fission products in irradiated nuclear material;

   (b) To enrich plutonium-239 in plutonium by any isotopic separation process; or

   (c) To enrich uranium-233 or uranium-235 in uranium to an enrichment of 20 percent or greater in those isotopes, separately or in combination, by any isotopic separation process.

3. The term "produce fissile material" does not include activities involving fissile material produced prior to entry into force of the Treaty, provided that such activities do not increase the total quantity of plutonium, uranium-233, or uranium-235 in such fissile material.

Article III

1. Each Party shall take the necessary measures to ensure that all persons and entities anywhere on its territory or in any other place under its jurisdiction or control do not produce fissile material for use in nuclear weapons or other nuclear explosive devices, and do not use fissile material produced after entry into force of this Treaty for that Party in nuclear weapons or other nuclear explosive devices.

2. For the purposes of this Treaty, no Party shall be precluded from using information obtained by national means and methods in a manner consistent with generally recognized principles of international law, including that of respect for the sovereignty of States.

3. Any questions that arise regarding the implementation by a Party of the provisions of this Treaty shall be addressed through consultations between that Party and the Party or Parties seeking clarification.

4. In addition, any Party may bring to the attention of the Parties to this Treaty concerns regarding compliance with the provisions of this Treaty by another Party or Parties and may request the depositary to convene the Parties to this Treaty to consider the matter.

5. If, in connection with the implementation of this Treaty, any Party believes that questions have arisen that are within the competence of the Security Council of the United Nations as the organ bearing the main responsibility for the maintenance of international peace and security, that Party may request consideration of such questions by the Security Council. The requesting Party should provide evidence related to the matter.

Article IV

1. This Treaty shall be open to all States for signature until its entry into force in accordance with paragraph 1 of Article VI.

2. After its entry into force, this Treaty shall remain open for accession by States that have not signed it.

3. This Treaty shall be subject to ratification by States Signatories in accordance with their respective constitutional processes.

Article V

1. Instruments of ratification and accession shall be deposited with [_____].

2. The depositary shall inform all States Signatories and acceding States promptly of the date of each signature, the date of deposit of each instrument of ratification or accession, the date of the entry into force of this Treaty and of any amendments and changes there to, and the receipt of other notices.

3. The depositary shall send duly certified copies of this Treaty to the Governments of the States Signatories and acceding States.

Article VI

1. This Treaty shall enter into force on the date on which an instrument of ratification has been deposited by all of the following States: the People's Republic of China, the French Republic, the Russian Federation, the United Kingdom of Great Britain and Northern Ireland, and the United States of America.

2. For a State that deposits an instrument of ratification or accession after the conditions set out in paragraph 1 above for entry into force have been fulfilled, the Treaty shall enter into force on the date of the deposit by that State of its instrument of ratification or accession.

Article VII

1. Each Party shall, in exercising its national sovereignty, have the right to withdraw from the Treaty if it decides that extraordinary events, related to the subject matter of this Treaty, have jeopardized its supreme interests. A Party shall deliver notice of such withdrawal in writing to the depositary no less than three months in advance of the date of withdrawal from the Treaty. Such notice shall include a statement of the extraordinary events that the notifying Party regards as having jeopardized its supreme interests.

2. This Treaty shall remain in force for a period of 15 years from the date of its entry into force. No later than six months before the expiration of

the Treaty, the Parties shall meet to consider whether it will be extended. By consensus of the Parties, this Treaty may be extended.

Article VIII

This Treaty, of which the Arabic, Chinese, English, French, Russian, and Spanish language texts are equally authentic, shall be registered by the depositary pursuant to Article 102 of the Charter of the United Nations.

IN WITNESS WHEREOF, the undersigned, being duly authorized thereto by their respective Governments, have signed this Treaty opened for signature at [_____] on [date].

APPENDIX II

The Baruch Plan

(PRESENTED TO THE UNITED NATIONS ATOMIC ENERGY COMMISSION, JUNE 14, 1946)

My Fellow Members of the United Nations Atomic Energy Commission, and My Fellow Citizens of the World:

We are here to make a choice between the quick and the dead.

That is our business.

Behind the black portent of the new atomic age lies a hope which, seized upon with faith, can work our salvation. If we fail, then we have damned every man to be the slave of Fear. Let us not deceive ourselves: We must elect World Peace or World Destruction.

Science has torn from nature a secret so vast in its potentialities that our minds cower from the terror it creates. Yet terror is not enough to inhibit the use of the atomic bomb. The terror created by weapons has never stopped man from employing them. For each new weapon a defense has been produced, in time. But now we face a condition in which adequate defense does not exist.

Science, which gave us this dread power, shows that it *can* be made a giant help to humanity, but science does *not* show us how to prevent its baleful use. So we have been appointed to obviate that peril by finding a meeting of the minds and the hearts of our peoples. Only in the will of mankind lies the answer.

It is to express this will and make it effective that we have been assembled. We must provide the mechanism to assure that atomic energy is used for peaceful purposes and preclude its use in war. To that end, we must provide immediate, swift, and sure punishment of those who violate the agreements that are reached by the nations. Penalization is essential if peace is to be more than a feverish interlude between wars. And, too, the United Nations can prescribe individual responsibility and punishment on the principles applied at Nuremberg by the Union of Soviet Socialist Republics, the United Kingdom, France and the United States - a formula certain to benefit the world's future.

In this crisis, we represent not only our governments but, in a larger way, we represent the peoples of the world. We must remember that the peoples do not belong to the governments but that the governments belong to the peoples. We must answer their demands; we must answer the world's longing for peace and security.

In that desire the United States shares ardently and hopefully. The search of science for the absolute weapon has reached fruition in this country. But she stands ready to proscribe and destroy this instrument - to lift its use from death to life - if the world will join in a pact to that end.

In our success lies the promise of a new life, freed from the heart-stopping fears that now beset the world. The beginning of victory for the great ideals for which millions have bled and died lies in building a workable plan. Now we approach fulfillment of the aspirations of mankind. At the end of the road lies the fairer, better, surer life we crave and mean to have.

Only by a lasting peace are liberties and democracies strengthened and deepened. War is their enemy. And it will not do to believe that any of us can escape war's devastation. Victor, vanquished, and neutrals alike are affected physically, economically and morally.

Against the degradation of war we can erect a safeguard. That is the guerdon for which we reach. Within the scope for the formula we outline here there will be found, to those who seek it, the essential elements of our purpose. Others will see only emptiness. Each of us carries his own mirror in which is reflected hope - or determined desperation -courage or cowardice.

There is a famine throughout the world today. It starves men's bodies. But there is a greater famine - the hunger of men's spirit. That starvation can be cured by the conquest of fear, and the substitution of hope, from which springs faith - faith in each other, faith that we want to work together toward salvation, and determination that those who threaten the peace and safety shall be punished.

The peoples of these democracies gathered here have a particular concern with our answer, for their peoples hate war. They will have a heavy exaction to make of those who fail to provide an escape. They are not afraid of an internationalism that protects; they are unwilling to be fobbed off by mouthings about narrow sovereignty, which is today's phrase for yesterday's isolation.

The basis of a sound foreign policy, in this new age, for all the nations here gathered, is that anything that happens, no matter where or how, which menaces the peace of the world, or the economic stability, concerns each and all of us.

That roughly, may be said to be the central theme of the United Nations. It is with that thought we begin consideration of the most important subject that can engage mankind – life itself.

Let there be no quibbling about the duty and the responsibility of this group and of the governments we represent. I was moved, in the afternoon of my life, to add my effort to gain the world's quest, by the broad mandate under which we were created. The resolution of the General Assembly, passed January 24, 1946 in London reads:

Section V. Terms of References of the Commission

The Commission shall proceed with the utmost despatch and enquire into all phases of the problem, and make such recommendations from time to time with respect to them as it finds possible. In particular the Commission shall make specific proposals:

a. For extending between all nations the exchange of basic scientific information for peaceful ends;

b. For control of atomic energy to the extent necessary to ensure its use only for peaceful purposes;

c. For the elimination from national armaments of atomic weapons and of all other major weapons adaptable to mass destruction;

d. For effective safeguards by way of inspection and other means to protect complying States against the hazards of violations and evasions.

The work of the Commission should proceed by separate stages, the successful completion of each of which will develop the necessary confidence of the world before the next stage is undertaken. . . .

Our mandate rests, in text and spirit, upon the outcome of the Conference in Moscow of Messrs Molotov of the Union of Soviet Socialist Republics, Bevin of the United Kingdom, and Byrnes of the United States of America. The three Foreign Ministers on December 27, 1945 proposed the establishment of this body.

Their action was animated by a preceding conference in Washington on November 15, 1945, when the President of the United States, associated with Mr Attlee, Prime Minister of the United Kingdom, and Mr Mackenzie King, Prime Minister of Canada, stated that international control of the whole field of atomic energy was immediately essential. They proposed the

formation of this body. In examining that source, the Agreed Declaration, it will be found that the fathers of the concept recognized the final means of world salvation - the abolition of war. Solemnly they wrote:

> We are aware that the only complete protection for the civilized world from the destructive use of scientific knowledge lies in the prevention of war. No system of safeguards that can be devised will of itself provide an effective guarantee against production of atomic weapons by a nation bent on aggression. Nor can we ignore the possibility of the development of other weapons, or of new methods of warfare, which may constitute as great a threat to civilization as the military use of atomic energy.

Through the historical approach I have outlined, we find ourselves here to test if man can produce, through his will and faith, the miracle of peace, just as he has, through science and skill, the miracle of the atom.

The United States proposes the creation of an International Atomic Development Authority, to which should be entrusted all phases of the development and use of atomic energy, starting with the raw material and including:

1. Managerial control or ownership of all atomic-energy, activities potentially dangerous to world security.

2. Power to control, inspect, and license all other atomic activities.

3. The duty of fostering the beneficial uses of atomic energy.

4. Research and development responsibilities of an affirmative character intended to put the Authority in the forefront of atomic knowledge and thus to enable it to comprehend, and therefore to detect, misuse of atomic energy. To be effective, the Authority must itself be the world's leader in the field of atomic knowledge and development and thus supplement its legal authority with the great power inherent in possession of leadership in knowledge.

I offer this as a basis for beginning our discussion. But I think the peoples we serve would not believe – and without faith nothing counts – that a treaty, merely outlawing possession or use of the atomic bomb, constitutes effective

fulfillment of the instructions to this Commission. Previous failures have been recorded in trying the method of simple renunciation, unsupported by effective guaranties of security and armament limitation. No one would have faith in that approach alone.

Now, if ever, is the time to act for the common good. Public opinion supports a world movement toward security. If I read the signs aright, the peoples want a program not composed merely of pious thoughts but of enforceable sanctions - an international law with teeth in it.

We of this nation, desirous of helping to bring peace to the world and realizing the heavy obligations upon us arising from our possession of the means of producing the bomb and from the fact that it is part of our armament, are prepared to make our full contribution toward effective control of atomic energy.

When an adequate system for control of atomic energy, including the renunciation of the bomb as a weapon, has been agreed upon and put into effective operation and condign punishments set up for violations of the rules of control which are to be stigmatized as international crimes, we propose that:

1. Manufacture of atomic bombs shall stop;

2. Existing bombs shall be disposed of pursuant to the terms of the treaty; and

3. The Authority shall be in possession of full information as to the know-how for the production of atomic energy.

Let me repeat, so as to avoid misunderstanding: My country is ready to make its full contribution toward the end we seek, subject of course to our constitutional processes and to an adequate system of control becoming fully effective, as we finally work it out.

Now as to violations: In the agreement, penalties of as serious a nature as the nations may wish and as immediate and certain in their execution as possible should be fixed for:

1. Illegal possession or use of an atomic bomb;
2. Illegal possession, or separation, of atomic material suitable for use in an atomic bomb;
3. Seizure of any plant or other property belonging to or licensed by the Authority;
4. Willful interference with the activities of the Authority;
5. Creation or operation of dangerous projects in a manner contrary to, or in the absence of, a license granted by the international control body.

It would be a deception, to which I am unwilling to lend myself, were I not to say to you and to our peoples that the matter of punishment lies at the very heart of our present security system. It might as well be admitted, here and now, that the subject goes straight to the veto power contained in the Charter of the United Nations so far as it relates to the field of atomic energy. The Charter permits penalization only by concurrence of each of the five great powers - the Union of Soviet Socialist Republics, the United Kingdom, China, France, and the United States.

I want to make very plain that I am concerned here with the veto power only as it affects this particular problem. There must be no veto to protect those who violate their solemn agreements not to develop or use atomic energy for destructive purposes.

The bomb does not wait upon debate. To delay may be to die. The time between violation and preventive action or punishment would be all too short for extended discussion as to the course to be followed.

As matters now stand several years may be necessary for another country to produce a bomb, *de novo*. However, once the basic information is generally known, and the Authority has established producing plants for peaceful purposes in the several countries, an illegal seizure of such a plant might permit a malevolent nation to produce a bomb in 12 months, and if preceded by secret preparation and necessary facilities perhaps even in a much shorter time. The time required - the advance warning given of the possible use of a bomb - can only be generally estimated but obviously will depend upon many factors, including the success with which the Authority has been able to introduce elements of safety in the design of its plants and the degree to which illegal and secret preparation for the military use of atomic energy will have been eliminated. Presumably no nation would think of starting a war with only one bomb.3.

This shows how imperative speed is in detecting and penalizing violations.

The process of prevention and penalization - a problem of profound statecraft - is, as I read it, implicit in the Moscow statement, signed by the Union of Soviet Socialist Republics, the United States and the United Kingdom a few months ago.

But before a country is ready to relinquish any winning weapons it must have more than words to reassure it. It must have a guarantee of safety, not only against the offenders in the atomic area but against the illegal users of other weapons - bacteriological, biological, gas -perhaps - why not! - against war itself.

In the elimination of war lies our solution, for only then will nations cease to compete with one another in the production and use of dread 'secret' weapons which are evaluated solely by their capacity to kill. This devilish program takes us back not merely to the Dark Ages but from cosmos to chaos. If we succeed in finding a suitable way to control atomic weapons, it is reasonable to hope that we may also preclude the use of other weapons adaptable to mass destruction. When a man learns to say 'A' he can, if he chooses, learn the rest of the alphabet too.

Let this be anchored in our minds:

> Peace is never long preserved by weight of metal or by an armament race. Peace can be made tranquil and secure only by understanding and agreement fortified by sanctions. We must embrace international cooperation or international disintegration.

> Science has taught us how to put the atom to work. But to make it work for good instead of for evil lies in the domain dealing with the principles of human duty. We are now facing a problem more of ethics than of physics.

The solution will require apparent sacrifice in pride and in position, but better pain as the price of peace than death as the price of war.

I now submit the following measures as representing the fundamental features of a plan which would give effect to certain of the conclusions with I have epitomized.

1. *General.* The Authority should set up a thorough plan for control of the field of atomic energy, through various forms of ownership, dominion, licenses, operation, inspection, research, and management by competent personnel. After this is provided for, there should be as little interference as may be with the economic plans and the present private, corporate and state relationships in the several countries involved.

2. *Raw Materials.* The Authority should have as one of its earliest purposes to obtain and maintain complete and accurate information on world supplies of uranium and thorium. and to bring them under its dominion. The precise pattern of control for various types of deposits of such materials will have to depend upon the geological, mining, refining and economic facts involved

in different situations. The Authority should conduct continuous surveys so that it will have the most complete knowledge of the world geology of uranium and thorium. Only after all current information on world sources of uranium and thorium. is known to us all can equitable plans be made for their productions, refining, and distribution.

3. *Primary Production Plants.* The Authority should exercise complete managerial control of the production of fissionable materials in dangerous quantities and must own and control the product of these plants.

4. *Atomic Explosives.* The Authority should be given sole and exclusive right to conduct research in the field of atomic explosives. Research activities in the field of atomic explosives are essential in order that the Authority may keep in the forefront of knowledge in the field of atomic energy and fulfill the objective of preventing illicit manufacture of bombs. Only by maintaining its position as the best-informed agency will the Authority be able to determine the line between intrinsically dangerous and non-dangerous activities.

5. *Strategic Distribution of Activities and Materials.* The activities entrusted exclusively to the Authority because they are intrinsically dangerous to security should be distributed throughout the world. Similarly, stockpiles of raw materials and fissionable materials should not be centralized.

6. *Non-Dangerous Activities.* A function of the Authority should be promotion of the peacetime benefits of atomic energy. Atomic research (except in explosives), the use of research reactors, the production of radioactive tracers by means of non-dangerous reactors, the use of such tracers, and to some extent the production of power should be open to nations and their citizens under reasonable licensing arrangements from the Authority. Denatured materials, whose use we know also requires suitable safeguards, should be furnished for such purposes by the Authority under lease or other arrangement. Denaturing seems to have been overestimated by the public as a safety measure.

7. *Definition of Dangerous and Non-Dangerous Activities.* Although a reasonable dividing line can be drawn between dangerous and non-dangerous activities, it is not hard and fast. Provision should, therefore, be made to assure constant re-examination of the questions and to permit revision of the dividing line as changing conditions and new discoveries may require.

8. *Operations of Dangerous Activities.* Any plant dealing with uranium or thorium after it once reaches the potential of dangerous use must be not only subject to the most rigorous and competent inspection by the Authority, but its actual operation shall be under the management, supervision, and control of the Authority.

9. *Inspection. By* assigning intrinsically dangerous activities exclusively to the Authority, the difficulties of inspection are reduced. If the Authority is the only agency which may lawfully conduct dangerous activities, then visible

operation by others than the Authority will constitute an unambiguous danger signal. Inspection will also occur in connection with the licensing functions of the Authority.

10. *Freedom of Access.* Adequate ingress and egress for all qualified representatives of the Authority must be assured. Many of the inspection activities of the Authority should grow out of and be incidental to, its other functions. Important measures of inspection will be associated with the tight control of raw materials, for this is a keystone of the plan. The continuing activities of prospecting, survey, and research in relation to raw materials will be designed not only to serve the affirmative development functions of the Authority but also to assure that no surreptitious operations are conducted in the raw-materials field by nations or their citizens.

11. *Personnel.* The personnel of the Authority should be recruited on a basis of proven competence but also so far as possible on an international basis.

12. *Progress by Stages.* A primary step in the creation of the system of control is the setting forth, in comprehensive terms, of the functions, responsibilities, powers, and limitations of the Authority. Once a charter for the Authority has been adopted, the Authority and the system of control for which it will be responsible will require time to become fully organized and effective. The plan of control will, therefore, have to come into effect in successive stages. These should be **specifically fixed in the charter or** means should be otherwise **set forth in the charter for transitions** from one stage to another, as contemplated in the resolution of the United Nations Assembly which created this Commission.

13. *Disclosures.* In the deliberations of the United Nations Commission on Atomic Energy, the United States is prepared to make available the information essential to a reasonable understanding of the proposals which it advocates. Further disclosures must be dependent, in the interests of all, upon the effective ratification of the treaty. When the Authority is actually created, the United States will join the other nations in making available the further information essential to that organization for the performance of its functions. As the successive stages of international control are reached, the United States will be prepared to yield, to the extent required by each stage, national control of activities in this field to the Authority.

14. *International Control.* There will be questions about the extent of control to be allowed to national bodies, when the Authority is established. Purely national authorities for control and development of atomic energy should to the extent necessary for the effective operation of the Authority be subordinate to it. This is neither an endorsement nor a disapproval of the creation of national authorities. The Commission should evolve a clear demarcation of the scope of duties and responsibilities of such national authorities.

And now I end. I have submitted an outline for present discussion. Our consideration will be broadened by the criticism of the United States proposals and by the plans of the other nations, which, it is to be hoped, will be submitted at their early convenience. I and my associates of the United States Delegation will make available to each member of this body books and pamphlets, including the Acheson-Lilienthal report, recently made by the United States Department of State, and the McMahon Committee Monograph No. I entitled 'Essential Information on Atomic Energy' relating to the McMahon bill recently passed by the United States Senate, which may prove of value in assessing the situation.

All of us are consecrated to making an end of gloom and hopelessness. It will not be an easy job. The way is long and thorny, but supremely worth traveling. All of us want to stand erect, with our faces to the sun, instead of being forced to burrow into the earth, like rats.

The pattern of salvation must be worked out by all for all.

The light at the end of the tunnel is dim, but our path seems to grow brighter as we actually begin our journey. We cannot yet light the way to the end. However, we hope the suggestions of my Government will be illuminating.

Let us keep in mind the exhortation of Abraham Lincoln, whose words, uttered at a moment of shattering national peril, form a complete text for our deliberation. I quote, paraphrasing slightly:

> We cannot escape history. We of this meeting will be remembered in spite of ourselves. No personal significance or insignificance can spare one or another of us. The fiery trial through which we are passing will light us down in honor or dishonor to the latest generation.

> We say we are for Peace. The world will not forget that we say this. We know how to save Peace. The world knows that we do. We, even we here, hold the power and have the responsibility.

> We shall nobly save, or meanly lose, the last, best hope of earth. The way is plain, peaceful, generous, just - a way which, if followed, the world will forever applaud.

My thanks for your attention.

APPENDIX III

Address by Dwight D. Eisenhower (December 1953) ["Atoms for Peace" speech]

General Assembly President: Mrs. Vijaya Lakshmi Pandit (India)

MADAM PRESIDENT AND MEMBERS OF THE GENERAL ASSEMBLY;

When Secretary General Hammarskjold's invitation to address the General Assembly reached me in Bermuda, I was just beginning a series of conferences with the prime Ministers and Foreign Ministers of the United Kingdom and France. Our subject was some of the problems that beset our world. During the remainder of the Bermuda Conference, I had constantly in mind that ahead of me lay a great honour. That honour is mine today as I stand here, privileged to address the general Assembly of the United Nations.

At the same time that I appreciate the distinction of addressing you, I have a sense of exhilaration as I look upon this Assembly. Never before in history has so much hope for so many people been gathered together in a single organization. Your deliberations and decisions during these sombre years have already realized part of those hopes.

But the great tests and the great accomplishments still lie ahead. And in the confident expectation of those accomplishments, I would use the office which, for the time being, I hold, to assure you that the Government of the United States will remain steadfast in its support of this body. This we shall do in the conviction that you will provide a great share of the wisdom, of the courage and of the faith which can bring to this world lasting peace for all nations, and happiness and well-being for all men.

Clearly, it would not be fitting for me to take this occasion to present to you a unilateral American report on Bermuda. Nevertheless, I assure you that in our deliberations on that lovely island we sought to invoke those same great concepts of universal peace and human dignity which are so clearly etched in your Charter. Neither would it be a measure of this great opportunity to recite, however hopefully, pious platitudes. I therefore decided that this occasion warranted my saying to you some of the things that have been on the minds and hearts of my legislative and executive associates, and on mine, for a great many months: thoughts I had originally planned to say primarily to the American people.

I know that the American people share my deep belief that if a danger exists in the world, it is a danger shared by all; and equally, that if hope exists in the mind of one nation, that hope should be shared by all. Finally, if there is to be advanced any proposal designed to ease even by the smallest measure the tensions of today's world, what more appropriate audience could there be than the members of the General Assembly of the United Nations.

I feel impelled to speak today in a language that in a sense is new, one which I, who have spent so much of my life in the military profession, would have preferred never to use. That new language is the language of atomic warfare.

The atomic age has moved forward at such a pace that every citizen of the world should have some comprehension, at least in comparative terms, of the extent of this development, of the utmost significance to every one of us. Clearly, if the peoples of the world are to conduct an intelligent search for peace, they must be armed with the significant facts of today's existence.

My recital of atomic danger and power is necessarily stated in United States terms, for these are the only incontrovertible facts that I know, I need hardly point out to this Assembly, however, that this subject is global, not merely national in character.

On 16 July 1945, the United States set off the world's biggest atomic explosion. Since that date in 1945, the United States of America has conducted forty-two test explosions. Atomic bombs are more than twenty-five times as powerful as the weapons with which the atomic age dawned, while hydrogen weapons are in the ranges of millions of tons of TNT equivalent.

Today, the United States stockpile of atomic weapons, which, of course, increases daily, exceeds by many times the total equivalent of the total of all bombs and all shells that came from every plane and every gun in every theatre of war in all the years of the Second World War. A single air group whether afloat or land based, can now deliver to any reachable target a destructive cargo exceeding in power all the bombs that fell on Britain in all the Second World War.

In size and variety, the development of atomic weapons has been no less remarkable. The development has been such that atomic weapons have virtually achieved conventional status within our armed services. In the United States, the Army, the Navy, the Air Force and the Marine Corps are all capable of putting this weapon to military use.

But the dread secret and the fearful engines of atomic might are not ours alone.

In the first place, the secret is possessed by our friends and allies, the United Kingdom and Canada, whose scientific genius made a tremendous contribution to our original discoveries and the designs of atomic bombs.

The secret is also known by the Soviet Union. The Soviet Union has informed us that, over recent years, it has devoted extensive resources to atomic weapons. During this period the Soviet Union has exploded a series of atomic devices, including at least one involving thermo-nuclear reactions.

If at one time the United States possessed what might have been called a monopoly of atomic power, that monopoly ceased to exist several years ago. Therefore, although our earlier start has permitted us to accumulate what is today a great quantitative advantage, the atomic realities of today comprehend two facts of even greater significance. First, the knowledge now possessed by several nations will eventually be shared by others, possibly all others.

Second, even a vast superiority in numbers of weapons, and a consequent capability of devastating retaliation, is no preventive, of itself, against the fearful material damage and toll of human lives that would be inflicted by surprise aggression.

The free world, at least dimly aware of these facts, has naturally embarked on a large programme of warning and defence systems. That programme will be accelerated and extended. But let no one think that the expenditure of vast sums for weapons and systems of defence can guarantee absolute safety for the cities and citizens of any nation. The awful arithmetic of the atomic bomb doesn't permit of any such easy solution. Even against the most powerful defence, an aggressor in possession of the effective minimum number of atomic bombs for a surprise attack could probably place a sufficient number of his bombs on the chosen targets to cause hideous damage.

Should such an atomic attack be launched against the United States, our reactions would be swift and resolute. But for me to say that the defence capabilities of the United States are such that they could inflict terrible losses upon an aggressor, for me to say that the retaliation capabilities of the United States are so great that such an aggressor's land would be laid waste, all this, while fact, is not the true expression of the purpose and the hopes of the United States.

To pause there would be to confirm the hopeless finality of a belief that two atomic colossi are doomed malevolently to eye each other indefinitely across a trembling world. To stop there would be to accept helplessly the probability of civilization destroyed, the annihilation of the irreplaceable heritage of mankind handed down to us from generation to generation, and the condemnation of mankind to begin all over again the age-old struggle upward from savagery towards decency, and right, and justice. Surely no sane member of the human race could discover victory in such desolation. Could anyone wish his name to be coupled by history with such human degradation and destruction? Occasional pages of history do record the faces of the "great destroyers", but the whole book of history reveals mankind's never-ending quest for peace and mankind's God-given capacity to build.

It is with the book of history, and not with isolated pages, that the United States will ever wish to be identified. My country wants to be constructive, not destructive. It wants agreements, not wars, among nations. It wants itself to live in freedom and in the confidence that the peoples of every other nation enjoy equally the right of choosing their own way of life.

So my country's purpose is to help us to move out of the dark chamber of horrors into the light, to find a way by which the minds of men, the hopes of men, the souls of men everywhere, can move forward towards peace and happiness and well-being.

In this quest, I know that we must not lack patience. I know that in a world divided, such as ours today, salvation cannot be attained by one dramatic act. I know that many steps will have to be taken over many months before the world can look at itself one day and truly realize that a new climate of mutually peaceful confidence is abroad in the world. But I know, above all else, that we must start to take these steps - now.

The United States and its allies, the United Kingdom and France, have over the past months tried to take some of these steps. Let no one say that we shun the conference table. On the record has long stood the request of the United States, the United Kingdom and France to negotiate with the Soviet Union the problems of a divided Germany. On that record has long stood the request of the same three nations to negotiate an Austrian peace treaty. On the same record still stands the request of the United Nations to negotiate the problems of Korea.

Most recently we have received from the Soviet Union what is in effect an expression of willingness to hold a four-Power meeting. Along with our allies, the United Kingdom and France, we were pleased to see that this note did not contain the unacceptable pre-conditions previously put forward. As you already know from our joint Bermuda communique, the United States, the United Kingdom and France have agreed promptly to meet with the Soviet Union.

The Government of the United States approaches this conference with hopeful sincerity. We will bend every effort of our minds to the single purpose of emerging from that conference with tangible results towards peace, the only true way of lessening international tension.

We never have, and never will, propose or suggest that the Soviet Union surrender what rightly belongs to it. We will never say that the peoples of the USSR are an enemy with whom we have no desire ever to deal or mingle in friendly and fruitful relationship.

On the contrary, we hope that this coming conference may initiate a relationship with the Soviet Union which will eventually bring about a freer mingling of the peoples of the East and of the West - the one sure, human way of developing the understanding required for confident and peaceful relations.

Instead of the discontent which is now settling upon Eastern Germany,occupied Austria and the countries of Eastern Europe, we seek a harmonious family of free European nations, with none a threat to the other, and least of all a threat to the peoples of the USSR. Beyond the turmoil and strife and misery of Asis, we seek peaceful opportunity for these peoples to develop their natural resources and to elevate their lot.

These are not idle words or shallow visions. Behind them lies a story of nations lately come to independence, not as a result of war, but through free grant or peaceful negotiation. There is a record already written of assistance gladly given by nations of the West to needy peoples and to those suffering the temporary effects of famine, drought and natural disaster. These are deeds of peace. They speak more loudly than promises or protestations of peaceful intent.

But I do not wish to rest either upon the reiteration of past proposals or the restatement of past deeds. The gravity of the time is such that every new avenue of peace, no matter how dimly discernible, should be explored. There is at least one new avenue of peace which has not been well explored –an avenue now laid out by the General Assembly of the United Nations.

In its resolution of 28 November 1953 (resolution 715 (VIII)) this General Assembly suggested: "that the Disarmament Commission study the desirability of establishing a sub-committee consisting of representatives of the Powers principally involved, which should seek in private an acceptable solution and report . . . on such a solution to the General Assembly and to the Security Council not later than 1 September 1954.

The United States, heeding the suggestion of the General Assembly of the United Nations, is instantly prepared to meet privately with such other countries as may be "principally involved", to seek "an acceptable solution" to the atomic armaments race which overshadows not only the peace, but the very life, of the world.

We shall carry into these private or diplomatic talks a new conception. The United States would seek more than the mere reduction or elimination of atomic materials for military purposes. It is not enough to take this weapon out of the hands of the soldiers. It must be put into the hands of those who will know how to strip its military casing and adapt it to the arts of peace.

The United States knows that if the fearful trend of atomic military build-up can be reversed, this greatest of destructive forces can be developed into a great boon, for the benefit of all mankind. The United States knows that peaceful power from atomic energy is no dream of the future. The capability, already proved, is here today. Who can doubt that, if the entire body of the world's scientists and engineers had adequate amounts of fissionable material with which to test and develop their ideas, this capability would rapidly be transformed into universal, efficient and economic usage?

To hasten the day when fear of the atom will begin to disappear from the minds the people and the governments of the East and West, there are certain steps that can be taken now.

I therefore make the following proposal.

The governments principally involved, to the extent permitted by elementary prudence, should begin now and continue to make joint contributions from their stockpiles of normal uranium and fissionable materials to an international atomic energy agency. We would expect that such an agency would be set up under the aegis of the United Nations. The ratios of contributions, the procedures and other details would properly be within the scope of the "private conversations" I referred to earlier.

The United States is prepared to undertake these explorations in good faith. Any partner of the United States acting in the same good faith will find the United States a not unreasonable or ungenerous associate.

Undoubtedly, initial and early contributions to this plan would be small in quantity. However, the proposal has the great virtue that it can be undertaken without the irritations and mutual suspicions incident to any attempt to set up a completely acceptable system of world-wide inspection and control.

The atomic energy agency could be made responsible for the impounding, storage and protection of the contributed fissionable and other materials. The ingenuity of our scientists will provide special safe conditions under which such a bank of fissionable material can be made essentially immune to surprise seizure.

The more important responsibility of this atomic energy agency would be to devise methods whereby this fissionable material would be allocated to serve the peaceful pursuits of mankind. Experts would be mobilized to apply atomic energy to the needs of agriculture, medicine and other peaceful activities. A special purpose would be to provide abundant electrical energy in the powerstarved areas of the world.

Thus the contributing Powers would be dedicating some of their strength to serve the needs rather than the fears of mankind.

The United States would be more than willing - it would be proud to take up with others "principally involved" the development of plans whereby such peaceful use of atomic energy would be expedited.

Of those "principally involved" the Soviet Union must, of course, be one.

I would be prepared to submit to the Congress of the United States, and with every expectation of approval, any such plan that would, first, encourage worldwide investigation into the most effective peacetime uses of fissionable material, and with the certainty that the investigators had all the material needed for the conducting of all experiments that were appropriate; second, begin to diminish the potential destructive power of the world's atomic stockpiles; third, allow all peoples of all nations to see that, in this enlightened age, the great Powers of the earth, both of the East and of the West, are interested in human aspirations first rather than in building up the armaments of war; fourth, open up a new channel for peaceful discussion and initiative at least a new approach to the many difficult problems that must be solved in both private and public conversations if the world is to shake off the inertia imposed by fear and is to make positive progress towards peace.

Against the dark background of the atomic bomb, the United States does not wish merely to present strength, but also the desire and the hope for peace. The coming months will be fraught with fateful decisions. In this Assembly, in the capitals and military headquarters of the world, in the hearts of men everywhere, be they governed or governors, may they be the decisions which will lead this world out of fear and into peace.

To the making of these fateful decisions, the United States pledges before you, and therefore before the world, its determination to help solve the fearful atomic dilemma - to devote its entire heart and mind to finding the way by which the miraculous inventiveness of man shall not be dedicated to his death, but consecrated to his life.

I again thank representatives for the great honour they have done me ininviting me to appear before them and in listening to me so graciously.

APPENDIX IV

Treaty on the Non-Proliferation of Nuclear Weapons (March 1970)

Signed at Washington, London, and Moscow July 1, 1968

Ratification advised by U.S. Senate March 13, 1969

Ratified by U.S. President November 24, 1969

U.S. ratification deposited at Washington, London, and Moscow March 5, 1970

Proclaimed by U.S. President March 5, 1970

The States concluding this Treaty, hereinafter referred to as the "Parties to the Treaty",

Considering the devastation that would be visited upon all mankind by a nuclear war and the consequent need to make every effort to avert the danger of such a war and to take measures to safeguard the security of peoples,

Believing that the proliferation of nuclear weapons would seriously enhance the danger of nuclear war,

In conformity with resolutions of the United Nations General Assembly calling for the conclusion of an agreement on the prevention of wider dissemination of nuclear weapons,

Undertaking to cooperate in facilitating the application of International Atomic Energy Agency safeguards on peaceful nuclear activities,

Expressing their support for research, development and other efforts to further the application, within the framework of the International Atomic Energy Agency safeguards system, of the principle of safeguarding effectively the flow of source and special fissionable materials by use of instruments and other techniques at certain strategic points,

Affirming the principle that the benefits of peaceful applications of nuclear technology, including any technological by products which may be derived by nuclear-weapon States from the development of nuclear explosive devices, should be available for peaceful purposes to all Parties of the Treaty, whether nuclear-weapon or non-nuclear weapon States,

Convinced that, in furtherance of this principle, all Parties to the Treaty are entitled to participate in the fullest possible exchange of scientific information for, and to contribute alone or in cooperation with other States to, the further development of the applications of atomic energy for peaceful purposes, Declaring their intention to achieve at the earliest possible date the cessation of the nuclear arms race and to undertake effective measures in the direction of nuclear disarmament,

Urging the cooperation of all States in the attainment of this objective,

Recalling the determination expressed by the Parties to the 1963 Treaty banning nuclear weapon tests in the atmosphere, in outer space and under water in its Preamble to seek to achieve the discontinuance of all test explosions of nuclear weapons for all time and to continue negotiations to this end,

Desiring to further the easing of international tension and the strengthening of trust between States in order to facilitate the cessation of the manufacture of nuclear weapons, the liquidation of all their existing stockpiles, and the elimination from national arsenals of nuclear weapons and the means of their delivery pursuant to a Treaty on general and complete disarmament under strict and effective international control,

Recalling that, in accordance with the Charter of the United Nations, States must refrain in their international relations from the threat or use of force against the territorial integrity or political independence of any State, or in any other manner inconsistent with the Purposes of the United Nations, and that the establishment and maintenance of international peace and security are to be promoted with the least diversion for armaments of the worlds human and economic resources,

Have agreed as follows:

Article I

Each nuclear-weapon State Party to the Treaty undertakes not to transfer to any recipient whatsoever nuclear weapons or other nuclear explosive devices or control over such weapons or explosive devices directly, or indirectly; and not in any way to assist, encourage, or induce any non-nuclear weapon State to manufacture or otherwise acquire nuclear weapons or other nuclear explosive devices, or control over such weapons or explosive devices.

Article II

Each non-nuclear-weapon State Party to the Treaty undertakes not to receive the transfer from any transferor whatsoever of nuclear weapons or other nuclear explosive devices or of control over such weapons or explosive devices directly, or indirectly; not to manufacture or otherwise acquire nuclear weapons or other nuclear explosive devices; and not to seek or receive any assistance in the manufacture of nuclear weapons or other nuclear explosive devices.

Article III

1. Each non-nuclear-weapon State Party to the Treaty undertakes to accept safeguards, as set forth in an agreement to be negotiated and concluded with the International Atomic Energy Agency in accordance with the Statute of the International Atomic Energy Agency and the Agencys safeguards system, for the exclusive purpose of verification of the fulfillment of its obligations assumed under this Treaty with a view to preventing diversion of nuclear energy from peaceful uses to nuclear weapons or other nuclear explosive devices. Procedures for the safeguards required by this article shall be followed with respect to source or special fissionable material whether it is being produced, processed or used in any principal nuclear facility or is outside any such facility. The safeguards required by this article shall be applied to all source or special fissionable material in all peaceful nuclear activities within the territory of such State, under its jurisdiction, or carried out under its control anywhere.

2. Each State Party to the Treaty undertakes not to provide: (a) source or special fissionable material, or (b) equipment or material especially designed or prepared for the processing, use or production of special fissionable material, to any non-nuclear-weapon State for peaceful purposes, unless the source or special fissionable material shall be subject to the safeguards required by this article.

3. The safeguards required by this article shall be implemented in a manner designed to comply with article IV of this Treaty, and to avoid hampering the economic or technological development of the Parties or international cooperation in the field of peaceful nuclear activities, including the international exchange of nuclear material and equipment for the processing, use or production of nuclear material for peaceful purposes in accordance with the provisions of this article and the principle of safeguarding set forth in the Preamble of the Treaty.

4. Non-nuclear-weapon States Party to the Treaty shall conclude agreements with the International Atomic Energy Agency to meet the requirements of this article either individually or together with other States in accordance with the Statute of the International Atomic Energy Agency. Negotiation of such agreements shall commence within 180 days from the original entry into force of this Treaty. For States depositing their instruments of ratification or accession after the 180- day period, negotiation of such agreements shall commence not later than the date of such deposit. Such agreements shall enter into force not later than eighteen months after the date of initiation of negotiations.

Article IV

1. Nothing in this Treaty shall be interpreted as affecting the inalienable right of all the Parties to the Treaty to develop research, production and use of nuclear

energy for peaceful purposes without discrimination and in conformity with articles I and II of this Treaty.

2. All the Parties to the Treaty undertake to facilitate, and have the right to participate in, the fullest possible exchange of equipment, materials and scientific and technological information for the peaceful uses of nuclear energy. Parties to the Treaty in a position to do so shall also cooperate in contributing alone or together with other States or international organizations to the further development of the applications of nuclear energy for peaceful purposes, especially in the territories of non-nuclear-weapon States Party to the Treaty, with due consideration for the needs of the developing areas of the world.

Article V

Each party to the Treaty undertakes to take appropriate measures to ensure that, in accordance with this Treaty, under appropriate international observation and through appropriate international procedures, potential benefits from any peaceful applications of nuclear explosions will be made available to non-nuclear-weapon States Party to the Treaty on a nondiscriminatory basis and that the charge to such Parties for the explosive devices used will be as low as possible and exclude any charge for research and development. Non-nuclear-weapon States Party to the Treaty shall be able to obtain such benefits, pursuant to a special international agreement or agreements, through an appropriate international body with adequate representation of non-nuclear-weapon States. Negotiations on this subject shall commence as soon as possible after the Treaty enters into force. Non-nuclear-weapon States Party to the Treaty so desiring may also obtain such benefits pursuant to bilateral agreements.

Article VI

Each of the Parties to the Treaty undertakes to pursue negotiations in good faith on effective measures relating to cessation of the nuclear arms race at an early date and to nuclear disarmament, and on a Treaty on general and complete disarmament under strict and effective international control.

Article VII

Nothing in this Treaty affects the right of any group of States to conclude regional treaties in order to assure the total absence of nuclear weapons in their respective territories.

Article VIII

1. Any Party to the Treaty may propose amendments to this Treaty. The text of any proposed amendment shall be submitted to the Depositary Governments which shall circulate it to all Parties to the Treaty. Thereupon, if requested to do so by

onethird or more of the Parties to the Treaty, the Depositary Governments shall convene a conference, to which they shall invite all the Parties to the Treaty, to consider such an amendment.

2. Any amendment to this Treaty must be approved by a majority of the votes of all the Parties to the Treaty, including the votes of all nuclear-weapon States Party to the Treaty and all other Parties which, on the date the amendment is circulated, are members of the Board of Governors of the International Atomic Energy Agency. The amendment shall enter into force for each Party that deposits its instrument of ratification of the amendment upon the deposit of such instruments of ratification by a majority of all the Parties, including the instruments of ratification of all nuclear-weapon States Party to the Treaty and all other Parties which, on the date the amendment is circulated, are members of the Board of Governors of the International Atomic Energy Agency. Thereafter, it shall enter into force for any other Party upon the deposit of its instrument of ratification of the amendment.

3. Five years after the entry into force of this Treaty, a conference of Parties to the Treaty shall be held in Geneva, Switzerland, in order to review the operation of this Treaty with a view to assuring that the purposes of the Preamble and the provisions of the Treaty are being realized. At intervals of five years thereafter, a majority of the Parties to the Treaty may obtain, by submitting a proposal to this effect to the Depositary Governments, the convening of further conferences with the same objective of reviewing the operation of the Treaty.

Article IX

1. This Treaty shall be open to all States for signature. Any State which does not sign the Treaty before its entry into force in accordance with paragraph 3 of this article may accede to it at any time.

2. This Treaty shall be subject to ratification by signatory States. Instruments of ratification and instruments of accession shall be deposited with the Governments of the United States of America, the United Kingdom of Great Britain and Northern Ireland and the Union of Soviet Socialist Republics, which are hereby designated the Depositary Governments.

3. This Treaty shall enter into force after its ratification by the States, the Governments of which are designated Depositaries of the Treaty, and forty other States signatory to this Treaty and the deposit of their instruments of ratification. For the purposes of this Treaty, a nuclear-weapon State is one which has manufactured and exploded a nuclear weapon or other nuclear explosive device prior to January 1, 1967.

4. For States whose instruments of ratification or accession are deposited subsequent to the entry into force of this Treaty, it shall enter into force on the date of the deposit of their instruments of ratification or accession.

5. The Depositary Governments shall promptly inform all signatory and acceding States of the date of each signature, the date of deposit of each instrument of ratification or of accession, the date of the entry into force of this Treaty, and the date of receipt of any requests for convening a conference or other notices.

6. This Treaty shall be registered by the Depositary Governments pursuant to article 102 of the Charter of the United Nations.

Article X

1. Each Party shall in exercising its national sovereignty have the right to withdraw from the Treaty if it decides that extraordinary events, related to the subject matter of this Treaty, have jeopardized the supreme interests of its country. It shall give notice of such withdrawal to all other Parties to the Treaty and to the United Nations Security Council three months in advance. Such notice shall include a statement of the extraordinary events it regards as having jeopardized its supreme interests.

2. Twenty-five years after the entry into force of the Treaty, a conference shall be convened to decide whether the Treaty shall continue in force indefinitely, or shall be extended for an additional fixed period or periods. This decision shall be taken by a majority of the Parties to the Treaty.

Article XI

This Treaty, the English, Russian, French, Spanish and Chinese texts of which are equally authentic, shall be deposited in the archives of the Depositary Governments. Duly certified copies of this Treaty shall be transmitted by the Depositary Governments to the Governments of the signatory and acceding States.

IN WITNESS WHEREOF the undersigned, duly authorized, have signed this Treaty.

DONE in triplicate, at the cities of Washington, London and Moscow, this first day of July one thousand nine hundred sixtyeight. [Also see **material** from the 2010 NPT Review Conference and its Preparatory Meetings.]

APPENDIX V

Convention on the Prohibition of the Development, Production and Stockpiling of Bacteriological (Biological) and Toxin Weapons and on Their Destruction (March 1975)

Signed at London, Moscow and Washington on 10 April 1972.

Depositaries: UK, US and Soviet governments.

The States Parties to this Convention,

Determined to act with a view to achieving effective progress towards general and complete disarmament, including the prohibition and elimination of all types of weapons of mass destruction, and convinced that the prohibition of the development, production and stockpiling of chemical and bacteriological (biological) weapons and their elimination, through effective measures, will facilitate the achievement of general and complete disarmament under strict and effective international control,

Recognizing the important significance of the Protocol for the Prohibition of the Use in War of Asphyxiating, Poisonous or Other Gases, and of Bacteriological Methods of Warfare, signed at Geneva on June 17, 1925, and conscious also of the contribution which the said Protocol has already made, and continues to make, to mitigating the horrors of war,

Reaffirming their adherence to the principles and objectives of that Protocol and calling upon all States to comply strictly with them,

Recalling that the General Assembly of the United Nations has repeatedly condemned all actions contrary to the principles and objectives of the Geneva Protocol of June 17, 1925,

Desiring to contribute to the strengthening of confidence between peoples and the general improvement of the international atmosphere,

Desiring also to contribute to the realization of the purposes and principles of the United Nations,

Convinced of the importance and urgency of eliminating from the arsenals of States, through effective measures, such dangerous weapons of mass destruction as those using chemical or bacteriological (biological) agents,

Recognizing that an agreement on the prohibition of bacteriological (biological) and toxin weapons represents a first possible step towards the achievement of agreement on effective measures also for the prohibition of the development, production and stockpiling of chemical weapons, and determined to continue negotiations to that end,

Determined for the sake of all mankind, to exclude completely the possibility of bacteriological (biological) agents and toxins being used as weapons,

Convinced that such use would be repugnant to the conscience of mankind and that no effort should be spared to minimize this risk,

Have agreed as follows:

Article I

Each State Party to this Convention undertakes never in any circumstances to develop, produce, stockpile or otherwise acquire or retain:

(1) Microbial or other biological agents, or toxins whatever their origin or method of production, of types and in quantities that have no justification for prophylactic, protective or other peaceful purposes;

(2) Weapons, equipment or means of delivery designed to use such agents or toxins for hostile purposes or in armed conflict.

Article II

Each State Party to this Convention undertakes to destroy, or to divert to peaceful purposes, as soon as possible but not later than nine months after entry into force of the Convention, all agents, toxins, weapons, equipment and means of delivery specified in article I of the Convention, which are in its possession or under its jurisdiction or control. In implementing the provisions of this article all necessary safety precautions shall be observed to protect populations and the environment.

Article III

Each State Party to this Convention undertakes not to transfer to any recipient whatsoever, directly or indirectly, and not in any way to assist, encourage, or induce any State, group of States or international organizations to manufacture or otherwise acquire any of the agents, toxins, weapons, equipment or means of delivery specified in article I of this Convention.

Article IV

Each State Party to this Convention shall, in accordance with its constitutional processes, take any necessary measures to prohibit and prevent the development, production, stockpiling, acquisition, or retention of the agents, toxins, weapons, equipment and means of delivery specified in article I of the Convention, within the territory of such State, under its jurisdiction or under its control anywhere.

Article V

The States Parties to this Convention undertake to consult one another and to cooperate in solving any problems which may arise in relation to the objective of, or in the application of the provisions of, the Convention. Consultation and Cooperation pursuant to this article may also be undertaken through appropriate international procedures within the framework of the United Nations and in accordance with its Charter.

Article VI

(1) Any State Party to this convention which finds that any other State Party is acting in breach of obligations deriving from the provisions of the Convention may lodge a complaint with the Security Council of the United Nations. Such a complaint should include all possible evidence confirming its validity, as well as a request for its consideration by the Security Council.

(2) Each State Party to this Convention undertakes to cooperate in carrying out any investigation which the Security Council may initiate, in accordance with the provisions of the Charter of, the United Nations, on the basis of the complaint received by the Council. The Security Council shall inform the States Parties to the Convention of the results of the investigation.

Article VII

Each State Party to this Convention undertakes to provide or support assistance, in accordance with the United Nations Charter, to any Party to the Convention which so requests, if the Security Council decides that such Party has been exposed to danger as a result of violation of the Convention.

Article VIII

Nothing in this Convention shall be interpreted as in any way limiting or detracting from the obligations assumed by any State under the Protocol for the Prohibition of the Use in War of Asphyxiating, Poisonous or Other Gases, and of Bacteriological Methods of Warfare, signed at Geneva on June 17, 1925.

Article IX

Each State Party to this Convention affirms the recognized objective of effective prohibition of chemical weapons and, to this end, undertakes to continue negotiations in good faith with a view to reaching early agreement on effective measures for the prohibition of their development, production and stockpiling and for their destruction, and on appropriate measures concerningequipment and means of delivery specifically designed for the productionor use of chemical agents for weapons purposes.

Article X

(1) The States Parties to this Convention undertake to facilitate, and have the right to participate in, the fullest possible exchange of equipment, materials and scientific and technological information for the use of bacteriological (biological) agents and toxins for peaceful purposes. Parties to the Convention in a position to do so shall also cooperate in contributing individually or together with other States or international organizations to the further development and application of scientific discoveries in the field of bacteriology (biology) for prevention of disease, or for other peaceful purposes.

(2) This Convention shall be implemented in a manner designed to avoid hampering the economic or technological development of States Parties to the Convention or international cooperation in the field of peaceful bacteriological (biological) activities, including the international exchange of bacteriological (biological) and toxins and equipment for the processing, use or production of bacteriological (biological) agents and toxins for peaceful purposes in accordance with the provisions of the Convention.

Article XI

Any State Party may propose amendments to this Convention. Amendments shall enter into force for each State Party accepting the amendments upon their acceptance by a majority of the States Parties to the Convention and thereafter for each remaining State Party on the date of acceptance by it.

Article XII

Five years after the entry into force of this Convention, or earlier if it is requested by a majority of Parties to the Convention by submitting a proposal to this effect to the Depositary Governments, a conference of States Parties to the Convention shall be held at Geneva, Switzerland, to review the operation of the Convention, with a view to assuring that the purposes of the preamble and the provisions of the Convention, including the provisions concerning negotiations on chemical weapons, are being realized. Such review shall take into account any new scientific and technological developments relevant to the Convention.

Article XIII

(1) This Convention shall be of unlimited duration.

(2) Each State Party to this Convention shall in exercising its national sovereignty have the right to withdraw from the Convention if it decides that extraordinary events, related to the subject matter of the Convention, have jeopardized the supreme interests of its country. It shall give notice of such withdrawal to all other States Parties to the Convention and to the United Nations Security Council three months in advance. Such notice shall include a statement of the extraordinary events it regards as having jeopardized its supreme interests.

Article XIV

(1) This Convention shall be open to all States for signature. Any State which does not sign the Convention before its entry into force in accordance with paragraph (3) of this Article may accede to it at any time.

(2) This Convention shall be subject to ratification by signatory States. Instruments of ratification and instruments of accession shall be deposited with the Governments of the United States of America, the United Kingdom of Great Britain and Northern Ireland and the Union of Soviet Socialist Republics, which are hereby designated the Depositary Governments.

(3) This Convention shall enter into force after the deposit of instruments of ratification by twenty-two Governments, including the Governments designated as Depositaries of the Convention.

(4) For States whose instruments of ratification or accession are deposited subsequent to the entry into force of this Convention, it shall enter into force on the date of the deposit of their instruments of ratification or accession.

(5) The Depositary Governments shall promptly inform all signatory and acceding States of the date of each signature, the date of deposit or each instrument of ratification or of accession and the date of entry into force of this Convention, and of the receipt of other notices.

(6) This Convention shall be registered by the Depositary Governments pursuant sto Article 102 of the Charter of the United Nations.

Article XV

This Convention, the English, Russian, French, Spanish and Chinese texts of which are equally authentic, shall be deposited in the archives of the Depositary Governments. Duly certified copies of the Convention shall be transmitted by the Depositary Governments to the Governments of the signatory and acceding states.

APPENDIX VI

Agreement Between the Government of the United States of America and the USSR on Principles of Implementing Trial Verification of Stability that Would Be Carried Out Pending the Conclusion of the Soviet Treaty on the Reduction and Elimination of Strategic Offensive Arms (September 1989)

Entered into force September 23, 1989.

The Government of the United States of America and the Government of the Union of Soviet Socialist Republics, hereinafter referred to as the Parties,

Proceeding from their mutual interest in using every opportunity to strengthen international security and reduce the risk of war,

Seeking to provide, through stability and predictability in the military sphere, a solid foundation for concluding the Treaty on the Reduction and Limitation of Strategic Offensive Arms and with a view to expediting agreement on effective verification procedures for this Treaty,

Desiring to achieve maximum confidence that the measures being negotiated at the Nuclear and Space Talks in Geneva to verify compliance with the obligations assumed under this Treaty will be both practical and sufficient for effective verification,

Have agreed as follows:

1. In the framework of the Geneva Nuclear and Space Talks, the Parties agree to develop verification and stability measures to be implemented pending the conclusion of the Treaty on the Reduction and Limitation of Strategic Offensive Arms.

The purpose of the above measures is to conduct pilot trials with the aim of subsequently refining, during negotiations, the verification procedures to be included in the Treaty on the Reduction and Limitation of Strategic Offensive Arms, as well as enhancing confidence in order to facilitate early finalization of the Treaty text for signature.

2. Trial verification and stability measures shall involve agreed kinds of strategic offensive arms to be covered by the Treaty being drawn up and agreed facilities for such arms.

3. These measures shall be selected with a view to examining, refining and trying out agreed on-site inspection and continuous monitoring procedures from among those proposed by the Parties for consideration and inclusion in the Treaty being drawn up.

4. Trial verification and stability measures shall be worked out on the basis of reciprocity and in light of the procedures agreed upon in the draft Treaty on Reduction and Limitation of Strategic Offensive Arms as applied to some designated locations, facilities and arms of both Parties.

5. These measures shall be agreed upon concurrently with continuing efforts to work out the draft Treaty on the Reduction and Limitation of Strategic Offensive Arms and must not slow down this work in any way whatsoever. The implementation of these measures must not be a precondition for finalizing and concluding the Treaty on the Reduction and Limitation of Strategic Offensive Arms.

6. Trial verification and stability measures shall be implemented as they are agreed upon, within the time periods established by the Parties.

7. Each specific measure may be formalized either through agreements concluded by the Parties or through other means as appropriate.

8. This Agreement shall enter into force upon signature.

IN WITNESS WHEREOF, the undersigned, being duly authorized by their respective Governments, have signed this Agreement.

DONE at Jackson Hole, Wyoming, in duplicate, this 23rd day of September 1989, in the English and Russian languages, each text being equally authentic.

FOR THE GOVERNMENT OF THE UNITED STATES OF AMERICA:

FOR THE GOVERNMENT OF THE UNION OF SOVIET SOCIALIST REPUBLICS:

_____

James A. Baker III

_____

Eduard Shevardnadze

APPENDIX VII

Signing Statement of the President for the Fiscal Year 1993 Energy and Water Development Appropriations Act (October 1992)

Today I have signed into law H.R. 5373, the "Energy and Water Development Appropriations Act, 1993." The Act provides funding for the Department of Energy. The Act also provides funds for the water resources development activities of the Corps of Engineers and the Department of the Interior's Bureau of Reclamation, as well as funds for various related independent agencies such as the Appalachian Regional Commission, the Nuclear Regulatory Commission, and the Tennessee Valley Authority.

I am pleased that the Congress has provided funding for the Superconducting super collider (SSC). This action will help us to maintain U.S. leadership in the field of high-energy physics. SSC-related research has spawned, and will continue to spawn, advances in many fields of technology, including accelerators, cryogenics, superconductivity, and computing. The program serves as a national resource for inspiring students to pursue careers in math and science. SSC-related work will support 7,000 first tier jobs in the United States. In addition, 23,000 contracts have been awarded to businesses and universities around the country.

I must, however, note a number of objectionable provisions in the Act. Specifically, Section 507 of H.R. 5373, which concerns nuclear testing, is highly objectionable. It may prevent the United States from conducting underground nuclear tests that are necessary to maintain a safe and reliable nuclear deterrent. This provision unwisely restricts the number and purpose of U.S. nuclear tests and will make future U.S. nuclear testing dependent on actions by another country, rather than on our own national security requirements. Despite the dramatic reductions in nuclear arsenals, the United States continues to rely on nuclear deterrence as an essential element of our national security. We must ensure that our forces are as safe and reliable as possible. To do so, we must continue to conduct a minimal number of underground nuclear tests, regardless of the actions of other countries. Therefore, I will work for new legislation to permit the conduct of a modest number of necessary underground nuclear tests.

In July 1992, I adopted a new nuclear testing policy to reflect the changes in the international security environment and in the size and nature of our nuclear deterrent. That policy imposed strict new limits on the purpose, number, and yield of U.S. nuclear tests, consistent with our national security and safety requirements and with our international obligations. It remains the soundest approach to U.S. nuclear testing.

Sections 304 and 505 of the Act also raise constitutional concerns. Section 304 would establish certain racial, ethnic, and gender criteria for businesses and other organizations seeking Federal funding for the development, construction, and operation of the Superconducting super collider. A congressional grant of Federal money or benefits based solely on the recipient's race, ethnicity, or gender is presumptively unconstitutional under the equal protection standards of the Constitution.

Accordingly, I will construe this provision consistently with the demands of the Constitution and, in particular, monies appropriated by this Act cannot be awarded solely on the basis of race, ethnicity, or gender.

Section 505 of the Act provides that none of the funds appropriated by this or any other legislation may be used to conduct studies concerning "the possibility of changing from the currently required 'at cost' to a 'market rate' or any other noncost-based method for the pricing of hydroelectric power" by Federal power authorities.

Article II, section 3, of the Constitution grants the President authority to recommend to the Congress any legislative measures considered "necessary and expedient." Accordingly, in keeping with the well-settled obligation to construe statutory provisions to avoid constitutional questions, I will interpret section 505 so as not to infringe on the Executive's authority to conduct studies that might assist in the evaluation and preparation of such measures.

George Bush
The White House,
October 2, 1992.

APPENDIX VIII

The U.N. Disarmament Commission's Sixteen Principles of Verification (1996)

In the General Assembly's 1996 resolution A/51/182 G, the Disarmament Commission created a list of general verification principles:

" Adequate and effective verification is an essential element of all arms limitation and disarmament agreements.

Verification is not an aim in itself, but an essential element in the process of achieving arms limitation and disarmament agreements. Verification should promote the implementation of arms limitation and disarmament measures, build confidence among States and ensure that agreements are being observed by all parties.

Adequate and effective verification requires employment of different techniques, such as national technical means, international technical means and international procedures, including on-site inspections.

Verification in the arms limitation and disarmament process will benefit from greater openness.

Arms limitation and disarmament agreements should include explicit provisions whereby each party undertakes not to interfere with the agreed methods, procedures and techniques of verification, when these are operating in a manner consistent with the provisions of the agreement and generally recognized principles of international law.

Arms limitation and disarmament agreements should include explicit provisions whereby each party undertakes not to use deliberate concealment measures which impede verification of compliance with the agreement.

To assess the continuing adequacy and effectiveness of the verification system, an arms limitation and disarmament agreement should provide for procedures and mechanisms for review and evaluation. Where possible, time-frames for such reviews should be agreed in order to facilitate this assessment.

Verification arrangements should be addressed at the outset and at every stage of negotiations on specific arms limitation and disarmament agreements.

All States have equal rights to participate in the process of international verification of agreements to which they are parties.

Adequate and effective verification arrangements must be capable of providing, in a timely fashion, clear and convincing evidence of compliance or non-compliance. Continued confirmation of compliance is an essential ingredient to building and maintaining confidence among the parties.

Determinations about the adequacy, effectiveness and acceptability of specific methods and arrangements intended to verify compliance with the provisions of an arms limitation and disarmament agreement can only be made within the context of that agreement.

Verification of compliance with the obligations imposed by an arms limitation and disarmament agreement is an activity conducted by the parties to an arms limitation and disarmament agreement or by an organization at the request and with the explicit consent of the parties, and is an expression of the sovereign right of States to enter into such arrangements.

Requests for inspections or information in accordance with the provisions of an arms limitation and disarmament agreement should be considered as a normal component of the verification process. Such requests should be used only for the purposes of the determination of compliance, care being taken to avoid abuses.

Verification arrangements should be implemented without discrimination, and, in accomplishing their purpose, avoid unduly interfering with the internal affairs of State parties or other States, or jeopardizing their economic, technological and social development.

To be adequate and effective, a verification regime for an agreement must cover all relevant weapons, facilities, locations, installations and activities."

APPENDIX IX

U.S. Working Paper on the Convention on Biological Weapons (October 1998)

BWC/AD HOC GROUP/WP.319

Twelfth session

Geneva, 14 September - 9 October 1998

Working paper submitted by the United States of America

I. PROPOSED TEXT FOR ARTICLE III – DECLARATIONS
CURRENT BIOLOGICAL DEFENCE DECLARATION

8 bis. Each State Party shall submit to the Organization, not later than [. . .] days after this Protocol enters into force for it and on an annual basis thereafter, not later than . . . of each successive year, a declaration, in which it shall:

(National Activities)

(a) Declare, in accordance with Appendix [X], whether, at any time during the previous calendar year, it has conducted activities which directly protect or directly defend humans, animals, or plants against the use of microbial or other biological agents and toxins for hostile purposes or in armed conflict;[1]

(b) Declare the following information, in accordance with Appendix [X], regarding any research or development activities that were a part of the activities declared pursuant to subparagraph (a) of this paragraph:

  (i) the general objectives of such research or development activities; and

  (ii) a summary of research or development activities on prophylaxis, pathogenicity and virulence, diagnostic techniques, aerobiology, medical treatment, or toxinology/toxicology;

(Government Facilities)

(c) For each site where more than [. . .] person years of technical or professional staff effort were devoted to activities referred to in subparagraph (b) (ii) of

---

1 Format would require a Yes/No answer.

this paragraph, declare, in accordance with Appendix [X], each government facility[2] where such activities were conducted;

(Non-Government Facilities)

(d) List, and provide general information on, in accordance with Appendix [Y], each non-governmental facility that received government funds or resources to support, and devoted more than [. . .] person years of its technical or professional staff effort to, activities referred to in subparagraph (b) (ii) of this paragraph;

(e) If fewer than [. . .] non-governmental facilities were subject to listing pursuant to subparagraph (d) of this paragraph, the provisions of this subparagraph shall apply. List, and provide general information on, in accordance with Appendix [Y], the [. . .] nongovernmental facilities, or all non-governmental facilities if there were fewer than [. . .], that received government funds or resources and where the greatest number of person years of technical or professional staff effort were devoted to activities referred to in subparagraph (b) (ii) of this paragraph;

(Minimum Declaration Requirement)

(f) If fewer than [. . .] facilities are subject to declaration under subparagraph (c) of this paragraph, the provisions of this subparagraph shall apply. Declare in accordance with Appendix [X], the [. . .] facilities (whether governmental or non-governmental), or all such facilities if there were fewer than [. . .], where the greatest number of person years of technical or professional staff effort were devoted to activities referred to in subparagraph (b) (ii) of this paragraph.

(Definitions)

8 ter. For purposes of paragraph 8 bis:

(a) "Site" means the local integration of one or more facilities, with any intermediate administrative levels, under one operational control, including common infrastructure such as administration and other offices, repair and maintenance shops, medical centre, utilities, central analytical laboratory, research and development laboratories, central effluent and waste treatment area, and warehouse storage, which is located on the territory of a State Party or in any other place under the jurisdiction or control of a State Party;

---

2 For the purposes of this Protocol, the term "facility" means the room(s), laboratory(ies), or structure(s) that are used, either individually or in combination, to conduct an activity or activities, and that are located on the territory of a State Party or in any other place under the jurisdiction or control of a State Party.

(b) "Government facility" means a facility that is wholly or partially government owned or that is wholly or partially government operated;

(c) "Non-governmental facility" means a facility that is not wholly or partially government owned and that is not wholly or partially government operated.

II. PROPOSED TEXT FOR APPENDIX [Y]: INFORMATION TO BE PROVIDED IN CURRENT BIOLOGICAL DEFENCE LISTING FORMAT

Non-Governmental Facilities

1. Do you have a non-governmental facility or facilities that received government funds or resources to support, and that devoted more than [. . .] person years of its technical or professional staff effort to research and development activities on prophylaxis, pathogenicity and virulence, diagnostic techniques, aerobiology, medical treatment, or toxinology/toxicology activities, and which directly protect or directly defend human, animals, or plants against the use of microbial or other biological agents and toxins for hostile purposes or in armed conflict?

    ___Yes   ___No

2. If yes, provide the following information on each listed facility:
    - Name of the non-governmental facility:
    - Address:
    - Postal address, if different than above:
    - Estimate the number of person years of technical or professional staff effort devoted to the activities noted above:
    - Estimate the monetary amount of government funding in the calendar year:
    - Provide a brief description of the objective(s) of the work (ten lines or less):
    - Estimate the duration of the contract or grant:

    ___less than one year   ___1 to 3 years   ___more than 3 years

APPENDIX X

United Nations Security Council
Resolution 1718 (October 2006)

Adopted by the Security Council at its 5551st meeting, on 14 October 2006

The Security Council,

Recalling its previous relevant resolutions, including resolution 825 (1993), resolution 1540 (2004) and, in particular, resolution 1695 (2006), as well as the statement of its President of 6 October 2006 (S/PRST/2006/41),

Reaffirming that proliferation of nuclear, chemical and biological weapons, as well as their means of delivery, constitutes a threat to international peace and security,

Expressing the gravest concern at the claim by the Democratic People's Republic of Korea (DPRK) that it has conducted a test of a nuclear weapon on 9 October 2006, and at the challenge such a test constitutes to the Treaty on the Non-Proliferation of Nuclear Weapons and to international efforts aimed at strengthening the global regime of non-proliferation of nuclear weapons, and the danger it poses to peace and stability in the region and beyond,

Expressing its firm conviction that the international regime on the non-proliferation of nuclear weapons should be maintained and recalling that the DPRK cannot have the status of a nuclear-weapon state in accordance with the Treaty on the Non-Proliferation of Nuclear Weapons,

Deploring the DPRK's announcement of withdrawal from the Treaty on the Non-Proliferation of Nuclear Weapons and its pursuit of nuclear weapons,

Deploring further that the DPRK has refused to return to the Six-Party talks without precondition,

Endorsing the Joint Statement issued on 19 September 2005 by China, the DPRK, Japan, the Republic of Korea, the Russian Federation and the United States,

Underlining the importance that the DPRK respond to other security and humanitarian concerns of the international community,

Expressing profound concern that the test claimed by the DPRK has generated increased tension in the region and beyond, and *determining* therefore that there is a clear threat to international peace and security,

Acting under Chapter VII of the Charter of the United Nations, and taking measures under its Article 41,

1. *Condemns* the nuclear test proclaimed by the DPRK on 9 October 2006 in flagrant disregard of its relevant resolutions, in particular resolution 1695 (2006), as well as of the statement of its President of 6 October 2006 (S/PRST/2006/41), including that such a test would bring universal condemnation of the international community and would represent a clear threat to international peace and security;

2. *Demands* that the DPRK not conduct any further nuclear test or launch of a ballistic missile;

3. *Demands* that the DPRK immediately retract its announcement of withdrawal from the Treaty on the Non-Proliferation of Nuclear Weapons;

4. *Demands* further that the DPRK return to the Treaty on the Non-Proliferation of Nuclear Weapons and International Atomic Energy Agency (IAEA) safeguards, and *underlines* the need for all States Parties to the Treaty on the Non-Proliferation of Nuclear Weapons to continue to comply with their Treaty obligations;

5. *Decides* that the DPRK shall suspend all activities related to its ballistic missile programme and in this context re-establish its pre-existing commitments to a moratorium on missile launching;

6. *Decides* that the DPRK shall abandon all nuclear weapons and existing nuclear programmes in a complete, verifiable and irreversible manner, shall act strictly in accordance with the obligations applicable to parties under the Treaty on the Non-Proliferation of Nuclear Weapons and the terms and conditions of its International Atomic Energy Agency (IAEA) Safeguards Agreement (IAEA INFCIRC/403) and shall provide the IAEA transparency measures extending beyond these requirements, including such access to individuals, documentation, equipments and facilities as may be required and deemed necessary by the IAEA;

7. *Decides* also that the DPRK shall abandon all other existing weapons of mass destruction and ballistic missile programme in a complete, verifiable and irreversible manner;

8. *Decides* that:

   (a) All Member States shall prevent the direct or indirect supply, sale or transfer to the DPRK, through their territories or by their nationals, or using their flag vessels or aircraft, and whether or not originating in their territories, of:

   (i) Any battle tanks, armoured combat vehicles, large calibre artillery systems, combat aircraft, attack helicopters, warships, missiles or missile systems as defined for the purpose of the United Nations Register on Conventional Arms, or related materiel including spare parts, or items as determined by the Security Council or the Committee established by paragraph 12 below (the Committee);

(ii) All items, materials, equipment, goods and technology as set out in the lists in documents S/2006/814 and S/2006/815, unless within 14 days of adoption of this resolution the Committee has amended or completed their provisions also taking into account the list in document S/2006/816, as well as other items, materials, equipment, goods and technology, determined by the Security Council or the Committee, which could contribute to DPRK's nuclear-related, ballistic missile-related or other weapons of mass destructionrelated programmes;

(iii) Luxury goods;

(b) The DPRK shall cease the export of all items covered in subparagraphs (a) (i) and (a) (ii) above and that all Member States shall prohibit the procurement of such items from the DPRK by their nationals, or using their flagged vessels or aircraft, and whether or not originating in the territory of the DPRK;

(c) All Member States shall prevent any transfers to the DPRK by their nationals or from their territories, or from the DPRK by its nationals or from its territory, of technical training, advice, services or assistance related to the provision, manufacture, maintenance or use of the items in subparagraphs (a) (i) and (a) (ii) above;

(d) All Member States shall, in accordance with their respective legal processes, freeze immediately the funds, other financial assets and economic resources which are on their territories at the date of the adoption of this resolution or at any time thereafter, that are owned or controlled, directly or indirectly, by the persons or entities designated by the Committee or by the Security Council as being engaged in or providing support for, including through other illicit means, DPRK's nuclear-related, other weapons of mass destruction-related and ballistic missilerelated programmes, or by persons or entities acting on their behalf or at their direction, and ensure that any funds, financial assets or economic resources are prevented from being made available by their nationals or by any persons or entities within their territories, to or for the benefit of such persons or entities;

(e) All Member States shall take the necessary steps to prevent the entry into or transit through their territories of the persons designated by the Committee or by the Security Council as being responsible for, including through supporting or promoting, DPRK policies in relation to the DPRK's nuclear-related, ballistic missile-related and other weapons of mass destruction-related programmes, together with their family members, provided that nothing in this paragraph shall oblige a state to refuse its own nationals entry into its territory;

(f) In order to ensure compliance with the requirements of this paragraph, and thereby preventing illicit trafficking in nuclear, chemical or biological weapons, their means of delivery and related materials, all Member States are called upon to take, in accordance with their national authorities and legislation, and consistent with international law, cooperative action including through inspection of cargo to and from the DPRK, as necessary;

9. *Decides* that the provisions of paragraph 8 (d) above do not apply to financial or other assets or resources that have been determined by relevant States:

(a) To be necessary for basic expenses, including payment for foodstuffs, rent or mortgage, medicines and medical treatment, taxes, insurance premiums, and public utility charges, or exclusively for payment of reasonable professional fees and reimbursement of incurred expenses associated with the provision of legal services, or fees or service charges, in accordance with national laws, for routine holding or maintenance of frozen funds, other financial assets and economic resources, after notification by the relevant States to the Committee of the intention to authorize, where appropriate, access to such funds, other financial assets and economic resources and in the absence of a negative decision by the Committee within five working days of such notification;

(b) To be necessary for extraordinary expenses, provided that such determination has been notified by the relevant States to the Committee and has been approved by the Committee; or

(c) To be subject of a judicial, administrative or arbitral lien or judgement, in which case the funds, other financial assets and economic resources may be used to satisfy that lien or judgement provided that the lien or judgement was entered prior to the date of the present resolution, is not for the benefit of a person referred to in paragraph 8 (d) above or an individual or entity identified by the Security Council or the Committee, and has been notified by the relevant States to the Committee;

10. *Decides* that the measures imposed by paragraph 8 (e) above shall not apply where the Committee determines on a case-by-case basis that such travel is justified on the grounds of humanitarian need, including religious obligations, or where the Committee concludes that an exemption would otherwise further the objectives of the present resolution;

11. *Calls upon* all Member States to report to the Security Council within thirty days of the adoption of this resolution on the steps they have taken with a view to implementing effectively the provisions of paragraph 8 above;

12. *Decides* to establish, in accordance with rule 28 of its provisional rules of procedure, a Committee of the Security Council consisting of all the members of the Council, to undertake the following tasks:

(a) To seek from all States, in particular those producing or possessing the items, materials, equipment, goods and technology referred to in paragraph 8 (a) above, information regarding the actions taken by them to implement effectively the measures imposed by paragraph 8 above of this resolution and whatever further information it may consider useful in this regard;

(b) To examine and take appropriate action on information regarding alleged violations of measures imposed by paragraph 8 of this resolution;

(c) To consider and decide upon requests for exemptions set out in paragraphs 9 and 10 above;

(d) To determine additional items, materials, equipment, goods and technology to be specified for the purpose of paragraphs 8 (a) (i) and 8 (a) (ii) above;

(e) To designate additional individuals and entities subject to the measures imposed by paragraphs 8 (d) and 8 (e) above;

(f) To promulgate guidelines as may be necessary to facilitate the implementation of the measures imposed by this resolution;

(g) To report at least every 90 days to the Security Council on its work, with its observations and recommendations, in particular on ways to strengthen the effectiveness of the measures imposed by paragraph 8 above;

13. *Welcomes and encourages further* the efforts by all States concerned to intensify their diplomatic efforts, to refrain from any actions that might aggravate tension and to facilitate the early resumption of the Six-Party Talks, with a view to the expeditious implementation of the Joint Statement issued on 19 September 2005 by China, the DPRK, Japan, the Republic of Korea, the Russian Federation and the United States, to achieve the verifiable denuclearization of the Korean Peninsula and to maintain peace and stability on the Korean Peninsula and in north-east Asia;

14. *Calls upon* the DPRK to return immediately to the Six-Party Talks without precondition and to work towards the expeditious implementation of the Joint Statement issued on 19 September 2005 by China, the DPRK, Japan, the Republic of Korea, the Russian Federation and the United States;

15. *Affirms* that it shall keep DPRK's actions under continuous review and that it shall be prepared to review the appropriateness of the measures contained in paragraph 8 above, including the strengthening, modification, suspension or lifting of the measures, as may be needed at that time in light of the DPRK's compliance with the provisions of the resolution;

16. *Underlines* that further decisions will be required, should additional measures be necessary;

17. *Decides* to remain actively seized of the matter.

APPENDIX XI

United Nations Security Council Resolution 1874
(June 2009)

Adopted by the Security Council at its 6141st meeting, on 12 June 2009

The Security Council,

Recalling its previous relevant resolutions, including resolution 825 (1993), resolution 1540 (2004), resolution 1695 (2006), and, in particular, resolution 1718 (2006), as well as the statements of its President of 6 October 2006 (S/PRST/2006/41) and 13 April 2009 (S/PRST/2009/7),

Reaffirming that proliferation of nuclear, chemical and biological weapons, as well as their means of delivery, constitutes a threat to international peace and security,

Expressing the gravest concern at the nuclear test conducted by the Democratic People's Republic of Korea ("the DPRK") on 25 May 2009 (local time) in violation of resolution 1718 (2006), and at the challenge such a test constitutes to the Treaty on Non-Proliferation of Nuclear Weapons ("the NPT") and to international efforts aimed at strengthening the global regime of non-proliferation of nuclear weapons towards the 2010 NPT Review Conference, and the danger it poses to peace and stability in the region and beyond,

Stressing its collective support for the NPT and commitment to strengthen the Treaty in all its aspects, and global efforts towards nuclear non-proliferation and nuclear disarmament, and *recalling* that the DPRK cannot have the status of a nuclear-weapon state in accordance with the NPT in any case,

Deploring the DPRK's announcement of withdrawal from the NPT and its pursuit of nuclear weapons,

Underlining once again the importance that the DPRK respond to other security and humanitarian concerns of the international community,

Underlining also that measures imposed by this resolution are not intended to have adverse humanitarian consequences for the civilian population of the DPRK,

Expressing its gravest concern that the nuclear test and missile activities carried out by the DPRK have further generated increased tension in the region and beyond, and *determining* that there continues to exist a clear threat to international peace and security,

Reaffirming the importance that all Member States uphold the purposes and principles of the Charter of the United Nations,

Acting under Chapter VII of the Charter of the United Nations, and taking measures under its Article 41,

1. *Condemns* in the strongest terms the nuclear test conducted by the DPRK on 25 May 2009 (local time) in violation and flagrant disregard of its relevant resolutions, in particular resolutions 1695 (2006) and 1718 (2006), and the statement of its President of 13 April 2009 (S/PRST/2009/7);

2. *Demands* that the DPRK not conduct any further nuclear test or any launch using ballistic missile technology;

3. *Decides* that the DPRK shall suspend all activities related to its ballistic missile programme and in this context re-establish its pre-existing commitments to a moratorium on missile launches;

4. *Demands* that the DPRK immediately comply fully with its obligations under relevant Security Council resolutions, in particular resolution 1718 (2006);

5. *Demands* that the DPRK immediately retract its announcement of withdrawal from the NPT;

6. *Demands* further that the DPRK return at an early date to the NPT and International Atomic Energy Agency (IAEA) safeguards, bearing in mind the rights and obligations of States Parties to the NPT, and *underlines* the need for all States Parties to the NPT to continue to comply with their Treaty obligations;

7. *Calls upon* all Member States to implement their obligations pursuant to resolution 1718 (2006), including with respect to designations made by the Committee established pursuant to resolution 1718 (2006) ("the Committee") pursuant to the statement of its President of 13 April 2009 (S/PRST/2009/7);

8. *Decides* that the DPRK shall abandon all nuclear weapons and existing nuclear programs in a complete, verifiable and irreversible manner and immediately cease all related activities, shall act strictly in accordance with the obligations applicable to parties under the NPT and the terms and conditions of the IAEA Safeguards Agreement (IAEA INFCIRC/403) and shall provide the IAEA transparency measures extending beyond these requirements, including such access to individuals, documentation, equipment and facilities as may be required and deemed necessary by the IAEA;

9. *Decides* that the measures in paragraph 8 (b) of resolution 1718 (2006) shall also apply to all arms and related materiel, as well as to financial transactions, technical training, advice, services or assistance related to the provision, manufacture, maintenance or use of such arms or materiel;

10. *Decides* that the measures in paragraph 8 (a) of resolution 1718 (2006) shall also apply to all arms and related materiel, as well as to financial transactions, technical training, advice, services or assistance related to the provision, manufacture, maintenance or use of such arms, except for small arms and light weapons and their related materiel, and *calls upon* States to exercise vigilance over the direct or indirect supply, sale or transfer to the DPRK of small arms or light weapons, and further *decides* that States shall notify the Committee at least five days prior to selling, supplying or transferring small arms or light weapons to the DPRK;

11. *Calls upon* all States to inspect, in accordance with their national authorities and legislation, and consistent with international law, all cargo to and from the DPRK, in their territory, including seaports and airports, if the State concerned has information that provides reasonable grounds to believe the cargo contains items the supply, sale, transfer, or export of which is prohibited by paragraph 8 (a), 8 (b), or 8 (c) of resolution 1718 or by paragraph 9 or 10 of this resolution, for the purpose of ensuring strict implementation of those provisions;

12. *Calls upon* all Member States to inspect vessels, with the consent of the flag State, on the high seas, if they have information that provides reasonable grounds to believe that the cargo of such vessels contains items the supply, sale, transfer, or export of which is prohibited by paragraph 8 (a), 8 (b), or 8 (c) of resolution 1718 (2006) or by paragraph 9 or 10 of this resolution, for the purpose of ensuring strict implementation of those provisions;

13. *Calls upon* all States to cooperate with inspections pursuant to paragraphs 11 and 12, and, if the flag State does not consent to inspection on the high seas, *decides* that the flag State shall direct the vessel to proceed to an appropriate and convenient port for the required inspection by the local authorities pursuant to paragraph 11;

14. *Decides* to authorize all Member States to, and that all Member States shall, seize and dispose of items the supply, sale, transfer, or export of which is prohibited by paragraph 8 (a), 8 (b), or 8 (c) of resolution 1718 or by paragraph 9 or 10 of this resolution that are identified in inspections pursuant to paragraph 11, 12, or 13 in a manner that is not inconsistent with their obligations under applicable Security Council resolutions, including resolution 1540 (2004), as well as any obligations of parties to the NPT, the Convention on the Prohibition of the Development, Production, Stockpiling and Use of Chemical Weapons and on Their Destruction of 29 April 1997, and the Convention on the Prohibition of the Development, Production and Stockpiling of Bacteriological (Biological) and Toxin Weapons and on Their Destruction of 10 April 1972, and *decides* further that all States shall cooperate in such efforts;

15. *Requires* any Member State, when it undertakes an inspection pursuant to paragraph 11, 12, or 13, or seizes and disposes of cargo pursuant to paragraph 14, to submit promptly reports containing relevant details to the Committee on the inspection, seizure and disposal;

16. *Requires* any Member State, when it does not receive the cooperation of a flag State pursuant to paragraph 12 or 13 to submit promptly to the Committee a report containing relevant details;

17. *Decides* that Member States shall prohibit the provision by their nationals or from their territory of bunkering services, such as provision of fuel or supplies, or other servicing of vessels, to DPRK vessels if they have information that provides reasonable grounds to believe they are carrying items the supply, sale, transfer, or export of which is prohibited by paragraph 8 (a), 8 (b), or 8 (c) of resolution 1718 (2006) or by paragraph 9 or 10 of this resolution, unless provision of such services is necessary for humanitarian purposes or until such time as the cargo has been inspected, and seized and disposed of if necessary, and *underlines* that this paragraph is not intended to affect legal economic activities;

18. *Calls upon* Member States, in addition to implementing their obligations pursuant to paragraphs 8 (d) and (e) of resolution 1718 (2006), to prevent the provision of financial services or the transfer to, through, or from their territory, or to or by their nationals or entities organized under their laws (including branches abroad), or persons or financial institutions in their territory, of any financial or other assets or resources that could contribute to the DPRK's nuclear-related, ballistic missile-related, or other weapons of mass destruction-related programs or activities, including by freezing any financial or other assets or resources on their territories or that hereafter come within their territories, or that are subject to their jurisdiction or that hereafter become subject to their jurisdiction, that are associated with such programs or activities and applying enhanced monitoring to prevent all such transactions in accordance with their national authorities and legislation;

19. *Calls upon* all Member States and international financial and credit institutions not to enter into new commitments for grants, financial assistance, or concessional loans to the DPRK, except for humanitarian and developmental purposes directly addressing the needs of the civilian population, or the promotion of denuclearization, and also *calls upon* States to exercise enhanced vigilance with a view to reducing current commitments;

20. *Calls upon* all Member States not to provide public financial support for trade with the DPRK (including the granting of export credits, guarantees or insurance to their nationals or entities involved in such trade) where such financial support could contribute to the DPRK's nuclear-related or ballistic missile-related or other WMD-related programs or activities;

21. *Emphasizes* that all Member States should comply with the provisions of paragraphs 8 (a) (iii) and 8 (d) of resolution 1718 (2006) without prejudice

to the activities of the diplomatic missions in the DPRK pursuant to the Vienna Convention on Diplomatic Relations;

22. *Calls upon* all Member States to report to the Security Council within forty-five days of the adoption of this resolution and thereafter upon request by the Committee on concrete measures they have taken in order to implement effectively the provisions of paragraph 8 of resolution 1718 (2006) as well as paragraphs 9 and 10 of this resolution, as well as financial measures set out in paragraphs 18, 19 and 20 of this resolution;

23. *Decides* that the measures set out at paragraphs 8 (a), 8 (b) and 8 (c) of reso-lution 1718 (2006) shall also apply to the items listed in INFCIRC/254/Rev.9/Part 1a and INFCIRC/254/Rev.7/Part 2a;

24. *Decides* to adjust the measures imposed by paragraph 8 of resolution 1718 (2006) and this resolution, including through the designation of entities, goods, and individuals, and directs the Committee to undertake its tasks to this effect and to report to the Security Council within thirty days of adoption of this resolution, and further *decides* that, if the Committee has not acted, then the Security Council will complete action to adjust the measures within seven days of receiving that report;

25. *Decides* that the Committee shall intensify its efforts to promote the full implementation of resolution 1718 (2006), the statement of its Presi-dent of 13 April 2009 (S/PRST/2009/7) and this resolution, through a work programme covering compliance, investigations, outreach, dialogue, assistance and cooperation, to be submitted to the Council by 15 July 2009, and that it shall also receive and consider reports from Member States pursuant to paragraphs 10, 15, 16 and 22 of this resolution;

26. *Requests* the Secretary-General to create for an initial period of one year, in consultation with the Committee, a group of up to seven experts ("Panel of Experts"), acting under the direction of the Committee to carry out the following tasks: (a) assist the Committee in carrying out its mandate as specified in resolution 1718 (2006) and the functions specified in paragraph 25 of this resolution; (b) gather, examine and analyze information from States, relevant United Nations bodies and other interested parties regarding the implementation of the measures imposed in resolution 1718 (2006) and in this resolution, in particular incidents of non-compliance; (c) make recommendations on actions the Council, or the Committee or Member States, may consider to improve implementation of the measures imposed in resolution 1718 (2006) and in this resolution; and (d) provide an interim report on its work to the Council no later than 90 days after adoption of this resolution, and a final report to the Council no later than 30 days prior to termination of its mandate with its findings and recommendations;

27. *Urges* all States, relevant United Nations bodies and other interested parties, to cooperate fully with the Committee and the Panel of Experts, in particular

by supplying any information at their disposal on the implementation of the measures imposed by resolution 1718 (2006) and this resolution;

28. *Calls upon* all Member States to exercise vigilance and prevent specialized teaching or training of DPRK nationals within their territories or by their nationals, of disciplines which could contribute to the DPRK's proliferation sensitive nuclear activities and the development of nuclear weapon delivery systems;

29. *Calls upon* the DPRK to join the Comprehensive Nuclear-Test-Ban Treaty at the earliest date;

30. *Supports* peaceful dialogue, *calls upon* the DPRK to return immediately to the Six Party Talks without precondition, and *urges* all the participants to intensify their efforts on the full and expeditious implementation of the Joint Statement issued on 19 September 2005 and the joint documents of 13 February 2007 and 3 October 2007, by China, the DPRK, Japan, the Republic of Korea, the Russian Federation and the United States, with a view to achieving the verifiable denuclearization of the Korean Peninsula and to maintain peace and stability on the Korean Peninsula and in north-east Asia;

31. *Expresses* its commitment to a peaceful, diplomatic and political solution to the situation and welcomes efforts by Council members as well as other Member States to facilitate a peaceful and comprehensive solution through dialogue and to refrain from any actions that might aggravate tensions;

32. *Affirms* that it shall keep the DPRK's actions under continuous review and that it shall be prepared to review the appropriateness of the measures contained in paragraph 8 of resolution 1718 (2006) and relevant paragraphs of this resolution, including the strengthening, modification, suspension or lifting of the measures, as may be needed at that time in light of the DPRK's compliance with relevant provisions of resolution 1718 (2006) and this resolution;

33. *Underlines* that further decisions will be required, should additional measures be necessary;

34. *Decides* to remain actively seized of the matter.

ACRONYMS

ABM Treaty—Anti-Ballistic Missile Treaty

BWC—Biological Weapons Convention

CTBT—Comprehensive Test Ban Treaty

CTBTO—Preparatory Commission for the Comprehensive Test Ban
Treaty Organization

FMCT—Fissile Material Cut-Off Treaty

FMT—Fissile Material Treaty

HEU—Highly Enriched Uranium

IAEA—International Atomic Energy Agency

INF—Intermediate-Range Nuclear Forces

LEU—Lowly Enriched Uranium

NTM—National Technical Means (of verification)

NTMM—Natural Technical Means and Methods (of verification)

NPT—The Non-Proliferation Treaty

OPCW—Organisation for the Prohibition of Chemical Weapons

SALT—Strategic Arms Limitations Treaty

TTBT—Threshold Test Ban Treaty

U.N.—United Nations

U.S.—United States of America

WMD—Weapons of Mass Destruction

INDEX